EMPOWERING THE WEST

DEVELOPMENT OF WESTERN RESOURCES

The Development of Western Resources is an interdisciplinary series focusing on the use and misuse of resources in the American West. Written for a broad readership of humanists, social scientists, and resource specialists, the books in this series emphasize both historical and contemporary perspectives as they explore the interplay between resource exploitation and economic, social, and political experiences.

John G. Clark, University of Kansas, Founding Editor
Hal K. Rothman, University of Nevada, Las Vegas, Series Editor

EMPOWERING THE WEST

Electrical Politics Before FDR

Jay L. Brigham

 University Press of Kansas

Published by the University Press of Kansas (Lawrence, Kansas 66049), which was
organized by the Kansas Board of Regents and is operated and funded by
Emporia State University, Fort Hays State University, Kansas State University,
Pittsburg State University, the University of Kansas, and Wichita State University

Library of Congress Cataloging-in-Publication Data
Brigham, Jay L.
    Empowering the west : electrical politics before FDR / Jay L.
Brigham.
        p.   cm. — (Development of western resources)
    Includes bibliographical references and index.
    ISBN 0-7006-0920-2 (alk. paper)
    1. Rural electrification—Political aspects—West (U.S.)—History.
2. Electric utilities—West (U.S.)—History.   3. Rural
electrification—Law and legislation—West (U.S.)   4. West (U.S.)—
Politics and government.   5. West (U.S.)—Economic conditions.
I. Title.   II. Series.
HD9688.U53W33   1998
333.793'2—dc21   98-19379

British Library Cataloguing in Publication Data is available.

Printed in the United States of America

10 9 8 7 6 5 4 3 2 1

The paper used in this publication meets the minimum requirements of the
American National Standard for Permanence of Paper for Printed Materials
Z39.48-1984.

For Sue

Contents

Preface

Many of the most popular historical images of the 1920s involve electricity: lighted streets, movies, assembly lines, radios, and a multitude of labor-saving electrical appliances. People did not, however, suddenly become aware of electricity or its modernizing potential during the 1920s. Instead, since the beginning of the century American citizens, politicians, and reformers had started to see electricity as a necessity that would dramatically lift the country's standard of living. Simultaneously, engineers solved a series of perplexing problems that initially had limited the efficient transmission of electrical energy. In the 1920s it was technologically possible for every American to use electrical energy regardless if he or she lived in a major urban center or the most sparsely populated area of rural America. Yet, most Americans did not use electricity in a meaningful way on a daily basis, either in rural or urban America.

The lack of widespread electrical consumption and the emerging view that electricity was a necessity of modern life made electricity the focal point of a major political controversy on the local, state, and national level in the years before the New Deal. Essentially two opposing and often hostile groups developed. On one side stood the private utility companies, their spokesmen, and their trade associations, such as the National Electric Light Association. They steadfastly protected their enterprises, often noting that electrical rates had been falling for years. Private power advocates defended the formation of holding companies, heightened merger activity, and interlocking corporate directories in the 1920s as essential to the economies of scale that they believed their industry required. Opponents of the private utility industry scoffed at such claims: greed and questionable business practices caused high electrical rates and prevented widespread use. They believed that regulation was essentially worthless since unscrupulous utility executives either bribed or ignored regulators. The only alternative then was public ownership of at least some generation and transmission systems. Public ownership, they thought, would reveal the exorbitant rates that private power companies charged, since little actual difference existed in generation and transmission costs.

The great debate between public ownership proponents and private power spokesmen started to play itself out in the political arena early in the century. The debate gained momentum as the decades passed. On the local level the fight developed in small towns and larger cities. Two of the fiercest battles broke out in Seattle and Los Angeles. In each city, despite drastically different environments and histories, dual electrical systems—one privately owned, the other publicly owned—competed for customers. In each city, public power ultimately triumphed, but only after a long and acrimonious debate. On the state level the power fight influenced the establishment of regulatory commissions, the passage of laws allowing for the sale of publicly generated power across municipal borders, and the creation of public utility districts. Nationally, the call for public power influenced congressional debates regarding the status of Muscle Shoals, proposals for a Colorado River dam, demands to investigate the private utility industry, and the 1928 and 1932 presidential elections.

In the end both sides claimed victory. The federal government ultimately created public power agencies such as the Tennessee Valley Authority and Bonneville Power Administration. Public access to Hoover Dam power occurred. Numerous federal programs and organizations made power available to increasing numbers of people in rural and urban America after 1932. The private power industry—despite the damaging Federal Trade Commission investigation, the stock market plunge that brought holding company pyramids to the brink of collapse, and various pieces of New Deal legislation designed to limit the industry—remained intact. Public power and the intense political fight associated with it, however, emerged as a significant issue before either the Great Depression or FDR's election. The great promise of electricity coupled with the growing recognition that it was no longer a luxury made its control and allocation an issue of national political importance and ignited an intense political debate.

Many people made this project possible from its earliest days as a dissertation idea at the University of California, Riverside. Three people at UCR especially influenced my intellectual growth and ultimately this book. My dissertation adviser, Ronald Tobey, first introduced me to the potential of quantitative analysis. As the dissertation director he continually challenged me and shared his own considerable knowledge and research on the electrical modernization of the American home. He also introduced me to the important difference between electrification and electrical modernization that provides the crucial backdrop to this work. I owe Charles Wetherell an equally great intellectual debt. Besides reading an endless number of drafts of one paper or chapter after another, he introduced and instructed me on the meaning and significance of social science history. Not only did he provide constant guidance as I learned quantitative methodology, but he always seemed to have work for me in the university's Laboratory for Historical Research. Although he did not have as much direct influence on this project as Tobey or Wetherell, the late John Phillips always gave encouragement and provided valuable insight by drawing on his own considerable knowledge of quantitative history.

Other people played crucial roles when this book was in the research stage. Keith Olson of the University of Maryland at College Park took time to serve on my dissertation committee. Janet Mores and Richard Beaumont of the Thomas Rivera Library at the University of California, Riverside, always found the book or information that I sought. William Meyers shared with me his knowledge of Southern California Edison. Hal Rothman, the series editor, not only gave strong encouragement during the revision stage but also was a thoughtful colleague at UNLV who remains a good friend. Nancy Scott Jackson, my editor at the University Press of Kansas, gave an unending amount of support. Her help and ideas have made this a much stronger book. Carl Abbott of Portland State University and the press's anonymous reader deserve thanks for their critical, yet evenhanded reviews. I also want to thank the family of Hugo Black Jr. for allowing me access and publication rights to material contained in his papers. Charles Harris of Seattle City Light helped find the book jacket's photograph. The staffs at the State Historical Society of Wisconsin, the Library of Congress reading room, and Suzzallo Library's special collections room at the University of Washington helped me locate archival information.

People not directly involved in the research, writing, and publication of this book nevertheless helped it become a reality. Special thanks to those who made research trips a little easier. The number of friends who gave encouragement is too long to list, but that does not diminish the importance of their friendship. Most important is the constant encouragement that my family has always given to me. My parents, Jim and Ruby Brigham, have been a steady source of support for as long as I can remember. I also have drawn on my father's knowledge of electrical engineering in writing this book. My sisters and their spouses, Jamie and Dan Knodle and Nancy and Andy Pehl, always offered words of encouragement.

Three people deserve more thanks than I can ever attempt to express in words. Sue Brigham has been constantly at my side through the entirety of the project and much more. Without her support and patience neither this book nor the dissertation that it is built on would have become realities. It is for those reasons and many more that this book is dedicated to her. Our two children, Ellen Mae and Kelly Henry, provide an endless amount of joy and in doing so help keep everything in perspective.

CHAPTER ONE

Electricity and Politics:
The Battle First Fought

Lightning bolts are nature's most striking manifestation of electrical energy. Since time immemorial people have pondered the meaning of lightning, awestruck by its ability to momentarily turn night into day. The eighteenth-century Methodist minister John Wesley called electricity the "soul of the universe." As early as 1730 inquisitive Europeans experimented with electricity, and in 1746 a two-mile-long low-voltage wire transmitted electricity in England. Benjamin Franklin conducted his famous kite-and-key experiment in 1752. Still, several generations passed before people began to view electricity as anything more than an oddity. By the 1850s rudimentary forms of electrical lighting began to appear in Paris and London. Electricity also started to surface in popular literature; consider Jules Verne's electrically powered *Nautilus* submarine in *Twenty Thousand Leagues Under the Sea*.[1]

A brief review of the early history of electricity in the United States reveals two crucial aspects of the developing electrical utility industry. First, following early successful tests, electrical use expanded rapidly. Second, the generation, transmission, and allocation of electrical energy raised political concerns from the beginning. By the end of the nineteenth century, in some towns political debates developed over franchise rights and electrical rates leading to public takeover of private systems. Those political controversies that first appeared in the 1880s continued to fester and expand after the turn of the century, reaching a crescendo in the 1920s. Over forty years passed between the first successful lighting tests and the passage of the Federal Water Power Act in 1920; during those years issues related to electricity became entangled in the Progressive Era debates on the local, state, and federal level. Conservationist stalwarts battled to preserve public control of the nation's waterways to prevent the privatization of hydroelectric sites. Late in the 1910s the nation's leaders expressed concern about electrical development and its importance in fueling the wartime economy. It took several decades, however, for electrical development to reach a point where it could drive a wartime economy. In the 1870s, when Americans gazed across the Atlantic they saw the bright flicker of electricity—not the violent energy of lightning strikes, but the harnessed electricity of the lightbulb burning in Paris and London.

1

In the United States, inventors worked feverishly to unlock the secrets of electricity during the 1870s. Charles Brush perfected a generator in 1876 and the arc light two years later. Engineers used both to light the streets of Cleveland in April 1879, suggesting the fabulous possibilities of electrical power. Even before this successful demonstration, Brush began to market his generator and arc light inventions. One system already lit a clothing store in Boston, another illuminated the front porch of a Cincinnati doctor, and a third powered a mill in Providence. After his Cleveland lighting success, Brush sold generators to business interests in San Francisco and to people in Lowell and Hartford. Finally, in 1880 Brush founded the Brush Electric Company and began construction of a central supply system for Cleveland.[2]

Other Americans worked as diligently as Brush to gain control of electricity. Thomas Edison, a name now synonymous with electric lighting, was one of those individuals. People already recognized Edison as an accomplished inventor for his pioneering work on the phonograph, telegraph, and telephone. The electric shows in Europe had dazzled Edison's patent attorney, Grosevenor Lowrey, who encouraged the inventor to become involved in electric light projects. Working from his Menlo Park, New Jersey, labs with a well-financed staff, Edison designed a system of electrical generation and lighting. Not only an inventor but an accomplished salesperson as well, Edison demonstrated his lighting system for New York City business icons including J. P. Morgan, who had already made substantial financial investments in Edison's work. Before long Edison received a franchise agreement to operate a central power system in New York City. The resulting Pearl Street station lit buildings in the Wall Street district, including Morgan's offices. While Edison continued to work in New Jersey, his young assistant Samuel Insull traveled the country looking for investors and buyers. By 1883 he had sold 334 Edison generators.[3]

Though Edison's early systems proved the feasibility of a "limited-area-of-distribution system," they were only partial successes.[4] Technological barriers confined their application. Direct current systems worked well in populated urban areas but were inefficient over long distances because of their inherent energy loss. The development of alternating current and high-voltage transformers decreased energy loss over long distances and changed the nature of electrical transmission. William Stanley, with backing from the Westinghouse family, built the first successful alternating current system in the United States in Great Barrington, Massachusetts, in 1886. After transmitting electricity four thousand feet from his lab to the village center, Stanley's system provided power to stores, doctors' offices, a barbershop, and the post office. The Westinghouse Company quickly perfected Stanley's system and in a short time received twenty-five orders for alternating current plants.[5]

Both direct current and alternating current plants continued to operate throughout the 1890s and early 1900s. At the 1893 Chicago World's Exposition, the Westinghouse Company displayed a universal system of transmission that "completed the transition from the era of electric light to the era of electric light and power."[6] The universal system allowed engineers to join alternating and direct current systems together into one network. Coupled with high-voltage transmission lines the universal system permitted utilities to transmit electricity from remote generation sites to distant customers. In 1901, for example, the Bay Area Power Company completed a 60,000-volt transmission line that ran 140 miles from Colgate in the California Sierras to Oakland on the San Francisco Bay. Following that accomplishment, the company interconnected its various power sources creating a 14,000-square-mile service area.[7]

In the years between Brush's successful demonstration in Cleveland and the connection of the California transmission line, electricity became a political issue as city governments and private companies started to use electricity for public lighting and streetcars. In 1890 fifty-one municipalities had electrified their streetcar lines; by 1895 another eight hundred had followed. Simultaneously, arguments over fair electrical rates became entangled with the emerging debates over political corruption and municipal reform that characterized turn-of-the-century America. The small service areas of early electric companies helped create a situation ripe for graft and corruption; politicians often awarded electrical contracts according to political favor. With several firms operating in any given city, inefficient distribution systems and overlapping service areas were all but inevitable. In the face of this situation, some city leaders came to believe that municipal ownership would provide more efficient and less expensive street lighting. Although private utilities would always serve the majority of Americans, by 1888 fifty-three towns had created municipal power systems.[8]

On February 3, 1889, a *New York Record Guide* article compared private and public electric lighting rates. In five towns where the city assumed control of the street lighting system, the cost dropped nearly 70 percent. Although the article only examined five towns that had switched to municipal ownership, the importance of the article is that it identified ownership as the primary factor in determining electrical rates. Without using the word "trusts," the article pointed to corrupt private ownership that manipulated the political process as the chief impediment to cheaper electricity. Electrical corporations had become so entrenched that neither individuals nor cities could buy power at a fair cost, the article stated. A city found it nearly impossible to buy the holdings of a private company because of the political strength of private utilities.[9] Those ideas emerged in the late 1880s only ten years after Brush's success in Cleveland, not in the late 1920s at the height of the debates over the private utility industry.

Reformers and private utility officials soon realized that public utilities, including electricity as well as telegraphs, telephones, and railroads, required new forms of regulation. The technological nature of these utilities prevented effective direct competition, leading many to call them natural monopolies. During the early development of modern public utilities, expensive and wasteful duplication of systems occurred. It made little economic sense to have several electrical systems or railroads serving any given area. The development of natural monopolies and the increasing merger activity of public utilities were part of the bigger changes in American business taking place at the end of the nineteenth century.

Since the later decades of the nineteenth century, American business had been in a state of transformation from relatively small economic enterprises to nationwide, multiunit businesses. Little agreement exists among historians over how to interpret changes in the country's economic structure before World War I and how those changes influenced politics. Some historians consider the move to large corporations as a fundamental positive that improved the country's economic foundation and living standard. Other historians consider the emergence of corporations not as a positive, but as a threat to society because of the influence they could wield.[10] Despite disagreement over interpretation, few can deny that the emergence of large, national corporations like railroads and later electrical utilities altered America's economic landscape.

The transformation to an economy increasingly characterized by national firms spurred on the reform movements of the late nineteenth and early twentieth century. Railroads provide a useful analogy for understanding the political and social debates over electricity and the electrical utility industry. Technological breakthroughs made both possible, and both promised real improvement for most Americans, from the farmer to the industrialist. The physical growth of the electrical utility industry shared many features of the railroad's development. Both represented natural monopolies in that multiple and overlapping networks were impractical, inefficient, and expensive. Similar to the history of the railroads, as economies of scale developed in the electrical utility industry, a period of consolidation occurred that resulted in a few large corporations dominating the production and distribution of electrical energy along geographic lines. Just as the railroads became a major target of reformers, so too did the electrical utilities. Historians also have noted that the railroads drove American economic expansion from the 1850s into the twentieth century. Beginning in the 1890s, electricity played an increasingly important role in American economic growth.[11] By the 1920s the electrical power industry had replaced the railroads as the primary target of reformers.

Richard T. Ely was one of the leading reform intellectuals of the period. Ely, a cofounder of the American Economic Association and the father of land economics, wrote widely on the issue of natural monopolies and public ownership. Several of his papers were especially relevant to electricity, railroads, and all public utilities.[12] A monopoly, Ely affirmed, had the power to set the price of a commodity without fear of price-cutting from a competitor. The provider of a commodity or service need not control the entire market to dominate, only a substantial percentage—enough to dictate the marketing of the service or product by all proprietors. Without competition the consumer was subject to the profiteering of the monopolistic enterprise. Monopolies, in his and many others' eyes, threatened democracy because businesses were thereby able to eclipse government control and exert disproportionate influence on society.[13] Large industrial enterprises such as Standard Oil, the House of Morgan, U.S. Steel, and various railroads exerted increasing influence on the political process and on individual lives. At the end of the nineteenth century many Americans perceived economic trusts as threats to the common good.

Ely stressed that either public ownership or public regulation of private ownership must occur to abolish the advantage of monopolies—especially natural monopolies—so that "no privileged classes composed of monopolists" would exist. He argued that inheritance laws needed revising, tariff and patent reform must occur, and laws governing private corporations must change to allow more public control and to prevent concentrations of economic power. Public utilities—water, light, and transportation—represented the principal class of natural monopolies. These commodities and services naturally precluded competition and had become essential to modern society. Higher costs and inefficient service would result if multiple systems developed in providing these services. Ely did not favor public ownership of all enterprises but insisted on the need to balance private and public interests to avoid the extremes of plutocracy and socialism.[14] The yardstick principle—the belief that a few publicly owned systems would serve as the measuring rule for private rates—that public power advocates later proposed resembled the middle ground Ely sought. Endorsing neither complete public ownership nor absolute private control, progressives believed that the yardstick principle represented the best way of protecting both the public interest and free enterprise. Once established, municipal ownership would cause a "harmony of interests" resulting in good government.[15] Ely believed, moreover, that municipal ownership ultimately would increase competition among private businesses since none would receive special treatment from monopolistic utility companies. Before World War I, reformers primarily targeted railroads; after the war, the electrical power industry became the main target.

As the political debate over electrical utilities intensified at the turn of the century, a host of problems plagued electrical engineers and managers. Technological and managerial innovations finally allowed the electrical utility industry to overcome these early difficulties and embark on a period of profound growth.[16] The first and most basic concern was price; no one knew how to accurately determine the cost of electricity. Initially, Thomas Edison charged a flat rate for lighting per bulb, regardless of how much the customer used the bulb per billing cycle. At the time engineers had not yet invented demand meters, common in every household and business today, so a utility could not accurately measure the amount of current a customer used. The British engineer John Hopkinson made the first significant breakthrough when he divided the cost of generating electricity into two parts: fixed costs that remained constant, such as land, buildings, and equipment; and operating costs such as fuel, labor, and maintenance that fluctuated according to output.[17]

Hopkinson also introduced the idea of "load factor." Just as railroads profited from always having a full trainload of passengers or freight, electrical utilities made more money when their generating facilities constantly operated near full capacity. In their earliest years utilities had to supply great amounts of electricity during the evening hours for home lighting. During the day, however, little demand existed, and generators operated far below capacity. To meet increased evening demand a company might have to install more generators, although they still would have little daytime use when customer demand dropped.

Technology entered the picture in the form of the "Wright demand meter," named for its inventor Arthur Wright, which allowed for the precise measurement of electrical consumption. Expanding on Hopkinson's work Wright realized that if utilities could disperse load throughout a twenty-four-hour period, higher profits at little additional expense would soon follow. The key to success was finding customers whose peak levels of consumption occurred at different times of the day (or night). A daytime market would draw power from otherwise idle generating equipment at no extra cost to the utility company other than additional fuel and the expense of connecting the daytime customer to the generating system. Daytime business use would offset evening residential use, thus diversifying load. To lure large daytime business users, Samuel Insull first offered reduced rates making it unprofitable for businesses to generate their own electricity. Businesses soon began to buy the cheaper power, thereby diversifying the utility's load.[18] In time, utilities established rate scales with predetermined increments; as a customer's consumption increased from one increment to the next, the rate per kilowatt hour decreased.

Progressive reformers, trustbusters, and municipal power advocates were among Insull's early opponents. In response to their attacks he started to push for state regulation in 1898. Insull argued that the state should award territorial monopolies to achieve the economies of scale necessary for efficient electrical generation and distribution.[19] Every state but Delaware ultimately formed a regulatory commission of some type, but the effectiveness of state-level regulation was and remains questionable. From the beginning, reformers often considered state commissions corrupt, ineffective, or both. In 1907 Milwaukee's mayor called the legislation creating Wisconsin's commission "political humbuggery and downright fraud . . . legislation for the power oligarchy."[20] Journalists Richard Rudolph and Scott Ridley portray state commissions as understaffed and no match for private power. They note that in the fifty-two rate cases filed in Wisconsin between 1907 and 1912 the commission granted increases fifty times.[21] Historians Thomas Hughes and Richard Hirsh take a more favorable view of commissions, seeing them as necessary mechanisms that allowed economies of scale to flourish.[22] Merit exists in each argument. State commissions often did not regulate the electrical utility industry effectively. In fact, they could not when cases involved interstate commerce issues. At the same time, the industry was a natural monopoly and economies of scale did result in better service and cheaper rates. Reformers in the 1920s recognized both sides of the argument.

The state of the electrical industry in the first decade of the twentieth century was promising though problematic. Early attempts at lighting and traction had been successful. Engineers and managers solved many problems that initially hampered growth and interconnection. Resolution of these difficulties triggered a period of expansion that resulted in, at the invitation of the private utility industry, state-level regulation. The resolution of problems that marred the early years of electrical development occurred at the same time that Theodore Roosevelt initiated national-level reform efforts. The federal government soon started to express concern over the monopolistic control of water power sites, centralized control of transmission, and fair customer rates.

Reflecting the nation's growing interest in electricity, in 1906 Congress authorized the Census Bureau to conduct a quinquennial census of the electrical utility industry.[23] Congressional approval of the census shows the growing importance of electricity in American society. Congressman Edgar Crumpacker (R-Ind.), who sponsored the legislation in the House, called it "highly important" to take a census every five years because of the "almost sensational development of the electrical industries."[24] The nature of the 1907 census reflects the newness of electrical technology and hints at its great potential. The census contains twenty-six illustrations depicting household appliances such as electric coffee percolators, flatirons, and toasters. Lampposts featuring either tungsten or arc lighting from New York City are featured as are various types of light poles. Other sections of the census include illustrations of transformers, turbines, and switchboards. The census also contains a section entitled "Technical Aspects of the Period" that reported information on basic aspects of electrical generation including steam and water power, oil and gas engines, transmission and distribution, electric heating and cooking, and electric power.[25]

The censuses provide in-depth statistical information documenting the growth of the electrical industry in the United States in terms of number of plants, generation capacity, and type of generators. A look at the aggregate numbers reported by the Census Bureau reveals the extraordinary expansion of the electrical utility industry. After two decades of growth in the number of companies, a decade of merger activity followed. The amount of electricity generated in the United States increased in each five-year period between 1902 and 1932, although after 1927 generation grew at a much slower pace than in previous years. The data in Table 1.1 show the amount of electricity generated in the United States between 1902 and 1932. Both commercial and public enterprises generated expanding quantities of power in each five-year period. Except during the 1927 to 1932 period, after the onset of the Great Depression, the five-year expansion in generated electricity for both private and public plants always surpassed 50 percent and several times approached or exceeded 100 percent.

The great expansion in generated output early in the century is not surprising since the industry itself was still in its formative years. One would expect to find high percentages of increases since the actual beginning amounts were relatively small. The rate of growth slowed somewhat during the period that encompassed the post–World War I economic slowdown in the United States. What is more revealing is the tremendous growth during the 1922 to 1927 period, when the increase in total output surpassed 85 percent. The great expansion in the amount of electricity generated in the mid-1920s contributed to the political fight over its con-

Table 1.1 Generated Output of Electrical Energy in the United States, 1902–1932 in Kilowatt Hours (000,000)

Year	Total	Percent Change	Commercial	Percent Change	Municipal	Percent Change
1902	2507.0	—	2311.1	—	195.9	—
1907	5862.3	113.8	5572.8	141.1	289.5	47.8
1912	11569.1	97.3	11031.6	98.0	537.5	85.7
1917	25438.3	119.9	24399.0	121.2	1039.3	93.4
1922	40291.5	58.4	38413.2	57.4	1878.3	80.7
1927	74686.4	85.4	71306.8	85.6	3379.5	79.9
1932	79657.5	6.7	75692.7	6.2	3964.8	17.3
1902–27	—	2879.1	—	2958.4	—	3424.0
1902–32	—	3077.4	—	3175.2	—	4034.3

Source: U.S. Department of Commerce, Bureau of the Census, *Census of Electrical Industries, 1932, Central Electric Light and Power Stations* (Washington, DC, 1934), Table 36, "Current Generated, Commercial and Municipal Establishments, 1902 to 1932, with Type of Prime Mover: 1932 and 1927," 56.

trol. As electricity became ever more abundant and more apparent in popular culture, public power advocates thought that higher levels of electrical modernization also should occur. Those supporting public power argued that private utilities monopolized electrical generation for financial gain, preventing widespread usage despite the enormous increase in output. The data in Table 1.1 also show the small foothold that public power had created. Except for 1902, the percentages of electricity generated in the United States by municipal power plants fluctuated between 4 and 5 percent. Despite that relatively small percentage, the fight between public and private power remained potent from the turn of the century through the 1920s.

The data in Table 1.2 show the economies of scale that emerged in the electrical utility industry between 1902 and 1932. The total number of plants and the number of privately owned commercial plants increased through 1917, whereas the number of municipally owned plants grew through 1922. After those years the number of plants decreased, although the number of municipal plants declined at a slower rate than did privately owned plants, indicating the resilience of public power in the twenties. The average size of the primary movers, or generators, increased throughout the thirty-year period. Tables 1.1 and 1.2 vividly illustrate the economies of scale that dominated the electrical utility industry between 1902 and 1932: fewer plants using larger generators produced more electricity. From a generational perspective the electrical utility industry had come of age in the United States in the 1920s.

The attitude of public power advocates in the 1920s is best understood when the data in Tables 1.1 and 1.2 are considered together. The utility industry generated expanding amounts of electricity through the decade. Public power supporters applauded the increased output, which they considered essential for a modernized society, but expressed concern about the control of generation in a dwindling number of enterprises. Those in the public power movement feared that the concentration of control in a few electrical utility companies was quickly subverting the modernizing potential of electricity.

The great hope that people associated with electrical power in the first decades of the twentieth century sparked political controversy about its generation and distribution in an economy devoted to private enterprise. Progressive reformers expressed the worry that unfettered private enterprise would ultimately prevent widespread use of electricity thereby denying Americans a modernized future. Although state-level regulation eased some early fears, another controversy quickly developed over using the nation's rivers and streams to generate electricity. The national debates surrounding the use of the nation's waterways for hydroelectric production became intertwined with the conservation movement of the early

Table 1.2 Number of Electrical Establishments and Average Kilowatt Output of Prime Movers per Plant, 1902–1932

Year	No. Est.	Percent Change	Avg. Prime Mover	No. Comm. Est.	Percent Change	Comm. Avg. Prime Mover	No. Mun. Est.	Percent Change	Mun. Avg. Prime Mover
1902	3,620	–	380.2	2,805	–	448.1	815	–	146.5
1907	4,714	30.2	648.5	3,462	23.4	813.8	1,252	53.6	191.5
1912	5,221	10.8	1075.9	3,659	5.7	1421.2	1,562	24.8	267.1
1917	6,542	25.3	1475.9	4,224	15.4	2133.0	2,318	48.4	276.5
1922	6,355	(2.9)	2330.3	3,774	(10.7)	3670.8	2,581	11.3	370.0
1927	4,335	(31.8)	6145.3	2,137	(43.4)	11750.8	2,198	(14.8)	695.3
1932	3,429	(20.9)	10435.5	1,627	(23.9)	20720.8	1,802	(18.0)	1149.1

Source: U.S. Department of Commerce, Bureau of the Census, *Census of Electrical Industries, 1932, Central Electric Light and Power Stations* (Washington, DC, 1934), Table 30, "Number of Establishments and Horsepower of Prime Movers, Commercial and Municipal Establishments: 1902 to 1932," 49. Horsepower converted to kilowatt hours.

twentieth century. Private utility officials along with progressives and conservationists such as Theodore Roosevelt, Gifford Pinchot, and James Garfield considered "white coal" to be the inexhaustible energy source of the future, capable of facilitating dramatic social improvement. With the development of high-voltage transmission lines, faraway consumers could use hydroelectric power. A utility could conceivably dam any river or stream with enough current to spin a turbine for hydroelectric generation, regardless of how far the utility might have to transmit the electricity. Nowhere would this process become more important than in the expansive West with its growing and extraordinarily dispersed population, often located hundreds of miles from potential power sources.[26]

Hydroelectric power offered several major advantages over electricity produced from other sources. Utilities could generate water power without having to mine or transport fuel. In fact, most considered it a limitless source of energy because it did not require the burning of a fossil fuel. Instead, after construction of a dam many thought that the electrical generation would have no end. And, after the high initial cost of constructing dams and transmission lines, hydropower was inexpensive. Low operating costs eventually offset the high initial investments. In Los Angeles, people anticipated that the widespread use of electricity would help improve the region's air quality, while in Seattle people thought that easy access to nearby hydroelectric sites would make the region a major manufacturing center.

Early in the century three basic groups developed with regard to the politics of electricity. Private power proponents, usually political conservatives and utility representatives, argued that laissez-faire economics should apply: government should not be involved in the production and distribution of electricity. The regulatory group, which included many progressives, believed that electrical production and distribution should remain in private hands but be subject to state or federal regulation. That group believed private utilities should receive a fair return on their investment but should not overcharge consumers. Public ownership supporters insisted that only government ownership could guarantee fair electrical rates. This group was convinced that greed would prevail if laissez-faire economics prevailed. They also considered regulation inadequate; selfish and unscrupulous utility executives could easily buy off regulators and alter account books. As the years passed, those favoring regulation merged with those favoring public ownership.

Representatives for these three groups first did battle in the early debates over water power. Gifford Pinchot and other progressives in Theodore Roosevelt's administration voiced alarm over what they considered the monopolization of water power sites by a few private companies. From Roosevelt's second term until passage of the Federal Water Power

Act in 1920, public ownership advocates and their adversaries in the private utility industry vigorously debated whether state or federal government should approve hydroelectric projects.

Conservationists early in the century believed that the country should develop the nation's natural resources to benefit the greatest number of people possible.[27] A river, for example, in its natural state held certain aesthetic qualities, but those attributes benefited only the individuals who actually viewed the river. Conservationists reasoned that society should develop rivers to serve many uses including navigation, irrigation, flood control, and electrical power generation, thus using a river to its fullest extent. Electricity quickly assumed a special significance in multiuse projects since its generation and sale could finance the entire project.[28] Construction of a hydroelectric dam incorporated conservation's ideas by harnessing the water of a stream or river for the production of electricity, thereby developing a natural resource for widespread use. A large project, such as Boulder Dam, could not only generate electricity but also prevent flooding and provide water for reclamation projects and domestic consumption.[29] The development of the water and land resources would serve the greatest number of people in an entire basin.

The political debate over dam construction and control of water power sites revolved around the questions of who should control the sites and for how long. Some thought that state governments should grant franchise rights for hydroelectric dams, while others thought that only the federal government possessed the necessary authority. Yet another group desired no government involvement. Those who favored governmental input usually believed that a franchise holder should pay the government for the right to develop an area. The emerging national political debate over both the monopoly of electricity and the control of developed and undeveloped water power sites manifested itself in the National Conservation Association in the 1910s.

In 1913 the water power controversy split the Congress, as members of the water power committee hotly debated the issue of hydroelectric power. The sensitive political issues of compensation, development, and length of acquisition were at the center of the discussions. The water power committee's majority report favored compromise legislation to the extent that private utilities might escape paying any fees for the right to use water power sites. Gifford Pinchot, one of the nation's major political figures of the era, led the fight for franchise agreements and fee payment. The association ultimately rejected the water power committee's majority report and instead endorsed the minority report that Pinchot, Henry L. Stimson, and Joseph Neal wrote warning of a growing water power monopoly.[30]

The minority report concluded that ten business interests controlled 65 percent of the developed water power sites in the country through common officers and directors. Between 1911 and 1913 the energy that the ten interests controlled had doubled to 6.27 million horsepower, more than twice what Hoover Dam can generate today.[31] The minority report characterized the fight against the water power monopoly as developing over two issues. The first was the fight against monopoly itself. The second was to prevent the acquisition of sites for speculative purposes and instead to push for the immediate and "full development" of undeveloped, privately held sites. The country needed a water power policy based on three principles: "prompt development," "prevention of unregulated monopoly," and "good service and fair charges to the consumer."[32]

Other conservationists echoed Pinchot, Stimson, and Neal's call for federal control. Theodore Roosevelt's former secretary of the interior, James R. Garfield, son of the twentieth president, further articulated the conservationists' belief in the need for federal jurisdiction. In a letter to Utah senator Reed Smoot (R), who opposed federal regulation, Garfield argued that the government must treat as a unit any watershed that covered two or more states to realize the highest level of development while also protecting the public interest. Only the federal government could oversee full development and public protection of interstate watersheds. The interstate nature of electrical generation and transmission meant that electrical utilities could often ignore state laws. For that reason Garfield believed they would welcome any legislation excluding them from federal control.[33]

The water power debate reached Congress several times in the first decades of the twentieth century.[34] Since the federal government owned vast public lands in the West, Washington could decide the future of water power in the region.[35] Until the development of hydroelectric power, the federal government took little interest in inland waterways except for navigation matters. That began to change when individuals or companies gained control of water power sites through either land grants or purchases with little federal oversight.[36] Throughout the ensuing debate, the War Department expressed concern that construction of hydroelectric dams would prevent ship passage on the country's rivers.

A 1896 law empowered the secretary of the interior to grant permits for the use of public and forest service lands to generate and distribute electricity. Congress expanded that power five years later when it granted the Department of the Interior the power to authorize right-of-ways across federal land for the production and distribution of power. Together those laws meant that the executive branch had broad power over the nation's hydroelectric resources, especially in the western public domain. Yet, at a time when the Republican Roosevelt was increasing presidential power, Congress was clearly worried about relinquishing too much authority. Congress started to reassert its authority when it passed a bill in 1906 that gave it the authority to issue individual permits for electrical sites on navigable streams and rivers in the United States. The law required the secretary of war to approve any plans for hydroelectric dams and, if necessary, require the construction of locks and other navigational needs at the expense of the licensee. The Department of War could revoke the grant because of noncompliance or authorize the removal of any dam that impeded navigation. The law, however, did not place a time limit on the permit.[37]

The 1906 law meant, however, that every project on any navigable stream or river in the country required congressional approval. These early laws created a maze of federal authority. The executive branch through the Department of the Interior maintained broad authority over transmission and generation on Forest Service and other public lands. Congress influenced the debate through the legislative process required for projects on navigable rivers or streams. Any legislation Congress passed required the approval of the Department of War and the White House before it became law.

The convoluted set of laws governing water power faced a new challenge in 1908 when President Roosevelt exerted his influence, vetoing a bill that would authorize construction of a dam on the James River in Missouri. Roosevelt's veto message drew on conservationist themes with the criticisms that the bill granted an unconditional and monopolistic privilege without ensuring adequate public protection. He reiterated his belief that a great monopoly threatened the country and said he would veto any bill that lacked clauses specifying a time limit and financial charge for the private use of a water power site.[38] Roosevelt, who had signed the 1906 law expanding congressional power, said the growing influence of the conservationist movement, specifically Gifford Pinchot and Henry Graves of the Forest Service, influenced his veto decision.[39]

In 1910 President Taft signed a general law giving the secretary of war the authority, but not requiring him, to collect fees from any person or corporation that constructed a hydroelectric dam to maintain a river's navigability. Although the legislation did not require the payment of a yearly fee for the privilege of using a site for water power, it did establish a fifty-year franchise that meant the license would expire in fifty years, requiring the owner to reapply.[40] The ambiguous and often conflicting nature of the laws passed from 1896 to 1910 contributed to a ten-year battle over water power legislation. Congress held several hearings during the decade devoted to water power issues.

In November 1911 the National Waterways Commission, consisting of five House and seven Senate members, conducted hearings on the "development and control of water power." During the hearings a debate emerged regarding the relationship of reclamation projects to water power. John D. Ryan, president of the Great Falls Power Company in Montana, attacked what he perceived to be the existing law's narrow focus on irrigation as the primary reason for major dams. He believed that the current law's emphasis on reclamation prevented construction of dams in the mountains for the primary purpose of electrical generation. In his home state of Montana, Ryan envisioned a series of dams on the Missouri River as it flowed east. Dams on the river's mountainous western stretches would generate electricity, while those on the eastern plains would harness the river for reclamation. As more power markets developed, more hydroelectric dams would be built. This relationship, he believed, represented true conservationist principles. Ryan thought that little incentive existed for private development until the federal government sorted out the issues concerning ownership, licensing, fees, transmission lines, and right-of-ways.[41]

Committee members and witnesses alike expressed the need to determine accurately how much potential hydroelectric power existed in the United States. Although the exact amount of electrical energy that dams could generate remained a mystery, nearly everyone recognized that the West contained vast amounts of potential electricity that, if developed, would improve society. Gano Dunn, president of the American Institute of Electrical Engineers, said that dams could generate sixty-five million horsepower for commercial and manufacturing development. The Columbia River and other Pacific Northwest rivers could generate nearly one-third of that capacity. Dunn noted that electrical usage was accelerating more quickly than steam power, in part because manufacturing used an ever-increasing amount of electrical energy.[42] Marshall Leighton of the U.S. Geographical Survey later predicted that hydroelectric sources could eventually provide two hundred million horsepower.[43]

Though the exact amount of potential electricity was open to debate, few people doubted that wide-scale use of electrical energy would lead to a higher standard of living and increased industrial production. During the 1911 hearings Edward R. Taylor appeared for the American Electrochemical Society and said that in the United States ten thousand chemists were working on solutions to economic problems through better use of raw materials for material improvement. Hydroelectric power would make that task cheaper. Taylor specifically addressed the potential of electrical iron smelting and noted that a few plants using electricity from coal-burning steam plants operated in California, Chicago, Pittsburgh, and Syracuse. The cost of coal represented the major drawback. Returning to the low-cost potential of water power, he stated that one developed horsepower of water power produced as much energy as twelve tons of coal annually. Cheaper electricity meant cheaper steel.[44] Charles Wallace, representing the Boston-based utility conglomerate Stone and Webster, called water power development an "enterprise which contributes [to] . . . the public welfare."[45]

Gifford Pinchot and Secretary of the Interior Walter Fisher tempered the committee's enthusiasm for water power development and the associated improvement in the country's living standard. Each man warned that the growing water power monopoly would prevent widespread use of inexpensive hydropower. During his testimony Pinchot quickly summarized what he considered the essence of the problem: private companies that wanted as little government influence as possible versus the public good. He warned that consolidation of water power entities was rapidly occurring in many parts of the country. As the Pennsylvanian would say repeatedly in the following years, "the water belongs to all the people." Except for a few states that had established water power commissions (California, Oregon, Wisconsin, and soon New York), people had little recourse "against the monopolistic practices on the part of great water power combinations." Pinchot went on to declare the industry no different in nature from the sugar, tobacco, or oil industries. He said, as did nearly everyone, that the public needed water power based on efficient and equal service at a fair price. He also said the government needed to establish a reasonable franchise time limit.[46]

Secretary Fisher also sounded many conservationist tenets when he called for federal control of hydroelectric development on both navigable rivers and on the federal domain. The government, he said, must treat each river or stream as a unit. Fisher stated that "any stream should be developed in its entirety . . . for domestic uses . . . for navigation and for power, and for irrigation—all of these things ought to be so coordinated and worked out that we shall get the highest value out of each particular stream, and I believe that the Federal government will . . . be the most effective agency to bring that about." Finally, just as Pinchot drew analogies to the sugar, tobacco, and oil industries, Fisher said that in time electricity will become, like the railroads, an interstate business, and the states will want federal regulation.[47]

Testimony again highlighted the West on the last day of the 1911 hearings. James Adams, assistant forester of the U.S. Forest Service, testified that nearly all hydroelectric development in the West had occurred since 1901. Since then, the Forest Service had processed about sixty applications for dams and had received another one hundred inquiries regarding dam building. Most were or would be in the West; California had the most, followed by Washington and Oregon, then Idaho, Montana, and Colorado. One dam, in the Stanislaus National Forest, served part of the San Francisco power market two hundred miles away.[48]

As the promise of hydroelectricity became manifest, many in the Senate continued to worry about monopolistic tendencies in the industry. In 1915 the Senate passed a resolution sponsored by westerner William Borah (R-Idaho). It directed the secretary of agriculture to investigate the "ownership and control" of hydroelectric sites in the United States.[49] The investigation resulted in a voluminous three-part report that revealed the extent of the monopolistic control of the electrical utility industry and its extraordinary growth. According to the report, although water power accounted for only 16 percent of electricity generated in the United States in 1912, it was the fastest growing means of electrical production. The report said that eighteen private companies controlled 51 percent of the water power produced in the United States.[50] Forest Service officials wrote the report, based on the electrical utility census and their investigations. The first volume contained the actual text, while the second part included tables, charts, and other statistical information. The third part, the most damaging to private power interests, reported interconnection through holding companies and common directors.

The report revealed that western states far outpaced the rest of the country in the development of primary power between 1902 and 1912. Available primary power increased in the nonwestern sections of the country by 226 percent in those years, but in the West the figure was a staggering 440 percent. Examining water power alone, in the West production increased by 451 percent as compared with 98 percent in the remainder of the country. In the three years after the 1912 electrical census, the West completed primary power projects at an annual rate greater than the 1902–1912 period. In actual cost of construction since 1907, California led all states. The report underscored the importance of public lands to western electrical development: 56 percent of water power in the West originated on or was tied to public lands. Perhaps most important, the report stated that the greatest concentration of ownership occurred in the West.[51]

The massive size of the three-part report created a minor political controversy over whether the government should publish it as a public document. That controversy reveals the expanding political debate over electricity in the Senate. Senators sympathetic to private power interests, led by Utah's Reed Smoot, objected to publication, ostensibly because it was too expensive. Another westerner, the Democratic senator from Colorado, Charles Thomas, joined Smoot in objecting to printing the report as a government document and introduced an amendment to limit the printing to the first volume that contained only the text of the report. Thomas rejected charges that reasons other than cost saving motivated him to push for the amendment. George Norris (R-Nebr.), who soon would emerge as the most outspoken public power advocate in the Senate, led the charge against attempts to block printing of parts two and three. Norris announced on the Senate floor that Thomas objected to printing part three because it showed the extent of interconnections between utilities and banking institutions—information that Norris said the public had never seen. Norris and his supporters finally won when the Senate defeated Thomas's amendment and passed the resolution to print the entire report.[52]

While the Senate debated publication of the report, across the Atlantic war wrecked havoc in Europe, a war that the United States soon entered. American economic aid to the allies and then actual military participation in World War I contributed further to the idea that the nation needed to develop its hydroelectric resources rapidly.[53] During 1918 congressional hearings on water power, Chief U.S. Forester O. C. Merrill warned of the drain on fuel sources such as petroleum if water power remained untapped. He urged easterners to follow the example of California and create large-scale transmission systems. Merrill called eastern development "still in a large degree in the primitive state of isolated independent development" and said he saw no reason that it could not approach that of the West.[54] Regional development and boosterism entered the hearing when Harry Pierce of Seattle, president of the Washington Irrigation and Development Company, appeared before the committee. Pierce told the representatives that damming the Priest Rapids on the Columbia River would result in 250,000 horsepower of electricity for use in "the manufacture of electrochemicals, wood pulp, paper, abrasives, pottery . . . the smelting of lead and silver . . . and for the electrification of three transcontinental railroads." He further testified that a half million acres of desert could be reclaimed following power development.[55]

Other westerners or people representing western interests appeared and reflected the growing western interest in developing hydroelectricity sites. C. F. Kelley of New York, legal counsel for the Montana Power Company, claimed that Montana had the highest per capita amount of developed power at the cheapest rates of any state. The only problem Kelley identified was that of insufficient power markets. His testimony touched on a key issue that became a cornerstone of the public power fight throughout the 1920s—the responsibility of a private company that held a state-approved monopoly to provide power for everyone in its service area. He refuted allegations that Congressman John Raker of California (D) made that Montana Power had refused to service the surrounding territory.[56] Raker did not continue that line of questioning, although it touched on a fundamental aspect of extending the power grid. Many who supported public power believed if a private company controlled the power grid of a geographical region, it was obligated to provide service to every customer in the region, regardless of the customer's distance from generation sites or transmission lines. Private power representatives cited the expense of running lines for rural domestic service as prohibitive, while public power proponents charged that nearly all private costs were inflated and that high private rates resulted from stock watering, holding companies, and poor management.

Ultimately, the issue was not resolved until the New Deal, when the federal government became involved through the Rural Electrification Administration. The most important point in Kelley and Raker's exchange was that economic factors, not technological problems, blocked the widespread use of electrical energy. During his testimony Secretary of the Interior Franklin Lane tied together the high levels of electrical development that Kelley testified about to eastern economic growth and explicitly identified the possibility of a national power grid. Lane said that it was not really an East or West matter, but one of national importance, since a utility could transmit western power from Montana to Pittsburgh two thousand miles away.[57]

As the 1910s came to a close, Norris, Pinchot and other conservationists continued to push for strong national legislation requiring utilities to pay an annual usage fee and setting a definite franchise time limit for private development of water power sites. Senator Norris also wanted preference given to public entities over corporations in the granting of permits to develop hydroelectric power.[58] Conservatives and friends of the power interests opposed any time limits and fees, arguing instead that laissez-faire economics should prevail.[59] Those favoring a franchise time limit and fees finally won.

In 1920 Congress finally passed and President Wilson signed a comprehensive water power bill. The new law established the Federal Water Power Commission composed of the secretaries of the interior, war, and agriculture and gave the commission the authority to issue fifty-year permits for the construction of hydroelectric dams on any navigable waters in the United States. The legislation required an annual fee, established by the commission, to pay for the law's administration and for the use of the land and water. The law resolved the long-running debate over who controlled the nation's waterways by requiring any state, municipality, corporation, or individual planning to construct a dam on any nonnavigational body of water to notify the commission so it could launch an investigation to decide the project's impact on interstate or foreign commerce. If the project would not hamper commerce, dam construction could proceed.[60] Passage of the act took Congress out of the authorization process, though both houses would continue to exert influence through the appropriation process. The law guaranteed public guidance of water power policy, but it did not address the issues of multipurpose development, irrigation, or flood control.[61]

The Federal Water Power Act clarified many of the legal issues involved with the generation and transmission of electricity. The law brought a degree of coherence to the maze of federal laws that had governed the development of water power since the turn of the century. It clearly established the application and approval process for new dam construction and clarified the issues of time limits and fees, but despite those successes much remained unchanged. The law did not lessen the political battle being waged over electricity in the United States. In fact, resolution of the legal issues only heightened the fight and focused even more attention on the promise of electricity. More than ever it seemed to many that everyone should be able to use electricity on a daily basis. During the 1920s the merger activity that had started before World War I accelerated and became one of the major areas of debate between those favoring public ownership and those opposed to it.

Historians of electricity have viewed the development of the electrical utility industry and the use of electricity from several perspectives. Some consider the story of electricity to be that of system building in which engineers worked diligently to overcome technological problems. Another interpretation is that the electrification of America was essentially a social process that quickened in the 1920s. Still others consider electricity as part of a city building process.[62] All of these interpretations are compelling and contribute greatly to the historical understanding of electricity. Several things, however, are often overlooked in these interpretations. One is the political fight over electricity. Another is a clear distinction between electrification and electrical modernization and the related issue of load factor that had plagued the industry since its earliest days.

In the twenties public power advocates often used the term "modernization" when they discussed the great promise of electrical energy. Private utility spokesmen, however, did not discuss modernization as much as they discussed electrification. This differentiation was no surprise, since the terms held different meanings with distinct implications for how society allotted and consumed electricity. Electrification commonly referred to the ability to transmit electrical current to a given geographic region. A city or rural area could be considered electrified when a utility had connected most of the homes and businesses to a central power station. Accordingly, most of urban America had electrification in the 1920s, although it was not until the 1930s, after the establishment of the Rural Electrification Administration, that rural America started to become electrified. However, even if a house had access to electricity, it did not mean that it was electrically modernized.

Electrical modernization meant that people could and did use modern electrical appliances such as refrigerators, stoves, and heaters as well as smaller appliances including irons, coffee percolators, and of course electric lighting on a daily basis. In the modernized home, a family used electricity to its fullest benefit and was not merely connected to a distribution system. Electrical usage in the home took two forms. The first was for lighting and small appliances. The second was for large appliances, such as refrigerators, ranges, and washing machines, that used more current and required heavier wiring. Most homes in the twenties did not have heavy wiring and could not use large appliances. In 1929 *Electric World*, the major trade journal of private power, estimated that only about 20 percent of the

American households served by private power could be considered eligible for "complete electrical service."[63]

Recognizing the difference between electrification and electrical modernization is crucial to understanding the political fight over electricity and public power in the 1920s. Electrical modernization was not the everyday experience of most Americans before the Great Depression. A review of information in some recent works addressing the use of electricity underscores the lack of electrical modernization in the 1920s. In 1925 more than 90 percent of Chicago's families lived in dwellings connected to a central supply system, suggesting that the electrification of the city was nearly complete. The amount of electrical energy used in the city seems to support this view, as per capita electrical consumption doubled between 1915 and 1925. Commonwealth Edison, like many private utilities, actively encouraged electrical modernization through sales campaigns. Take, for example, the "Give Something Electrical" promotion during the 1925 holiday season: an aggressive advertising campaign resulted in the sale of more than 100,000 electrical appliances.[64] Despite such activity, however, Chicago clearly was not electrically modernized by 1930. Examining aggregate data on the percentage of Chicago households with specific types of appliances in 1929 reveals that although 90 percent of the homes had elec-

Table 1.3 Percentage of Chicago Homes with Select Electrical Appliances in 1929

Appliance	Percent
Iron	96.0
Vacuum Cleaner	87.0
Radio	53.0
Toaster	37.0
Washing Machine	36.0
Percolator	16.0
Refrigerator	10.0
Fan	10.0
Heater	10.0
Waffle Iron	9.0
Heating Pad	7.0
Ironing Machine	5.0
Curling Iron	4.0
Clock	1.0

Source: Commonwealth Edison Company, Statistical Department, "Wiring and Appliance Survey in Chicago Homes Reveals Extensive Future Market," Edison Round Table 21 (31 December 1929): 10. Data are drawn from Platt, The Electric City, 251, and are for central station customers only.

trical service, many had only a few small appliances. Very few homes enjoyed the luxury associated with electric refrigerators, heaters, and washing machines.

So, despite the beginnings of electrical modernization in Chicago by 1929, it was by no means complete before the time of the Great Depression. The same held true nationally. Although direct comparisons with other cities are difficult, one can compare the Chicago data with aggregate data for the entire United States. In Chicago in 1929, 36 percent of homes had electric washing machines; nationally, about 20 percent of Americans homes had electric washing machines. Counting only homes with electricity nationally in 1929 shows that 27 percent had washing machines. What these numbers indicate, of course, is that more than 70 percent of American homes in 1929 did not use electric washing machines.[65]

Other available evidence points to the same conclusion. A National Electric Light Association (NELA) survey of 1,300 Philadelphia homes in 1921 revealed that only electric irons were found in a majority of all categories of homes. Vacuum cleaners existed in most "Modern homes" (ten to twelve years old) and "Better Class" homes. In those two groups of homes, 28 and 32 percent of residences respectively had an electric washing machine, and 10 and 36 percent owned an electric fan. Another survey in 1920 revealed that residential customers owned only 200 refrigerators in Boston and in Baltimore, 150 in New York, and 15 in Philadelphia.[66] As of December 1, 1926, 11,027 of Seattle City Light's 74,616 residential customers owned electric ranges (14.8 percent). City Light claimed in 1929 to have the highest per capita number of electric ranges in the nation. Despite that claim, many in Seattle did not own an electric range. The Seattle information, like the Chicago data, illustrates an important factor: despite increased consumption of electricity throughout the 1910s and especially the 1920s, general use remained low.

Available data for smaller American cities show similar levels of electrical modernization. Ronald Tobey in his work on electrical modernization during the New Deal found relatively low levels in Riverside, California, in the early twenties that persisted for much of the decade. In 1922 the publicly owned utility that served the town conducted an appliance survey of Riverside's 4,338 electrified residential units. The electric iron was the most widely used appliance, found in nearly 82 percent of all homes. Next in the survey were kitchen appliances (other than refrigerators and ranges), found in 22 percent of all homes, followed by vacuum cleaners, 18 percent.[67]

That most American homes were not electrically modernized was not an accident. It reflected the priorities of the private utilities: cost and revenue.[68] In 1929, domestic customers accounted for nearly 83 percent of central station customers, yet they generated less than 30 percent of total revenue.[69] *Electric World* reported in 1930 that 40 percent of the nation's electrified homes used too little electricity to result in private utility profit.[70] Private power found a much more lucrative market in the sale of electricity to business and industry for three reasons. First, since many factories at one time had their own generators to drive electric motors, bringing a factory on-line only required stringing wires to the factory. The cost of wiring or rewiring did not exist since many businesses already had adequate wiring. Second, businesses and industries usually used larger motors that demanded more power than a residential customer would use, which meant larger sales per customer. Three, geographic concentrations of business and industry did not require the construction of an enormous power grid. Generally, a utility needed to build fewer miles of transmission lines to connect businesses and industries than homes, which further contributed to lower costs. These factors made the electrification of business and industry less expensive in the short term. Modernizing a home created a special set of circumstances. Most homes required new or upgraded wiring to support the greater electrical demands of heavy appliances. Private enterprise was understandably reluctant to provide the money for such improvements.[71] It is estimated that by 1930 only about 35 percent of all American homes were adequately wired to take full advantage of electrical appliances, large and small.[72]

Private utility officials knew that many homes lacked modernization. For example, during the public power debate in Sikeston, Missouri, in 1930, before the town voted to establish municipal power, a spokesman for the Missouri Utility Company estimated that 90 percent of the homes in the town did not have enough electrical outlets to be adequately lighted. In some homes, he said, there were not any outlets in some rooms, and in other homes a person could only use one appliance at a time because of the lack of outlets. Private utilities continued to resist spending money for basic household improvements until the onset of the Great Depression, when drastic drops in business and industrial power use forced private utilities to turn to the domestic market to cut their losses. In 1935, after private utilities had turned to the domestic market, *Electric World* stated: "Interest has centered in the home this year. . . . Because of the depression, neither factory, store nor office has presented a hopeful field for rapid development."[73]

Another and admittedly imperfect way of examining electrical modernization is through an examination of family radio ownership. Radios are often thought to be ubiquitous features of American life in the 1920s and early 1930s. At the end of the decade the radio, some argue, had become an "electric hearth" that families gathered around "to hear crackling reports from great distances, baseball games, and the latest music."[74] Despite the popularity of the radio in the late 1920s, most American families did not own one. Examining the actual number of families with radios rather than the total number of radios sold, since some families might have owned more than one radio, gives a better indication of the everyday experience of Americans regarding their access to electrical technology. In 1930, 40.3 percent of all American families had at least one radio. In the nation's urban areas the radio was just starting to become a common feature in many households. According to the Census Bureau, 58 percent of American families lived in areas defined as urban, and exactly half of those urban families owned at least one radio. In the households of the nation's largest ninety-three cities, those with populations greater than 100,000 in 1930, 53.1 percent of the families owned at least one radio. A much different situation existed in the nation's rural areas, where only 26.9 percent of the families had radios (and 21 percent of the farm families).[75] Given the differences between rural and urban America regarding family ownership of radios, it is not surprising that regional variations also existed. In the more urban East, 55.0 percent of families owned at least one radio, whereas in the North Central region the percentage dropped to 47.8 percent. Forty-four percent of families in the West owned a radio, but in the South only 16.4 percent did.[76]

There is no doubt that income and wealth influenced radio ownership. Lizabeth Cohen, for example, discovered lower levels of family radio ownership among working-class families than among middle-class families in 1930. In five working-class neighborhoods, 44.4 percent of families owned a radio; the percentage of middle-class families with a radio equaled 73.4.[77] These figures do indicate a relationship between income and radio ownership. The data on radios should only be viewed in the context of other available information on appliance ownership and the ability of the American home to technologically support appliance usage.[78] For example, 53 percent of homes in Chicago had a radio, but even fewer homes had less expensive appliances like toasters and percolators.

Public power supporters in the 1920s blamed the lack of widespread electrical modernization on high rates, not on low incomes, inadequate wiring, or some other household factor. They believed that little incentive existed for people to buy appliances as long as rates remained high. Appliance ownership and making structural improvements to their home, including wiring and retrofitting, meant little if people could not afford the energy that appliances required. Although many American homes may have been electrified, most were not modernized, not even in urban areas. Radios and appliances were not ubiquitous, and most Americans did not enjoy the fruits of electrical modernization. That is why the battle over electricity became so passionate in the 1920s. Those favoring public ownership believed that the private utility industry was subverting the promise of electricity and preventing more Americans from enjoying the benefits of electrical modernization. Distinguishing between electrification and electrical modernization provides the picture window through which to view the fight over public power in the 1920s.

People supporting public power believed that the state should intervene to bring the promise of electricity to the entire nation. The issue of load factor emerged again in the 1920s, though not in the same sense as it had several decades earlier. Public power advocates believed that an untapped load-diversifying market existed in urban and rural households. High private rates, however, impeded the development of the household market. When Gifford Pinchot prepared the Giant Power Plan, his idea for connecting all of Pennsylvania's generation and transmission systems into a statewide power grid, he recognized load factor, or what he called "capacity factor." Under Giant Power rural customers would have purchased power at the average rate, except at peak demand times when officials would adjust the rate accordingly. "Only at a few points in the United States," the Pennsylvania governor wrote, "has a sustained effort been made to develop a rural load." Pinchot argued that high domestic rates made low industrial rates possible. He claimed that although the "power trust" sold only 20 percent of its electricity for domestic use, that same 20 percent accounted for two-thirds of the private utility industry's revenue and carried nearly all of the industry's overhead charges. Pinchot reported that when he was Pennsylvania's governor the average wholesale customer paid on average 1.35 cents per kilowatt hour, but the average domestic user paid 8.4 cents per kilowatt hour. Creating a more equitable rate schedule, he believed, would increase evening and nighttime domestic electrical consumption.[79] George Norris echoed Pinchot when he stated that in order to cause widespread household use, the price of electricity must decline. Norris also discussed load factor and said that although most systems could supply peak daytime load, during much of a twenty-four-hour period utilities wasted power.[80] He too thought that lower rates would encourage domestic consumption. J. D. Ross, the longtime head of publicly owned Seattle City Light, said residential usage of electrical appliances including ranges and refrigerators created a "mighty load factor."[81] Ross consistently pointed to the relatively high degree of appliance use in Seattle as evidence that even cheaper power would stimulate the residential market.

Pinchot, Norris, Ross, and other private utility critics in the twenties charged that private utilities had to turn a quick profit to keep their shaky financial arrangements afloat. Public power advocates argued that if private utilities had wanted to, they could have made long-term investments in the domestic market that would have more efficiently diversified load factor, but at a reduced short-term profit. Yet, that is not where private utilities decided to invest, instead opting for the cheaper short-term investment in the nonresidential market. Public power advocates said the need for quick profits influenced that decision.

Since private power refused to take the initiative in lowering rates, the public power movement thought that the state must build projects to force down rates. Several examples underscore the way in which public power supporters thought state intervention could hasten a modernized future. Perhaps the most popular, and debated, in the 1920s involved Giant Power, a proposed dam on the Colorado River, and efforts to further develop the Muscle Shoals region. When Boulder Dam and the TVA finally started to generate electricity in the 1930s, they demonstrated to many the promise of publicly owned electrical generation and distribution systems. The TVA transmitted cheap electricity to homes and industries throughout the Tennessee River Valley. Boulder Dam power, although sold primarily to Southern California, was distributed in Nevada and Arizona. Norris also favored developing the hydroelectric potential of the Potomac River upstream from Washington, D.C., and tying the power into a regional network reaching into New Jersey and New York. These projects, many of which had their origins in the 1920s or earlier, reflected their supporters' belief in the need for public competition through the yardstick principle. Not all electrical systems needed to be publicly owned—only enough to reveal the high cost of privately produced electricity. People then would see that the private utilities overcharged and demand lower rates.

The yardstick principle discloses two more ideological components of the public power mind in the 1920s: they believed in private enterprise, and they did not want to nationalize the electrical utility industry in the United States. Despite the private utility industry's attempts to label public power advocates as socialists or "Bolsheviks," they did not hold such views, believing instead that only some public power networks needed to exist. The other important element of the public power ideology that the yardstick principle revealed is faith in the common citizen. Public power would expose high rates, and then people in towns that private power served could act to lower the private rates. Although public power supporters thought that the public utility industry threatened democracy, they also believed that society could ultimately rein in private power.

A final idea that reflects the public power proponents' attitudes toward reform was their attitudes toward efficiency and expertise. Morris L. Cooke, who heavily influenced the Giant Power Plan, J. D. Ross, and E. F. Scattergood, chief engineer of the Los Angeles public system, epitomized the definition of a new, urban, middle-class reformer. All three were electrical engineers who firmly believed that electrical technology would result in a better future. Each of them deemed electricity a neutral phenomenon that could be used either for or against the public good. Ross and Scattergood heavily influenced the development of public power in Seattle and Los Angeles and actively fought against the private utilities that operated in each city. Cooke became involved in reform politics in Philadelphia and was a strong supporter of Frederick Taylor and scientific management. In the 1920s, besides giving Pinchot engineering expertise, Cooke also conferred with other progressives such as Norris. During the New Deal he advised on TVA and became the Rural Electrification Administration's first administrator, while Ross assumed the same post in the Bonneville Power Administration. Roosevelt's appointment of Cooke and Ross revealed both their political views toward electricity and their knowledge of electrical engineering.[82]

Modernization was very much on the minds of many Americans as the country entered the 1920s. Despite a presidentially proclaimed "return to normalcy," the decade also brought fundamental and long-lasting change. Consumerism, credit, and advertising began to flourish.[83] Regardless of the distorted view that all Americans shared in the prosperity of the decade, the enduring popular image was one of abundance: the image of the roaring twenties. Electricity, electrical modernization, and the expanding electrical utility industry became central characters in the 1920s. Electricity lit downtown streets, powered amusement park rides, and energized factories. All across America people longingly read the advertisements for the latest radios, washing machines, and a host of other appliances. Others thought they could get rich quick by investing in the profitable if risky stock market growth that electrical utility and holding company stocks partially fueled. None of these things happened in a political vacuum. Instead, they became central points in the continuing fight over the control of electricity in the United States in the years before the Great Depression.

CHAPTER TWO

The Consolidation and Influence of the Electrical Utility Industry in the 1920s

In the 1920s Americans, it appeared, had good reason to anticipate a quick leap to an electrically modernized future. Technological and managerial problems that had hampered widespread access to electricity at the turn of the century had become distant memories by World War I. In the twenties economies of scales dominated the electrical utility industry. Expansion occurred in nearly all phases of the industry: there were more customers, greater generating capacity and output, and thousands of miles of new transmission lines. Private and public rates, which had been dropping since the turn of the century, continued to decline throughout the decade. Very much in line with the private utility industry's emphasis on technologically based growth and consolidation, fewer companies existed in the late 1920s than immediately after the war. Throughout the decade private power spokesmen applauded the growth that characterized their industry. Continued expansion in the amount of electricity generated that accompanied rate decreases served as strong testimony to the "grow and build" ideology that prevailed in the industry. Holding companies furthered the trend toward consolidation in the electrical utility industry. The growing public power movement's outcry over perceived monopolistic practices in the private power industry contributed to Congress authorizing the Federal Trade Commission's utility investigations beginning in 1926.

Technological advances, of course, made possible the long-distance transmission of electricity, and utilities were quick to use them. Between 1922 and 1932, utilities constructed sixty-five thousand miles of new transmission lines, an increase of 35.6 percent. Commercial utilities built most of these lines; before 1930, only a handful of states allowed publicly produced power to be sold beyond a municipality's geographic limits.[1] The expansion of the nation's power grid in the 1920s made it theoretically possible to interconnect all of the nation's private utilities into one giant "Super Power" network of electrical utilities.

"Super Power" became a popular term in the 1920s. Industry representatives explained its advantages in economic terms. Super Power, they said, would allow a utility to connect with other systems to meet peak load demands during times of temporary shortages, thereby reducing the need for costly emergency plants that the utility might otherwise need to construct. Thus utility operating costs and capital expenditures would decline and save consumers money.[2] Many electrical utilities also cited these reasons as the rationale for mergers.

Many mergers did occur during this period, but they alone do not explain the consolidation that occurred in the private utility industry. Utility holding companies were a central and controversial feature of the industry. Broadly defined, a holding company "is a company not directly engaged in the business of producing and distributing commodities or services, but which controls such a business through the ownership of stock in operating companies."[3] Through stock ownership and interlocking directorates, a single holding company might control the electrical supply of an entire region. Besides owning operating companies, holding companies often bought controlling stock in other holding companies. Ownership of multiple operating and holding companies resulted in an ownership structure similar in design to a pyramid. Through such a structure one holding company could control the generation, transmission, and marketing of great amounts of electricity.

Private utility spokesmen and their public power counterparts constantly fought over the intent of holding companies. Holding companies were one of the most compelling reasons that Norris, Pinchot, Ross, and many others thought that a "power trust" existed in the United States. They believed that holding companies existed for three simple reasons: to make money, to manipulate public opinion, and to elude state-level regulation of operating companies. Private utility representatives argued that economies of scale, the need for technological transfer, and corporate financing not only justified but demanded holding companies.

An example of the structure of holding companies is depicted in Figure 2.1. In the diagram each holding company controls 51 percent of the stock of the holding or operating companies on the tier below it. Holding and operating companies sold common stock, preferred stock, and bonds to raise capital. H. S. Raushenbush and Harry W. Laidler, in their 1928 book *Power Control*, provided examples of purchasing and marketing procedures that they believed typical to illustrate the breakdown in investment options and the enormous profits that holding companies could reap.

The eight hypothetical operating companies in Figure 2.1 "typically" invested $400,000 in 5.5 percent bonds, $120,000 in nonvoting 7.0 percent preferred stock, and $280,000 in common stock. The first holding company would purchase from the operating companies A, B, C, and D 14 percent of their bonds ($28,000), 50 percent of their preferred stock ($30,000), and 90 percent of their common stock ($126,000) for a total investment of $184,000. The first holding company would market its securities (those purchased from companies A, B, C, and D) by selling $46,000 in 5.5 percent bonds (25 percent of the total), $58,880 in 7.0 preferred bonds (32 per-

Figure 2.1 Model of Holding Company Structure

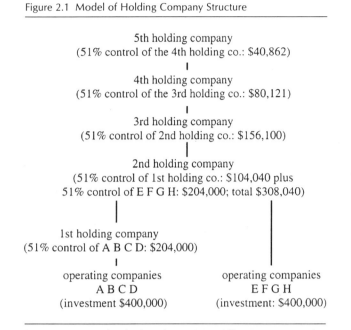

5th holding company
(51% control of the 4th holding co.: $40,862)

|

4th holding company
(51% control of the 3rd holding co.: $80,121)

|

3rd holding company
(51% control of 2nd holding co.: $156,100)

|

2nd holding company
(51% control of 1st holding co.: $104,040 plus
51% control of E F G H: $204,000; total $308,040)

|

1st holding company
(51% control of A B C D: $204,000)

|

operating companies   operating companies
A B C D   E F G H
(investment $400,000)   (investment: $400,000)

Source: H. S. Raushenbush and Harry W. Laidler, *Power Control* (New York, 1928), 61–64.

cent of the total), and finally the remaining $79,120 (43 percent) in common stock. If the four operating companies realized a profit of 8 percent (the amount that state regulatory commissions often allowed), the result would be a profit of $32,000. The first holding company would receive $18,760 on its investments in operating companies A, B, C, and D. After meeting the 5.5 percent bond obligation ($2,530) and paying 7.0 percent to preferred stockholders ($4,122), $12,108 remained for the first holding company to pay as dividends on its common stock, which translates into a return of 15.3 percent.

A second holding company would repeat the scenario by buying 14 percent of the bonds, 50 percent of the preferred stock, and 90 percent of the common stock that the first holding company and operating companies E, F, G, and H sold. It would market these investments, totaling $291,088, in bonds (25 percent), preferred stock (32 percent), and common stock (43 percent). The second holding company would receive the following profit from the first holding company and operating companies E, F, G, and H: $26,017 (90 percent of the common stock dividend), $4,161 (50 percent of the preferred stock dividend), and $1,894 (14 percent of the bond dividend) for a total return of $32,072. From that amount the second company would pay $4,002 on bond interest and $6,520 on preferred stock. It would pay the remaining $21,550 on the common stock, a 17 percent dividend. A third holding company could own the second holding company. If the third company followed the same purchasing and marketing percentages for bonds, preferred stock, and common stock, the common stock dividend would equal 23.5 percent. Before the establishment of the Securities and Exchange Commission, people could purchase stock on a 10 percent margin. That meant that the second holding company would need only about $6,400 to secure control of the first holding company and the four operating companies. If the fourth and fifth holding companies repeated the purchasing and marketing options, they would pay dividends of 33.1 and 48 percent respectively on their common stock.

As Raushenbush and Laidler discussed, the voting majority of the fifth holding company, which only would have to control 51 percent of that company's common stock ($605 if bought on a 10 percent margin), could dictate the actions of the eight operating companies whose total investment equaled $800,000.[4] In actuality a holding company could increase the number of holding or operating companies at the lower tiers of the model. Such action could be undertaken at little expense to the holding company at the top of the pyramid. The model used small sums of money and only a few companies, whereas actual holding companies often controlled tremendous amounts of money with very little investment (although that investment paid high dividends). Through holding companies, one analysis estimated, a $23,100 investment controlled the Standard Gas and Electric Company, which had a total net worth of $1.2 billion.[5]

Holding companies allowed a handful of utilities to control the electrical industry in the United States, although the Census Bureau reported that more than 2,100 operating companies existed in 1927. In 1925, for example, the five largest holding companies controlled 46.9 percent of electrical production in the United States, the next eight companies generated an additional 22.6 percent, and, finally, seven more companies produced 13.6 percent. Together, twenty holding companies controlled 83 percent of the nation's electrical production. In 1930 eleven holding companies were responsible for 85 percent of the generation capacity in the country.[6] That concentration led to the term "power trust."

On the regional, state, and local level, friends of public power believed that a power trust existed that manipulated both electrical rates and public opinion. Although Super Power never became a reality, public power proponents thought that a national power trust was present in a shared industry ideology. Norris and others, for example, believed such a shared industrial outlook emphasized avoidance of regulation, maximum profit, and hostility toward public power that linked together holding companies and independent operating companies. They also pointed to interlocking directorates and the National Electric Light Association (NELA), the national trade association of private electrical utilities, as additional evidence of common interests among private utility executives and managers.

Industry spokesmen and organizations friendly to private utilities disputed claims that holding companies ruled the industry. NELA maintained that no single holding company controlled more than 7 percent of the kilowatt hours produced in the United States.[7] A brief examination of one holding company, however, reveals the extent of their influence. Samuel Insull of Chicago oversaw the most famous holding company network of the era. The Insull empire was only one example of the large-scale financing and stock ownership that existed in the electrical utility industry in the 1920s.

In the mid-1920s the Insulls owned stock in five midwestern companies. Three were holding companies. In only one company, Midland United Company, did the Insulls maintain majority control of the voting stock. Yet, they retained influence through interlocking directorates, the practice of having a small group of individuals sit on the board of directors of several different companies. Samuel Insull, the family patriarch, served as chairman of the board for all five companies. His son, Samuel Jr., was vice chairman of four of the boards and president of the fifth. Martin Insull, Samuel Insull Sr.'s brother, was president of the largest of the five companies, Middle West Utilities, and a director of the other four. The Insulls were not the only people to hold several directorships. Two other men, who served as presidents of the Public Service Company of Northern Illinois and of Commonwealth Edison, also served on the boards of two of the companies of which an Insull was president. Nine other men held directorships on the boards of at least two of the five companies.[8] Thus a small group of people controlled the actions of the five companies.

In December 1928 the Insulls formed Insull Utility Investment Incorporated to extend their control. Less than a year later, they founded the Corporation Securities Company of Chicago. These companies bought substantial blocks of voting stock in the five other Insull companies.[9] Corporation Securities also owned 28.8 percent of Insull Utility Investment stock, and Insull Utility Investment held 19.7 percent of Corporation Securities' stock. Samuel Insull Sr. chaired each board, and Samuel Jr. served as president of both companies. Martin Insull held a directorship in each company. At the end of 1930 the two companies' assets totaled $400 million.[10] The structure of the Insulls' widespread geographic interests is illustrated in Figure 2.2.

In stock circulars Middle West Utilities Company executives defended the wide geographic distribution of their operating companies, arguing that it made the company financially secure. "The income of the Company is stabilized by a large diversity factor, resulting from the diversified nature of the communities and industries served by the subsidiaries."[11] The stock

Figure 2.2 Major Elements in the Insull System (in millions of dollars) as of December 31, 1930

		States Operating in
	Midland United, 50%+ (352.5)* 30 subsidiaries	DE, IL, IN, MI, OH
Insull Utility Investment Inc.	Public Service Co. of N. Illinois, 11.5% (210)* 1 subsidiary	DE, IL
	Middle West Utilities, 29.2% (1,200)* 111 subsidiaries	AL, AK, DE, FL, GA, IL, IN, KS, KY, LA, ME, MD, MI, MS, MO, NE, NH, NJ, NY, NC, ND, OH, OK, PA, SC, SD, TN, TX, VT, VA, WV, WI, and Canada
Corporation Securities of Chicago	Commonwealth Edison, 17.2% (450)* 6 subsidiaries	IL, KY, VA
	Peoples Gas Light and Coke, 28.8% (211)* 8 subsidiaries	IL

*Assets in millions of dollars
Total assets: $2,423,500,000
Total subsidiaries: 156
Percent figure is amount of company stock owned by parent company
Holding companies: Peoples Gas Light and Coke, Commonwealth Edison, and Public Service Co. of Northern Illinois
Sources: James C. Bonbright and Gardiner Means, *The Holding Company: Its Public Significance and Its Regulation* (New York, 1932), 109; U.S. Federal Trade Commission, *Annual Report,* 1932 (Washington, DC, 1932), 17; and Federal Trade Commission diagram, "Insull Group Corporate Relations, Approximately January 1, 1932," contained in M. L. Ramsay, *Pyramids of Power: The Story of Roosevelt, Insull, and the Utility Wars* (New York, 1975), diagram follows p. 244.

circular contained an illustration that equated growth in miles of transmission lines with increased stock value. In 1921 the company owned 4,446 miles of line; by 1926 the mileage had more than doubled to 12,071 miles. As proof of investment security the circular noted that the company's common stock increased in value from $8.22 in 1921 to $15.66 in 1925.[12] The language of the stock bulletin also underscores the growth culture of the electrical utility industry. Only continued expansion would ensure future success, especially in monetary terms.

The widespread geographical dispersion of the Insull operating companies appeared to rule out interconnected electrical distribution systems as the only reason for holding companies. The Insulls were not the exception to the rule. Smaller holding companies also controlled widely geographically dispersed properties. The Stone and Webster financial group of Boston, which controlled 2 percent of the nation's electrical supply, held majority stock in such geographically dispersed companies as Virginia Electric and Power, Puget Sound Power and Light, and Columbus (Ohio) Electric.[13] Defenders of holding companies explained the lack of contiguous properties as a result of acquisitions in exchange for expertise or equipment, something that did occur in the early days of the electrical utility industry. Their opponents cited less than altruistic reasons for such diverse ownership.

An examination of the largest stockholders of the Southern California Edison Company in 1930 shows the complex nature of public utility stock sales and control. SCE was the eighth largest electrical utility in the United States in 1928.[14] The company first began selling stock in June 1917 and in 1926 claimed to have 91,000 stockholders with holdings exceeding $83 million.[15] SCE officials quickly recognized the advantage that a monopoly provided when raising money. During each stock selling campaign, company officials constantly stressed the importance of investments to guarantee a person's economic future. In 1917 A. N. Kemp, the company's comptroller, wrote, "In these rapidly changing times, it behooves everyone to save, and then to make their savings work for them at the highest rate of interest commensurate with safety."[16]

The safe and conservative investment Kemp referred to was, of course, the purchase of SCE securities. Kemp then, apparently unknowingly, sketched out the basic arguments for one of the biggest political battles of the 1920s when he stated why SCE stock was such a safe investment. He first noted the rapid growth of the motion picture industry in the United States, claiming that it was the nation's fourth largest industry, and said that it was "dependent largely upon electricity in its many varied forms for its successful operation."[17] Kemp then put forth what would become the centerpiece of the debate over private power: SCE had a virtual regulated monopoly on the electric power business in Southern California, a monopoly that included control of most "street cars, railroads, industrial and residence [power], street and commercial lighting."[18] He finished by saying, "It is in this great public utility that we are permitting you to become a profit sharer."[19] Fred L. Greenhouse, investment department manager, displayed the same attitude in a letter to a potential investor several years later when he said, "The additional development of power is essential to the continued growth of this section, which in turn will be reflected in increased values for all."[20]

Kemp's letter contained all the elements needed to convince the potential investor to purchase stock. It also spelled out, in its briefest form, the debates over public utility stock sales and purchases. What is surprising is Kemp's clarity in describing the situation. His first point was that Hollywood's expanding motion picture industry depended on electricity and would need more power for continued expansion. Second, SCE enjoyed a regulated monopoly. The inference is clear: the growing population of Southern California generally, and the motion picture industry specifically, would need increased amounts of electricity that only SCE could provide. The third point revolved around the phrase "profit sharer." Public service appeared to go out the window. Profit was the company's motivating factor in convincing people to purchase stock, a profit that a society dependent on electricity nearly guaranteed and that a regulated monopoly provided. These three elements—indispensable electricity, monopoly, and profit—became the major points of public power attacks on private utilities.

Southern California Edison boasted more than 100,000 stockholders by the late 1920s, although a small group of individuals or investment corporations controlled most of the voting common stock. Of the top twenty shareholders of Edison common stock with voting privileges, only six were individuals; the remainder were businesses or corporations.[21] The top twenty shareholders controlled 389,094 shares of common stock at the close of 1930 (see Appendix 2.1). Of that number John Miller, chairman of SCE, owned 9.1 percent; Russell Ballard, president of SCE, owned 3.4 percent; Albert Harris, who was the voting trustee for both the Norman Harris estate and Harris Trust and Savings Bank, controlled 8.8 percent; and C. C. Ward, SCE's executive vice president, owned 2.6 percent. Both Ward and Harris served on SCE's board of directors as did Ballard, Miller, and A. N. Kemp. Together Miller, Ballard, Harris, and Ward controlled nearly 94,000 shares of SCE's common stock.[22] Equally important, these five individuals held five of the thirteen seats on the company's board of directors. Most of the fourteen business enterprises owning SCE stock were involved in banking or other businesses friendly to a private utility making a profit and probably would not oppose the actions of the five men. The officers of the company acquired proxies from other owners of common stock to augment their voting. SCE undertook to secure proxies from individuals who owned more than one hundred shares of common stock. When the shareholder signed the proxy, he gave John Miller, R. H. Ballard, George Cochran, and Henry Robinson the power to vote. Each proxy, unless revoked, remained in effect for seven years.[23] Cochran and Robinson also served on the company's board of directors. Thus, six individuals with either direct ownership or control of stock through proxies served on SCE's board of directors. The addition of Kemp gave the group a majority of votes.

Publicly, Southern California Edison tried to create the image of a locally owned utility through stock sales to the people of Southern California. A 1926 questionnaire, compiled for SCE stock sales agents, stated that the objective of stock sales was to "obtain as large a body as possible of

'Satisfied Stockholders' among our consumers, thereby keeping owner-ship of the company at home." The company "emphatically" denied any political reasons for selling stock, such as securing votes for unpopular measures.[24] Regardless of SCE's contention that it wanted local owner-ship, the list of the top twenty holders of common stock suggests other-wise. Seventeen of the twenty had mailing addresses outside California; of those, eleven were in New York City and the largest was in Quebec, Canada.[25] Only twenty-seven of the top sixty owners of Edison's origi-nal preferred, 6 percent preferred, and 7 percent preferred stock (twenty for each) resided in California.[26] Therefore, despite Edison's claims, the individuals and corporations with the greatest financial interests in the company were not located in its service area.

The issues of stock control and sales in relation to electrical holding companies provide insights into the entire debate over public power in the 1920s. Critics of holding companies did not accept that they were either inevitable or necessary. Instead, they thought that greed motivated indi-viduals to organize holding companies to maximize profits at the public's expense. Proponents of holding companies argued the opposite. They ac-cepted that technological factors and financial considerations required the widespread control that holding companies allowed. That issue stood at the center of the much larger debate over economic trusts that drove the entire public power fight before the New Deal.

Norris and his allies did not believe that holding companies were re-quired in modern industrial societies and vigorously expressed their op-position. Spokesmen for private utilities undertook an extensive campaign through their trade associations to persuade the public that the beliefs of public power advocates were misguided. The entire issue became a politi-cal one because of the need for society to decide how to generate and dis-tribute electricity in the United States. The two major concerns were: would generation and distribution occur through privately controlled holding companies or through other means; and who would benefit from electri-cal energy—society in general or business and industry? Public power spokesmen believed that public ownership would provide the most effi-cient and cheapest way for all society to benefit from electrical use. Begin-ning in the mid-1920s, holding companies came under fire as many books and articles started to examine them and their practices.

James C. Bonbright, professor of finance at Columbia, and Gardiner C. Means, also of Columbia, studied the history of holding companies in the United States and examined in depth several major industrial, public utility, and railroad holding companies in existence in the late 1920s. The authors concluded that in theory holding companies existed for four po-tential reasons: to centralize management or control; to unite two or more companies under the same financial structure; to refinance a company by exchanging holding company securities for an operating company's securities; and to pyramid voting to control subsidiary companies with a minimum investment.[27] Bonbright and Means also offered a list of the advantages for the holding company: ease of organization, ease of control by the organizers, ability to combine business that could not occur under direct ownership, secrecy of combinations, accounts and operation, freedom from regulation, decentralized management, lower liability to creditors, and ease of selling properties. The list of disadvantages included problems of complete integration because of minority stockholders and creditors; expensive, top-heavy financial structures; cost of creating and maintaining separate organizations; and possibilities of breakups against the wishes of controlling interests.[28]

Many advantages and disadvantages that Bonbright and Means discussed revolved around finances, secrecy, and ease of incorporation (often to sidestep the law). In their discussion of public utility holding companies, Bonbright and Means took a more critical view of the actual situation. To them, the two primary reasons for "centralized control" were the "greater financial strength" of large utility systems and the "efficiency and economy of centralized management or supervision by . . . highly skilled experts."[29] These were services not otherwise available to small companies. However, Bonbright and Means also stated that the desire of engineers and manufacturers to control utility properties in order to secure markets for the sale of goods and services resulted in holding company systems of such size that they "could not be justified on the grounds of engineering or managerial efficiency." They also questioned the involvement of bankers in utility management, which they believed exacerbated the situation.[30] Public utilities had avoided public service and regulation to such a degree that Bonbright and Means believed that they threatened the entire idea of government-regulated private ownership in the United States.[31]

The advocates of public power quickly agreed with Bonbright and Means's criticisms. New Republic Incorporated published the Raushenbush and Laidler book *Power Control* in 1928 on the heels of the first FTC investigation. Throughout the debate over public and private power, the *New Republic* favored public ownership and harshly criticized private power. Raushenbush and Laidler noted that the rationale often given for the creation of giant systems was to distribute electricity efficiently throughout the United States, but there was no particular manner in how holding companies brought operating companies under their control. Centralized systems existed, although some holding companies, such as the Insull network and Stone and Webster, controlled operating companies scattered throughout the country: "the planning had been competitive and haphazard."[32] Bonbright and Means also believed financial motives drove holding companies when they wrote that "all of the large holding-company systems to-day [sic] control properties which cannot be physically integrated even under the most ambitious plans for superpower transmission."[33] Lacking a unified plan for consolidation and arguing that (economic) competition drove the creation of holding companies, Raushenbush and Laidler said that the quest for quick and easy financial gain represented the real motivation behind the creation of utility holding companies.[34]

The desire for profit and the speculative nature of the entire enterprise was the weakness of the holding company pyramid. If growth and profits increased, holding companies and investors made money. Any economic slowdown might cause reverse leverage and result in losses.[35] A decline in an operating company's earnings meant that each holding company in the pyramid would show even bigger losses since it held more shares of common stock. If the common stock of the first holding company did not generate revenue, the holding company would be hard-pressed to meet its bond and preferred stock obligations, let alone pay handsome common stock dividends. Failure of the first holding company to meet its obligations caused the second and subsequent holding companies to default on their obligations.

The ever-increasing returns on common stock made holding companies financially possible. Essentially, the owners of holding company stock held "paper wealth." Only the original investors of the operating companies' stocks and bonds held safe stock. In most states, regulatory agencies supervised the allowable return on operating company bond and stock sales and the frequency of security sales, but they did not monitor either a holding company's security sales or returns. An example is Puget Sound Power and Light (PSP&L), then headquartered in Seattle. The state of Washington regulated PSP&L's rates and approved the company's stock and bond sales. However, the Stone and Webster Holding Company of Boston controlled PSP&L, and because Stone and Webster was a holding company and located outside the state, it eluded Washington state regulation. Stone and Webster evaded Massachusetts's regulators because it did not engage in the production of electricity. Of course, it was those regulations that holding companies often wanted to avoid in the first place, and avoiding regulation was one reason holding companies located themselves in states different from the operating companies that they controlled.[36]

Trade associations linked together many different operating and holding companies in the United States and contributed to a common business culture in the electrical utility business. In 1926 private utility companies with NELA memberships controlled more than 90 percent of the electricity generated in the country.[37] Besides the national organization, twelve divisional organizations existed in the United States and one in Canada. These divisional associations operated within NELA and mirrored the national organization's structure. The Northwest Electric Light and Power Association, consisting of the private utilities in Oregon, Washington, Idaho, Utah, Montana, and Alaska, was one of these regional organizations.

In 1923 the Northwest Electric Light and Power Association held its sixteenth annual convention in Seattle. In his opening address, A. W. Leonard, president of PSP&L, discussed the advantages of trade associations. He stated that standardization, improved service, cheaper rates, and better industry-wide conditions grew out of organizations such as NELA and its divisional associations.[38] No doubt Leonard's words contained much truth, as standardization of many products in the American economy contributed to economic growth in the 1920s.[39] Many industrial and professional organizations existed then, and continue to exist, which provided forums for exchanging new ideas and technology. Critics of private power, NELA, and its regional associations, however, charged that the organizations went beyond mere forums for exchanging ideas and operated as propaganda machines intent on destroying public power sentiment in the United States. Raushenbush and Laidler contended that a 1927 NELA bulletin stated that the organization planned to spend $10 million on advertising in 1927, while public utilities intended to spend about $28 million on advertising in the same year.[40]

An example of the activities that critics of the public utilities charged as propaganda occurred at the 1923 Seattle meeting. Northwest Electric Light and Power Association officials announced that they would award a $1,000 college scholarship to the Washington high school student who wrote the best essay on "Government Regulation of Public Utilities."[41] A *Seattle Star* editorial, the town's pro–public power newspaper, called the contest "insidious propaganda intended to fill the impressionable minds of our school children with partisanship and cheap advertising."[42] According to the *Star*, the contest organizers distributed three anti–public ownership pamphlets to each student as writing guides for the essay. Norwood Brockett of PSP&L denied any wrongdoing and said that the pamphlets were information sources available to every student interested in writing an essay. The pamphlets, he continued, prevented students in larger schools with better libraries from having an advantage over students with less access to source material. The scholarship, he said, not only would provide financial help to a student but also would encourage the study of utility regulation.[43] Washington's superintendent of public schools, Josephine C. Preston, supported the distribution of the pamphlets, but FTC investigators later discovered that PSP&L had paid her $150 to help prepare the pamphlets.[44]

The Washington essay contest and the distribution of pamphlet material were part of NELA's much larger effort to influence public opinion. In 1924 the organization allocated $500,000 as prize money for essays of junior and senior high school students. The purpose of the essay program was "'public good-will' and to 'render a definite educational service' to 12,000,000 homes through children in those homes, thus creating 'public relations possibilities.'"[45] NELA officials hoped that the campaign would dampen any enthusiasm that might exist for public power. Contest promoters advertised the competition in national magazines and in local and school newspapers. NELA considered the money well spent and admitted that the real purpose for the contest was to "disseminate information."[46]

NELA representatives actively worked to gain the support of university professors and students through direct payment and textbook contracts. Believing that only college professors could reach young people, NELA officials and representatives of Middle West Utilities Company developed a plan at a 1923 meeting to contract with college professors. They could obtain a professor's favor through a variety of employment options: supplementing salaries, offering professional employment, financing fellowships, commissioning special studies, giving speeches, attending conferences, or helping with book writing. NELA considered college professors members of the "Starveling Professions" and thus anxious to earn extra money. Dr. C. A. Eaton, president of the American Educational Association and manager of industrial relations for General Electric, put the plan into practice at the 1924 NELA convention when he told the utility people to put educators on salary during vacation periods. Eaton inferred that increased salaries would prevent low-paid educators from advocating socialism.[47]

Public power proponents voiced great alarm at NELA's attempts to bribe college professors, since they believed that a democracy depended on an educated citizenship. Any attempts to influence research and education toward a particular political view not only undermined the educational process but democracy as well. NELA's apparent attempts to influence college professors exceed any idea that corporations needed specialized education to support science-based industry.[48] Instead, NELA wanted to pay professors to present a specific political view to their students. Ironically, Richard Ely, who in 1899 thought that increased civic virtue through education would allow a person to identify economic problems and was one of the first to articulate the need for a middle ground between socialism and unrestrained capitalism, became involved in one of the most publicized accounts of alleged influence peddling involving public utilities, universities, and college professors in the 1920s.

Ely founded the Institute for Research in Land Economics in 1920 with the avowed purpose of scientifically studying the land economic issues of his day. Broadly defined, land economics involves the study of land and nature as an economic resource. Ely recognized that this definition encompassed a wide area of study but thought it necessary because of the different types and uses of land. He and his associates, for example, studied land taxation and how different types of land merited different forms of taxes. To explain his beliefs on the need for different taxation systems, Ely discussed farmland and forestland. Because of the vastly different maturity rates of grain and lumber, he held that the government needed to develop different tax codes. Ely included public utilities in the institute's research agenda because of the relation of land to utilities.[49] Hydroelectric and coal power may be the best examples of that relation: both originate in land and contribute directly to electrical production.

Critics from across the nation started to assail Ely and the institute in the mid-1920s when they began questioning NELA's propaganda activities. The central issue was the financing of the institute's research. Although affiliated first with the University of Wisconsin and then, beginning in the fall of 1925, with Northwestern University, Ely depended on private contributions to finance research projects. The institute moved to Evanston because of its proximity to Chicago. Ely believed that moving the institute to a large urban center would enhance its reputation and make it easier to secure financial support. Additionally, Chicago was the center of commercial activity in agricultural trade, real estate, and public utilities.[50] The Insulls, who Ely tapped for substantial contributions, also lived in the Chicago area.

Even before moving to Chicago, NELA and the Insulls agreed to fund the institute. Both parties contributed enthusiastically. Martin Insull, who personally gave $2,500 in 1924, acted for the Public Relations Section of NELA and secured funding for the institute before the move to Northwestern. In a letter to the dean of Northwestern's School of Commerce, Insull stated that NELA would contribute $25,000 per year for five years. He noted that the public relations committee believed that when the institute's research involved issues of "the electric light and power business," it should focus on "a study of government in business, especially municipal, state, and federal ownership of public utilities." Each year between 1927 and 1930, NELA gave Ely $25,000 for research.[51] The money that NELA contributed did not come from the association's general fund. Instead, NELA's Public Policy Committee controlled a yearly budget of $100,000 from which the institute received its support.[52] Although NELA did not say what the research should conclude, it is likely that the association would oppose advocacy of public power and frown on studies critical of private power. The institute also took money from other people or businesses with direct ties to the electrical utility industry, including Byllesby Engineering, the president of General Electric, and the Westinghouse Corporation.

Ely also solicited individual operating companies for financial support. In 1926 he asked the San Antonio Public Service Company for a contribution of between $100 and $1,000.[53] Ely requested a greater sum of money from Southern California Edison. In 1926 the institute began a study of municipal power in Los Angeles. William Thum, a strong advocate of municipal ownership and former mayor of Pasadena (which publicly distributed electricity), contributed $5,000 for the Los Angeles electrical system study. In December 1926 Ely requested an equal amount from R. H. Ballard, then vice president and general manager of SCE.[54]

Ely did not limit his correspondences with Ballard to the issue of studying power in Los Angeles. Later in December 1926 Ely wrote Ballard asking for any suggestions he might offer regarding a bibliography Ely was preparing. Morris Cooke's name appeared on the bibliography, and Ballard suggested that Ely remove his name, stating that Cooke had failed to make a contribution of "interest or importance" to the issue of public utilities and seemed "quite socialistic."[55] Ely responded that Cooke's work had "attracted some attention" and excluding it might give the impression of being biased.[56] In the letter enclosed with the bibliography, Ely again solicited money from Ballard but suggested that he avoid any reference to NELA.[57] The fact that Ely wanted the NELA involvement hidden suggests that he knew of the potential public relation risks if it became known that the institute received NELA money.

Ely also maintained contact with individuals from NELA on matters relating to studies the institute published. In 1927 G. F. Oxley of the NELA sent Ely a note regarding his introduction in an institute-sponsored textbook that University of Wisconsin professor Martin Glaeser wrote on public utilities. Oxley recommended that Ely delete a reference to the organization.[58] Ely wanted Glaeser to join him at Northwestern, but Glaeser refused because he feared that the public utilities might "unduly" influence the institute's work. Glaeser based his belief in part on the "rather substantial financial support" that NELA contributed to the institute.[59] He also reported that while preparing his manuscript Ely asked if he would accept a utility company official as the book's coauthor. The unnamed utility man believed that the book could become, in Glaeser's words, "a public utility bible." Later, someone suggested Ely as a possible coauthor, but Glaeser refused.

When the book neared completion, an unidentified person approached Glaeser about writing a special edition for NELA. The individual told him that NELA would buy forty thousand copies with part of the profits going to the institute. Glaeser, who intimated that Ely solicited the offer, refused the proposition. After the publisher received the manuscript, an NELA representative asked Glaeser to delete Ely's reference to the association. Glaeser instructed the organization to contact Ely. According to Glaeser, NELA threatened to obtain a court injunction to delay publication unless he deleted all references to the organization. The general counsel to NELA's Educational Committee, who obtained proofs of the book, called it "the most damaging book which has come out against the public utility industry in recent years."[60] It is not clear who gave Glaeser's manuscript to NELA, but Ely and the institute would have gained materially from a book friendly to the industry.

Several years later a similar incident occurred. In 1929 the institute published Herbert Dorau's *The Changing Character and Extent of Municipal Ownership in the Electric Light and Power Industry.* Before the actual publication Ely sent a copy of the book's proofs to Paul S. Clapp, the managing director of NELA. Ely said that Dorau wrote the book "'without fear or favor.' Indeed, we have tried to lean a little backward not to make it more favorable to private ownership than the facts warrant."[61] Ely also alluded to an earlier statement in which Clapp said he would use the NELA to try to secure sales of the book, as many as forty thousand copies, to the association's member companies.[62]

Although no prima facie evidence exists that links the solicitation of funds for the institute in exchange for preferential treatment of private utilities, it certainly seems that Ely went beyond merely asking for financial support. The fact that he knew Ballard, Oxley, and Clapp well enough to check bibliographies, request changes in introductions, read proofs, and most likely exchange manuscripts suggests a relationship that went beyond impartial support. Ely himself seemed to develop a split personality over the issue. Throughout the 1920s he maintained an uncompromising belief in the scientific inquiry of economic issues. He also seemed to have recognized that he had put himself in a tenuous position and probably violated his academic integrity when he accepted funding and suggestions from public utility interests. An episode in the winter of 1925–1926 disclosed Ely's uneasiness shortly after he moved to Evanston. In January 1926 he wrote the manager of the Public Service Company of Northern Illinois, the Insull-controlled private utility that served Evanston, to complain about his electric bill. He believed that his home had a faulty electric meter since his bill exceeded by several times what it had been in Madison the previous winter. In requesting service Ely said that he wanted to avoid appealing to the state regulatory commission because "of my relations to the public utilities, receiving support for our work from the National Electric Light Association and also from gentlemen prominently identified with various public utilities."[63] The implication is clear: Ely did not want to antagonize his supporters.

The definitive turning point for Ely and his relationship to public utilities may have been in April 1928 when he wrote an article, "Chicago: The Public Utility Capital of the United States," for the *Chicago Tribune Survey,* in which he did nothing but praise public utilities.[64] "The public utilities display some of the best qualities of youth waxing into maturity," Ely wrote. Later he commented, "One respect in which the public utilities of Chicago and elsewhere are exercising leadership is in the promotion of education and fearless research." The Institute for Research in Land and Public Utilities had "been encouraged to search for truth fearlessly." Ely quoted a Chicago utility executive who said "the truth shall make you free." With such high praise for private utilities when revelations regarding the electrical utilities' propaganda activities were making the national news, it is not surprising that Ely fell from grace among liberals and progressives.

In 1929 the Federal Trade Commission began investigating Ely and the institute as part of its general investigation of the electrical industry. Robert Healy, the FTC's chief counsel, wrote Ely asking for a statement detailing the extent of NELA's financial support of the institute.[65] In a long and angry reply to Healy, Ely denied any wrongdoing and lashed out at his critics. He disavowed that the institute received money for propaganda and said that "sensational writers" had manipulated information to undermine scientific economic research. Ely cited as an example the press portraying him as opposing Boulder Dam although he had not studied the issue sufficiently to formulate an opinion. He did add that he thought President Hoover's actions were praiseworthy regarding the dam. In concluding, Ely stated that he did not oppose municipal ownership and believed that the scientific study of economics guaranteed impartiality.[66]

Ely wrote Gifford Pinchot on the same day he replied to Healy to ascertain Pinchot's opinion on the subject of public utilities and universities. In his letter to Pennsylvania's governor, Ely enclosed a copy of the Healy letter.[67] Pinchot's response could hardly have pleased Ely since he wrote that to accept contributions from power companies for research "under the present circumstances is utterly wrong." Pinchot believed that ulterior motives influenced utility contributions and that they would not make contributions unless they produced favorable results. The governor said financial combinations and private utilities wanted to control public sentiment. In conclusion he said that he believed Northwestern University committed a serious mistake, one that he hoped it would not repeat.[68] The Pennsylvania governor had quickly recognized what Ely and his associates did not want to see.

The FTC and Pinchot may have been among the best known of Ely's critics, but they were not the only ones. In response to an institute questionnaire, the secretary-treasurer of the League of Iowa Municipalities said he was unsure if he wanted to help an organization that was backed by private utilities. The writer questioned the usefulness of any of the institute's studies, except for propaganda purposes, if private utilities financed it. He also expressed his dismay that Ely had surrendered his independence to the power companies.[69]

Ely's troubles had begun even before the institute moved to Evanston. In 1924 the Manufacturers and Merchants Federal Tax League charged that he received money from large corporations that opposed fair taxes and sought "privilege and monopoly." The league charged that propaganda, not research, motivated Ely and the institute. He dismissed the charges and claimed that the league merely wanted a single tax—a tax system he opposed.[70] Emil Jorgensen was probably one of the "sensational writers" Ely had referred to in his 1929 letter to Robert Healy. Jorgensen, of the Manufacturers and Merchants League, launched a highly critical attack on Ely and the institute. In 1924 and 1925 he penned a series of articles published in the league's monthly bulletin that castigated Ely for being an agent of the private utilities with the purpose of influencing public education and opinion. After the last article appeared, Jorgensen and the league republished them in book form. The book's title accurately sums up the tone of the articles: *False Education in Our Colleges and Universities.*[71] The main theme of the articles and book was that special interests, including the electrical utilities, controlled Ely and the institute. The public considered Ely an unbiased authority on the issues the institute studied because of his well-established academic reputation. Instead, he had sold himself out and was undermining the public good while hiding behind his academic reputation. Jorgensen and the league took it as their civic duty to expose the real Ely.

During the years that Jorgensen and others criticized Ely, public power spokesmen in the U.S. Senate, led by Senator Norris, began to voice alarm about the corruption and influence peddling of highly financed senatorial campaigns. The two most disputed Senate campaigns took place in 1926 in states where the fight over private utilities and public power held special significance, Illinois and Pennsylvania.[72] The 1926 Republican primary in Pennsylvania featured three candidates: Williams S. Vare, a congressman from Philadelphia who headed that city's political machine and opposed prohibition; the incumbent senator, George Pepper; and the progressive Republican Gifford Pinchot. Vare easily defeated Pepper and Pinchot and seemed a sure victor in November, as winning the Republican primary was tantamount to victory in the general election. Controversy ensued, however, when reports revealed that Vare spent between $2 million and $5 million during the primary.

Norris and others viewed that revelation as essentially an attempt to purchase a Senate seat, and they feared that the buyers would want preferential treatment. Although himself a Republican, the Nebraska senator called on Pennsylvania voters to break with precedent and vote for the Democratic candidate, William Wilson, in the general election. Norris called the expenditures "a threat 'to the fundamental principles that underlie every free government'" in an article entitled "Patriot's Duty in Pennsylvania." He also took to the political stump across Pennsylvania and called for Vare's defeat.[73] Vare ultimately won the election, although the Senate referred his credentials to the Privileges and Elections Committee and denied him his seat until the Senate resolved the controversy; consequently, only one senator represented Pennsylvania until December 1929. Then the Senate approved two resolutions; the first officially declared Vare ineligible and a second said Wilson had not been properly elected. Finally, Pennsylvania's governor appointed Joseph R. Grundy to the seat, ending the controversy.[74] Grundy was no friend of public ownership. During the 1924 presidential election, he referred to the Progressive ticket candidates Robert La Follette Sr. and Burton K. Wheeler as "Lenine [sic] and Trostky" and alleged that public ownership of utilities and natural resources and the destruction of property rights would follow their election.[75]

While the Vare controversy gained the attention of Pennsylvania voters, the candidacy of Frank Smith took center stage in Illinois. Smith, a Republican, had served as a congressman from Illinois from 1919 to 1921 and chaired the Illinois Commerce Commission, which regulated public utilities, from 1921 to 1926. During his senatorial bid Smith spent $400,000 on his campaign and received strong support from the Insulls, who contributed $125,000. Smith accepted the Insull campaign donation while continuing to chair the Illinois Commerce Commission, which constituted a conflict of interest and a violation of state law. Norris quickly charged that Insull had bought a Senate seat. The growing controversy took an odd twist when the incumbent, William B. McKinley, died in November 1926. The Illinois governor appointed Senator-elect Smith to fill the remainder of McKinley's term. The Senate then voted to deny Smith his seat while the Privileges and Elections Committee investigated his credentials.[76] Only one senator represented Illinois throughout 1927. In January 1928 Norris said that "it is not a question of Illinois being deprived of her two votes in the Senate . . . it is a question of Mr. Insull being deprived of his votes in the Senate." The controversy came to an abrupt end when Smith terminated his senator-elect status. In a special election in November 1928, Illinois voters elected Otis Glenn to the Senate.[77]

The dispute over the high financing of Senate campaigns unfolded at a time when some U.S. senators began to demand that the Federal Trade Commission investigate public utilities. Senator Norris had first introduced legislation during the 66th Congress in 1919, calling for an FTC investigation of the General Electric Company.[78] Norris wanted the FTC to investigate two things: one, the General Electric Company, to decide whether it was a monopoly or existed as part of a combination that dominated the electric power industry, and two, public utility corporations, to determine their attempts to control public opinion.[79]

In February 1925 the Senate finally authorized the investigation. The FTC's commissioners then examined the language and voted three to two to solicit the attorney general's office for a legal opinion. In making the request the FTC commissioners asked the attorney general to rule on the authority of the agency to carry out the four separate investigations requested by the Senate. The four resolutions all involved antitrust issues: the milling and baking industry, the tobacco and electrical businesses, the legality of price or trade associations, and the economic importance of cooperative associations.[80] The commissioners' request seemed to call into question the FTC's function as a regulatory agency to monitor antitrust infractions in American business. Specifically, they asked the attorney general to rule on the authority of the Senate to request investigations even though section six, part D, of the Federal Trade Commission Act read as follows: "That the commission shall also have power . . . upon the direction of the President or either House of Congress to investigate and report the facts relating to any alleged violations of the antitrust Acts by any corporation."[81] The FTC also asked the attorney general to rule on its current appropriation act that stated: "No part of this sum [FTC budget] shall be expended for investigations requested by either House of Congress, except those requested by concurrent resolution of Congress, but this limitation shall not apply to investigations and reports in connection with alleged violations of the antitrust acts by any corporations."[82]

The language of both the original act and the appropriation law appears to state concisely the duties of the commission. The attorney general's office denied the request and so reaffirmed the FTC's investigative power on all the resolutions except the second part of the tobacco and General Electric resolution that called for an investigation of General Electric's attempts to influence public opinion. The attorney general's opinion stated that even if facts existed that proved a corporation attempted to control public opinion, such actions did not presume a violation of antitrust laws.[83]

The behavior of the FTC commissioners appears unusual at best. In asking the Department of Justice to rule on their authority to investigate possible antitrust violations, they were potentially undermining their power and the intended purpose of the agency. The commissioners may have wanted the attorney general to rule against them. In 1925 critics of President Coolidge charged the administration with intentionally weakening the FTC, the Interstate Commerce Commission, and the Tariff Commission and making them probusiness agencies. The *Nation* reported that under Coolidge appointees the FTC would no longer work to regulate business but would help American business. In commenting on an interview with W. E. Humphrey, Coolidge's appointee to chair the FTC, the *Nation* quoted Humphrey as saying, "The commission wishes to be worthy of the confidence of the business interests of the country."[84] Under Coolidge, the *Nation* stated, the FTC "would be without teeth, and therefore will soon sink into innocuous desuetude."[85]

Norris wrote in the *Nation* that presidential actions would lead to the administration placing "big business" in charge of the federal government.

He said that Humphrey had devoted his entire life to big business and that the new commissioner held no sympathy for the small businessman fighting trusts and monopolies. Even worse, according to Norris, under Humphrey the FTC began conducting business in secrecy, which Norris believed threatened a central principle of liberty, the open exchange of information. Humphrey's appointment, Norris thought, gave the big business advocates a three to two majority on the FTC. The Nebraska senator concluded that big business also had subverted the Interstate Commerce Commission and the Tariff Commission.[86]

In February 1927 the FTC issued the first volume of its findings that covered the concentration of corporate control in the electrical industry. The commission investigated the entire electrical industry in an attempt to ascertain General Electric's influence nationwide. Despite the FTC's apparent hesitance to conduct the investigations, the agency found concentrations of power in the electrical utility industry, although it concluded that the problems identified required congressional action and not an FTC ruling.[87] Coolidge would have to sign any legislation. The report stated that no nationwide monopoly existed in the power industry although monopolies existed "within certain states and lesser territorial areas."[88] The four major holding companies that the FTC identified were the General Electric Corporation, the Electric Bond and Share Company, the Insull group, and the North American group.[89]

The commission found that economic gain represented the primary reason behind the holding company. Efficient operation through centralized management represented a second motivation. The report also examined the method of financing holding companies and found that their promoters heavily financed the companies with low-interest bonds and preferred stock while retaining ownership of common stock that paid high dividends. From available information, common stock dividends in 1924 ranged from 19 to 55 percent and in 1925 from 21 to 40 percent.[90] Bonbright and Means and Raushenbush and Laidler used the FTC's findings in their books that appeared soon after the completion of the investigation.

Private power spokesmen must have found the FTC findings painful. Even under a probusiness Federal Trade Commission, whose leadership tried to dodge the inquiry, investigators uncovered significant problems within the industry. These problems were the same ones that public power proponents said had existed for years: the existence of regional monopolies, profit as the primary reason for holding companies, and high common stock dividends. The findings released in 1927 soon fueled calls for additional investigations. In December Senator Thomas Walsh (D-Mont.) first introduced a resolution to establish a committee of five senators to investigate the power industry and its attempts to manipulate public opinion against public power. The Senate did not debate the resolution until the following February, when it ultimately voted to have the FTC conduct that investigation as well.[91] By that time the private utility industry had become front-page news across the United States.

By the mid-1920s the electrical power industry in the United States had become highly concentrated, extremely forceful, and very profitable. A handful of holding companies controlled the generation and marketing of electrical energy and reaped enormous profits in the process. The high level of concentration led to the charge that a power trust existed. The activities of holding companies and utility executives became major political issues in the 1920s. Those who opposed private utilities on the local and national level pushed for the development of public power to reveal the activities of private power. Both contemporary observers, such as FTC investigators, Bonbright and Means, and Raushenbush and Laidler, and historical evidence collected from personal letters, stock reports, and periodicals underscore the magnitude of the political fight.

The electrification versus electrical modernization issue was a crucial part of the entire debate throughout the 1920s. Those favoring public power clearly believed that government sponsorship of large-scale systems would contribute to increased electrical usage. In the 1920s public power advocates began to agitate for reform measures to address the problems created by the concentration of economic and political power in the private utility industry. On the national level, those activities included calls to federally develop the Tennessee Valley and the Colorado River. Senator Norris and others thought that those projects would provide the much needed "yardstick" to measure private rates. Public power would then demonstrate the low-cost potential of electricity and thus expose the profits that private utilities made. Another federal investigation of the private utility industry would reveal the many unsavory activities that private power officials undertook to manipulate public opinion. The call for public power echoed not only in the nation's capital but also across the West to the Pacific Ocean, in numerous small midwestern towns, Seattle, and Los Angeles.

Examining the fight over electricity in each of these areas reveals the depth and breadth of the public power conflict. On the national political level the battle grew in intensity as the decade passed, reaching a crescendo just as the Great Depression began to grip the country. In the last years of the twenties and the first years of the thirties, Congress voted numerous times on public power issues. Although presidential vetoes blocked enactment of much of the legislation, they did not obscure the political support for public power that existed in both houses of Congress among Democrats and Republicans from all regions of the country except the Northeast. The core issue in the national press and in all the legislative debates was fair rates and widespread electrical usage. Inexpensive public power, many believed, would expedite the use of electricity.

CHAPTER THREE

Public Power, National Politics, and Congress: 1927–1932

The long debate between public power advocates and the electrical utility industry reached a fevered pitch in the late 1920s. By the end of the decade Senator Norris and others had introduced numerous pieces of legislation in Congress as part of their attempt to minimize the private utility industry's influence in society. The most famous would publicly develop Muscle Shoals, construct a Colorado River Dam, and authorize another utility industry investigation. As Congress debated such legislation, media coverage of the power fight increased. Liberal magazines such as the *New Republic* and the *Nation* gave the issue heavy coverage, and William Randolph Hearst threw the weight of his newspaper chain behind the fight for public power. Various interest groups and public organizations also voiced alarm at the growing power of the private electrical utility industry.

In the nation's capital public power proponents on the national level thought that public construction and ownership of hydroelectric dams would be effective tools to fight private power's growing influence. Although they recognized that the projects would create other benefits, their main emphasis was battling private electrical utilities. Senators Norris, Walsh, Hiram Johnson (R-Calif.), and others believed that the industry's greedy quest for profit would never allow it to actively push for electrical modernization of the American home. They argued that construction of a Colorado River Dam and resolution of the Muscle Shoals situation—the two largest water power projects that Congress debated during the twenties—would do much to achieve widespread electrical modernization.

Agitation for a Colorado River Dam began shortly after the turn of the century by residents of California's Imperial Valley who were eager to secure irrigation water and protect themselves from the Colorado's devastating floods. Their demands coincided with the Bureau of Reclamation's plan to establish a comprehensive development program for the Colorado River Basin. For several decades when people discussed the possibility of a dam, flood protection and irrigation remained the primary reasons for such an undertaking.[1] Yet, as time passed, interest developed over hydroelectric production on the river.

In 1916 the Department of the Interior reported on the river's hydroelectric potential. The short fall on many parts of the river made much of it unfavorable for generating cheap energy. In some canyons, however, the river fell as much as fifteen feet per mile, making those areas suitable for hydroelectric production. The report's author estimated that dams could generate nearly 1.5 million kilowatts of electricity without interfering with irrigation.[2] Five years later, interest in the river's power potential had spread beyond the federal government.

In 1921 city officials in Los Angeles announced their intention to secure future water and power supplies from the Colorado River, even if the city had to build a dam on the river. Southern California Edison and Southern Sierras Power joined the battle when they agreed that SCE would sell power to Southern Sierra from proposed SCE dams. Southern California Edison filed four applications with federal and state officials to build dams on the river.[3] E. F. Scattergood, the chief electrical engineer of the Los Angeles Bureau of Power and Light, later wrote Senator Norris that a dam was "necessary to the continued growth of the southwest."[4]

In 1921 the Bureau of Reclamation again entered the picture. Bureau chief Arthur Powell Davis in his proposed comprehensive development program for the Colorado River Basin called for a high dam to generate electricity in addition to flood control and irrigation. Davis reasoned that the federal government should build the dam and then sell power for compensation. If that proved unfeasible, he thought the government should solicit public or private groups about constructing the dam. Davis's call for a high dam was important since irrigation and flood control did not require a dam as high as the one ultimately built.[5] Two years after the Bureau of Reclamation issued Davis's report, Department of the Interior officials predicted that the St. Lawrence, Columbia, and Colorado Rivers in the future would generate cheap energy for communities and industry. Damming the Colorado would provide flood protection, irrigation, and generate an "abundance of power."[6]

The river's hydroelectric potential received nationwide attention. William Randolph Hearst repeatedly used his national newspaper chain to blame private power companies for blocking passage of Colorado River legislation. In 1924, during congressional debate over the second Swing-Johnson bill, the Hearst press claimed that a Boulder Canyon Dam could generate 600,000 horsepower of electricity.[7] The newspaper chain, with papers in eighteen major cities, recognized flood control and irrigation as the principal reasons for building the dam but said that electrical production remained the major point of contention.[8] Other newspapers recognized the relationship between public power and a Boulder Canyon Dam as well. The *Seattle Union Record,* a strong advocate of public utility ownership, noted the immense amount of electricity that a Colorado River Dam could generate. Several years later, in 1927, the same paper blamed private power companies and sectional interests for the defeat of the third Swing-Johnson bill in Congress. The paper charged the power companies with attempting to amass vast profits by exploiting the country's natural resources.[9]

The Hearst papers tied municipal power in Los Angeles to the Colorado River controversy. Public power proponents attributed low electrical rates in Los Angeles, which were already half the national average of privately produced power, to the city's municipal ownership. Additional publicly generated energy from a Colorado River Dam would reduce the city's rates even more, creating intolerable competition for private companies. Such a situation would reveal the high rates of private utilities, which is why they opposed the legislation.[10] Without using the word "yardstick," the Hearst chain put forth that idea. Publicly owned hydroelectric projects would produce cheap energy that would expose the high cost of privately generated electricity.

In 1928, when Congress finally passed the Swing-Johnson legislation, the Hearst press called Boulder Dam the "billion dollar dam site"—and one of the biggest congressional prizes since Congress allocated railroad land tracts in the nineteenth century. If private power companies won the prize, the Hearst papers said, they would dictate the industrial development of the entire Southwest. Public ownership, on the other hand, would guarantee cheap electric power and thereby the region's industrial growth.[11]

Others saw the Colorado River debate and the Muscle Shoals controversy as linked. In 1930 Robert La Follette Jr. (R-Wis.) praised government ownership and operation of Muscle Shoals and the recent approval of the Boulder Dam legislation as "characteristic of the practical usefulness and achievement of the Progressive group in the U.S. Congress."[12] La Follette called Muscle Shoals a great source of power. The debate, he said, was whether the government should operate it for everyone's benefit or if private power should exploit it for their advantage. He added that public development would reveal private power's "exorbitant prices."[13] Senator Norris, in a letter to a Tennessee resident, clearly thought that cheap power was the primary purpose of Muscle Shoals. He noted that private power opposed Muscle Shoals because it would serve as a yardstick against which to measure electrical charges throughout the United States and to reveal the "exorbitant" rates charged for electricity.[14]

The Muscle Shoals debate grew out of World War I, when the federal government authorized the project's development for nitrate production. In peacetime nitrate would be used for national defense and fertilizer. Soon after the war ended, the issue of public versus private power became involved in the dispute. Senator Norris, the legislative father of the Tennessee Valley Authority, is often thought to have led a small group of congressional progressives in preventing private development of Muscle Shoals in the 1920s.[15]

Although Norris fought hard for Muscle Shoals, the project had strong support in the Senate. Like Boulder Dam, the debate aroused national interest. Hearst papers from across the country bitterly attacked those proposing the leasing or selling of Muscle Shoals. In 1924 when Senator Oscar Underwood (D-Ala.) sponsored legislation to lease Muscle Shoals to private interests, the newspaper chain stated that Underwood often served private corporations in their attempts to seek free privileges. If Congress passed Norris's public development bill, it would reveal the "extortionate electricity rates" that private utilities charged. The Hearst papers dismissed contentions that Muscle Shoals involved anything other than electrical production and called the project primarily a power issue.[16] America owned two great public utilities, the papers maintained: the first was the Panama Canal, the second Muscle Shoals. Federal development would mark the "twilight of the power trust." The newspaper chain cited the situation in Canada, where public power generated at Niagara Falls resulted in electrical rates that were 75 to 90 percent lower than those in the United States.[17]

After Congress passed the Muscle Shoals conference report in May 1928 authorizing public ownership, the National League of Women Voters praised the legislation. A league bulletin said that after ten years of controversy Muscle Shoals would "benefit all the people," and cheap electrical power for all citizens within transmission distance would soon become available.[18] The league did not mention the private utility industry's opposition to the legislation, but the allusion to cheap electricity is another reference to the yardstick theory of public power.

Norris himself received letters from around the country complimenting him for his efforts regarding public power. In response to one letter he reiterated his views on electricity. Electrical power was a necessity of life. Although produced from nature, efficient electrical production required a monopoly. He did not think, however, that a private monopoly was "a necessity of life," especially since private companies often produced electricity from public streams and rivers.[19]

Norris believed that concern related to electrical generation and distribution was the major issue in the 1928 presidential election. His thoughts on electricity were so strong that he broke with the Republican Party and endorsed Al Smith's run for the White House. The Nebraska senator told Senator Arthur Capper (R-Kans.) that "to save the country from the domination of the power trust" he could not support the Republican ticket and "satisfy his conscience."[20] When Norris wrote to Governor Pinchot, he called the power question the most important issue in the campaign, followed by the farm problem and prohibition.[21] La Follette joined Norris in emphasizing the importance of electricity in the 1928 election when he said whoever controlled electricity would control industry and transportation.

To guarantee low-cost electrical power, "such as the people of Ontario enjoy," public power had to break the monopoly of private power through public competition.[22]

La Follette traveled to South Dakota in 1930 in support of William McMaster's (R-S.Dak.) Senate reelection bid. In his speech, La Follette addressed the issues of Muscle Shoals, Boulder Dam, the private utility industry, and progressivism. The FTC utility industry hearings had revealed the "most powerful conspiracy ever known to dominate national and state government to selfish ends." Boulder Dam power would reveal how much private utilities overcharged. Revelations made during recent debates over businesses that controlled electrical energy struck at "the very foundation of representative government." The oil, banking, and railroad monopolies paled in comparison to the electrical monopoly trust, La Follette believed. The goal of public power advocates, he continued, was not complete public ownership but "sufficient competition" to reveal and then force down high private rates. Two-thirds of La Follette's speech endorsing McMaster's candidacy discussed private power, Muscle Shoals, Boulder Dam, and the growing importance of electricity in society.[23]

Not surprisingly, Norris also attacked the power monopoly repeatedly in his discussions of Muscle Shoals and water power. In one reference to Muscle Shoals, he said that the "balance of power ought to be taken into the homes of the people" through a government corporation that could coordinate Muscle Shoals power with privately produced electricity. Norris blamed the White House and big business for the defeat of the project and claimed that "too much manipulation of the electric business" existed in the United States.[24]

During his tenure as editor of the *World*, Walter Lippman asked Norris to discuss Muscle Shoals, Boulder Dam, and the hydroelectric possibilities of the Potomac River at Great Falls. Boulder Dam, Norris stated, would be to the Colorado River what Muscle Shoals was to the Tennessee River. Boulder Dam would be within transmission distance from Los Angeles and could control the river's floods and irrigate the Imperial Valley. Muscle Shoals power would eventually tie in with water power in Arkansas, Georgia, Alabama, and North Carolina. Electricity from Great Falls, "a miniature Niagara," would serve the District of Columbia, Baltimore, Virginia, and even New York and New Jersey. In each location dams would control devastating floods. Norris considered it "inconceivable" that control of the systems should not be in government hands.[25] He hit on the same theme several years later in a letter to an individual in Denver who praised him for his support of Boulder Dam; the Nebraska senator again tied together the proposed Boulder Dam and Muscle Shoals. He called the Colorado River Dam fight the same "proposition" as the Muscle Shoals battle. The private utility industry's influence extended throughout the United States, and not a single town could claim immunity from it. Norris did say, however, that in the Colorado River situation flood control gave that project additional impetus.[26]

The progressive political organization, the National Popular Government League, also saw Muscle Shoals and the Colorado River as parts of the same issue. A league bulletin noted that President Coolidge had one hydroelectric policy for "Alabama and the South *East* . . . [and one] for California and the South *West* [sic]." The bulletin said that the entire Southwest wanted Boulder Dam built in order to receive cheap electricity. Los Angeles especially needed the dam to secure an additional power supply.[27]

Three common themes run through the Muscle Shoals and Colorado River debates. The first was the development of the nation's waterways, at least in part, according to a conservation ideal. Each project would develop the natural resources to benefit the most people. Both projects had multiple purposes, although as time passed, electrical production became the major point of contention in each debate. Public power supporters believed that they had to save Muscle Shoals and the Colorado River from private power. The second theme was the yardstick principle. Public power advocates held that public ownership and production of electricity would reveal the high private utility rates. That discovery would force down private rates contributing to the electrical modernization of the United States.

The third major theme was the role of the federal government. Proponents believed that only the federal government should develop Muscle Shoals and build Boulder Dam. The Federal Water Power Act of 1920 legally mandated government approval for the projects, but other perceptions existed. Many public power spokesmen believed that only an entity the size of the federal government could fight private power on the national level. The willingness of public power advocates to use the federal government for Muscle Shoals and Boulder Dam transcended legal requirements and power relations. Norris, Walsh, and others maintained that the state could, and should, serve as a positive social agent. Using the federal government was not a last-gasp alternative; instead it was the effective means of exposing private power and forcing down electrical rates. These common themes reveal the political meaning of Muscle Shoals and Boulder Dam: development of natural resources for the public good, fighting private electrical utilities to ensure lower rates, and positive governmental intervention in the economy to further the social good through electrical modernization.

Investigating the electrical utility industry was the second major concern of public power backers in the late 1920s. Several themes that existed during the Muscle Shoals and Boulder Dam debates emerged in the attempts to investigate the private utility industry. Primary among those concerns was the concentration of corporate power. Public power proponents again believed that a power trust existed that monopolized the power industry, repeated enormous profits, and exploited the country's natural resources. Private power and NELA's attempt to manipulate public opinion through propaganda only heightened anxieties.

In the 1920s public power advocates considered state-level regulatory commissions worthless. Private power controlled commissions through the selection of commissioners and the manipulation of the political process and the media. Even the most honest men could not withstand the constant barrage of witnesses and experts that utilities retained, Norris hypothesized.[28] Others echoed the Nebraskan's words on the ineffectiveness of state regulation. An editorial in the St. Louis Post-Dispatch went so far as to argue that fair regulation would not be possible without amending the Constitution.[29]

Senator Thomas Walsh, who successfully investigated the Teapot Dome Scandal, sponsored the 1928 utility investigation resolution that came on the heels of the investigation authorized in 1926. Friends of public power supported Walsh and agreed that private power had backed the effort for the FTC to conduct the investigation instead of having Walsh chair a special Senate committee. Pinchot wrote Norris that if the FTC conducted the investigation, it would shroud the hearing in secrecy behind closed doors, and any findings would be lost in government reports. Removing the investigation from Senate control would allow the continuance of the "extortion in electricity."[30]

"Young Bob" La Follette called the Senate vote to have the FTC conduct the power investigation a victory for private power. He said that not having a special Senate committee investigate private utilities illustrated the "control of Big Business over the two political parties." Private power had improved on the methods of the railroads in the "public be dammed" period of federal land grants. Power executives, he continued, considered the U.S. Senate no different from a city council that could grant tax and franchise favors.[31] In Yankee from the West, Burton Wheeler, former Democratic senator from Montana, recalled that thirteen holding companies controlled 75 percent of the electricity generated in the United States in the late 1920s.[32]

Senator Hugo Black (D-Ala.) also spoke out against private power and said that it maintained "monopolistic control" of the nation's hydroelectric resources. He called Boulder Dam and Muscle Shoals "the storm centers around which this great controversy has raged for years." Black cited electric rates in Ontario, Canada, as evidence that American utilities overcharged. Municipal power in some towns provided relief, but private utilities had carried out a "tragic tale of nation-wide deception" that deluded the public to the possibilities of public ownership.[33]

The practice of U.S. senators drawing attention to Ontario, Canada, was common among all supporters of public power. Throughout the

1920s, besides citing the lower electrical rates of American towns and cities with public ownership, public power champions also looked to the publicly owned system in Ontario for confirmation that private utilities in the United States overcharged for electricity. Senator Norris often compared rates in Ontario with those in American cities as proof that public power could provide low-cost electrical energy. In 1926 he wrote: "There are wonderful possibilities in store for the state that will generate and distribute electricity to municipalities and farmers' organizations at cost. The Province of Ontario, in Canada, has given to the world a most comprehensive and extensive exhibition of what can be accomplished along this line." Later, Norris said that the average rate per kilowatt hour in Ontario was less than three cents, while it was between seven and eight cents in the United States.[34]

Judson King, of the National Popular Government League, prepared a bulletin in 1928 comparing rates in twenty-one cities and towns in Ontario with thirty-two cities in the United States with an average population of 703,031. The largest was New York City and the smallest was Mobile, Alabama. The average monthly bill for domestic customers in the American cities, who on average used thirty kilowatt hours of electricity, was $2.22. In Ontario, on average, customers paid $1.79 per month for ninety-eight kilowatt hours. On average, people in the Ontario cities paid 1.66 cents per kilowatt hour compared with 7.4 cents in the American cities.[35]

Governors also spoke out against private power during the late 1920s and early 1930s. At the time Gifford Pinchot was perhaps the most famous. In 1929 he wrote *The Power Monopoly: Its Make-up and Its Menace*. In the pamphlet he stated that six financial interests controlled 63.5 percent of the electricity generated in the United States, which served two-thirds of the American population. The danger, Pinchot argued, was not the monopoly itself, as he recognized the monopolistic nature of public utilities, but the financial institutions and recently created holding companies that controlled the generation and distribution of electricity for excessive profit.[36] Other governors also warned against the concentration of power in a few companies. Governor Franklin Roosevelt called for the establishment of the New York Power Authority, continuing the tradition of concern over electrical utilities in New York state. In 1931 the governor of Mississippi, Theodore Bilbo, recommended public ownership of that state's gas and electric utilities. In his message proposing public ownership, the governor blasted eastern companies, who controlled the state's utilities, for charging "conscienceless rates." He compared the Tennessee River to the Columbia, Colorado, and St. Lawrence Rivers and the proposed Wilson Dam on the Tennessee River to Boulder Dam. He blamed the defeat of Muscle Shoals legislation on the Republican Party, particularly the Coolidge and Hoover administrations, which wanted to prevent southern industrial development. Bilbo also noted the low rates in Ontario, Canada, as evidence of the advantages of public ownership.[37]

Complaints against the private utility industry and the FTC were not limited to Pinchot, Norris, Walsh, La Follette, Black, and the Hearst newspapers. The *Chattanooga News* referred to Walsh's call for an investigation as "a most commendable one." The paper reported that private power had become too involved in politics and had "indulged" in financial pyramiding and manipulation while "divorcing ownership and responsibility."[38] In a letter responding to an inquiry from the paper's editor, Norris again mentioned the ineffective nature of state regulation when he said that "the State Commission can no more contest with this gigantic octopus than a fly could interfere with the onward march of an elephant."[39] Norris's analogy to a "giant octopus" was reminiscent of the political cartoons used to describe Standard Oil and other turn-of-the-century trusts.

In 1929 J. W. Harreld of Oklahoma City wrote Norris requesting that the FTC investigate the activities of Fred Insull, Samuel Insull's cousin, in Oklahoma politics. Harreld charged that Insull had put members of the state legislature on utility payrolls. He further alleged that the utilities hid their campaign contributions by making them under other people's names. Harreld asked that Norris not make his name public because he feared the "wrath" that would come to him.[40] The mayor of Bradford, Pennsylvania, wrote a similar letter to Norris, in which he said that the "octopus" gripped his city. When Bradford voted to construct a public generating plant, the mayor claimed that the "octopus" bought the town's press and spread propaganda against public ownership. The mayor blamed the defeat of the measure on the influence and money of the private power.[41] It was these types of activities regarding the manipulation of state politics and the press that contributed to public power supporters concluding that only the federal government through public power projects and investigations could control the private utility industry.

Two of the country's most outspoken magazines, the *Nation* and the *New Republic*, repeatedly attacked private power in the 1920s. Both magazines favored Muscle Shoals, a Colorado River Dam, and another utility industry investigation. The *New Republic* was very blunt. In 1928 the magazine's editors attacked the power industry, saying that it had won the first of three battles that year after the Senate referred the utility investigation to the FTC. Private power's second and third goals were to block passage of the Swing-Johnson and Muscle Shoals legislation. Ultimately, the magazine believed the utilities would fail. The utility investigation was not a "flash in the pan" issue but had "been smoldering for several years." Private power had used its political influence in preventing Walsh from chairing a special Senate committee to investigate the industry. The *New Republic* praised Walsh for preventing the investigation from going to the Senate Committee on Interstate Commerce, which was under the control of the "reactionary chairmanship of Watson of Indiana." The magazine's editors claimed that the Senate was divided into two bipartisan voting blocs over public power and the "power trust." One bloc believed that government should subvert itself to business, while the other represented the public interest. If the power lobby successfully defeated the Swing-Johnson and the Muscle Shoals legislation, the Senate division would be "ineradicable [and] . . . in the Senate we shall have two new parties."[42]

Felix Frankfurter, writing in the *New Republic,* warned that presidential candidate Hoover's hands-off attitude regarding federal regulation would cause a repetition of the "disastrous history" that besieged the nation's transportation industry: "overcapitalization, wasteful competition, needless duplication of equipment, receiverships, [and] undesirable consolidations."[43] The *Nation* also labeled the change in the Walsh resolution a private power triumph. Although "Progressive Senators on both sides of the aisle" favored the legislation, private power prevailed. The magazine reported that senators were torn between their constituents and the electrical utilities to the point of hiding in "cloakrooms and corridors" to avoid voting.[44] During the Muscle Shoals debate in the spring of 1928, the magazine called Norris's efforts "a long fight for the preservation of popular rights."[45]

When Congress finally passed the Walsh resolution, it charged the FTC with investigating five areas of the power industry: the growth of capital, assets and liabilities, the method of security and bond issues, the role and importance of holding companies in the industry, the services that holding companies provided utility companies, and the "value or detriment" to the public of holding companies. The resolution also instructed the FTC to determine if private utilities had attempted "to influence or control public opinion on account of municipal or public ownership . . . [and] since 1923 to influence or control elections" of the executive branch and Senate.[46] The Senate's concern, reflected in the five areas of the FTC investigation, was the degree of financial manipulation and the extent of political corruption perpetuated by public utility holding companies.

Despite their initial worry that the FTC would bury its findings, public power champions could not have been displeased with the commission's conclusions. In 1929 and 1930, the FTC examined in depth seven holding companies. Investigators discovered that the seven companies controlled 45 percent of the electrical output in the United States and over 80 percent of the electricity that private companies sold in interstate business.[47] Investigators also examined the extent that utilities used propaganda to influence public opinion against municipally owned power. They found, for example, that a Salem, Oregon, firm had received $168,000 annually. Half of the money came from "public-utility organizations" to collect information regarding American industry and business. Corporations sympathetic to private power contributed the rest. The firm wrote "canned" editorials and sold them to newspapers around the country, which printed the editorials as if their editors had written them. The head of the firm, B. M. Hofter, told investigators that he sold more than eight hundred articles to over fourteen thousand editors in 1927.[48] When the FTC finally concluded its investigation in the 1930s, it printed the findings in a ninety-five-volume report.[49]

The discoveries of the FTC regarding electrical utilities and the broadsides of the *New Republic* and the *Nation* further contributed to the frontpage nature of the fight over electricity, a fight that partially emerged in both the 1928 and 1932 presidential campaigns. In 1928 Hoover believed that regulation should occur on the state level.[50] Alfred Smith, the Democratic presidential candidate that year, favored both public control and ownership of existing or potential water power sites on public land. He also supported the public's right to regulate the distribution and price of electricity when the producer sold it to the consumer.[51] Four years later President Hoover favored federal regulation of interstate power through the Federal Power Commission. He steadfastly opposed federal development of the Tennessee Valley, believing instead that only the people of the area should develop the region.[52] Franklin Roosevelt thought that the federal government must actively protect the liberty and welfare of the American people against what he believed was the greed of the utilities so that all Americans could enjoy the benefits of electricity. As a presidential candidate he most forcefully voiced that position in his water power speech in Portland, Oregon, when he referred to the "four great power developments in the United States," the Columbia, Colorado, and St. Lawrence Rivers, and Muscle Shoals.[53]

The explosive issue of public power headed the agenda at the National Progressive Conference in March 1931 in Washington, D.C. Senator Norris, who chaired the conference, stated that "monopoly, corruption and dishonesty must eventually be driven from power." He maintained that the conference organizers did not seek political advantage for themselves or any political party, nor did they want to create a third party.[54] Other prominent individuals who helped organize the conference included Senators La Follette, Wheeler, Edward Costigan (D-Colo.), and Bronston Cutting (D-N.Mex.). Ten other senators and eleven representatives attended the conference, as did individuals from the *Nation*, the *New Republic*, the American Federation of Labor, and the Popular Government League.[55] Obviously, merely attending the conference did not automatically make one a progressive or a supporter of public power, but it does show the breadth of interest in the debate over electricity. That interest revealed itself in other reform-minded organizations.

The National Popular Government League endorsed public power projects and candidates nationwide. In 1932 the league called the power debate one of the most important issues of the campaign and published a pamphlet reporting Hoover's and Roosevelt's views toward the electrical utility industry. The signers of the pamphlet included Norris and other major supporters of public power.[56] The Public Ownership League of America that Carl Thompson directed also lobbied for public power causes. The organization's stationery in 1932 featured pictures of public power projects or cities with municipal power throughout the United States, including Muscle Shoals, Boulder Dam, Los Angeles, Tacoma, and Seattle.[57]

Calls for developing Muscle Shoals, constructing a Colorado River Dam, investigating the private electrical industry, and general concerns about private power were not regionally isolated issues. Individuals from many different backgrounds and from all regions of the country expressed interest in public power and feared the growing strength of private power. Senators, representatives, governors, the press, several national organizations, and ordinary citizens voiced their concerns. Newspapers and magazines followed the debates over Muscle Shoals, the proposed Boulder Dam, and the FTC's investigation. Each issue received national attention from all strata of society; people from around the country considered them nationally important political issues.

George Norris is often considered to be the leader of a small but determined group of senators who stopped the sale or lease of Muscle Shoals before the New Deal.[58] La Follette's remarks about public and private power and the usefulness of reform-minded senators reveal that he considered their work important, as did others fighting for public power. Although at times they viewed themselves as the last few defenders of democracy against the encroaching power of the electrical utility industry, that image was an artificial one. Public power proponents did not believe that they were fighting a losing battle, only a difficult one. They knew, in fact, that many like-minded individuals existed in Congress and around the country. Norris's secretary, John Robertson, answered a letter in 1931 from a Mississippi resident regarding the FTC utility investigation. In response to the southerner's inquiry, the secretary sent the individual a list of thirty-one senators "in sympathy" with Norris regarding the "public utility problem." Robertson also said that "this is not a complete list." The list was bipartisan in nature with senators from every region of the country, except the East, represented.[59]

The letter from Norris's office suggests that more than a few senators expressed concern about private power. Studying congressional roll call votes reveals that Muscle Shoals, the Colorado River, and the electrical utility investigation legislation received support from sizable blocs of senators and representatives. Although presidential vetoes prevented Muscle Shoals development in the 1920s, the political stalemate between conservative presidents and Congress does not mean that significant pro–public power sentiment did not exist.

Between 1927 and 1931 the Senate cast several crucial votes dealing with public power. The House also voted a number of times between 1928 and 1931. On those votes, involving Muscle Shoals, the Colorado River, and a private utility investigation, senators and representatives revealed their attitudes toward public and private power. Roll call analysis allows for the systematic examination of the those attitudes (the analysis explores more Senate votes since the House conducted fewer roll call votes). Two obstacles preclude using more traditional scaling techniques for examining legislative voting behavior: turnover and unequal voting records. Because of turnover, the roll call analysis examines party seats instead of individual senators or representatives. If a person of the same party succeeded an incumbent, the analysis treats the seat as if no turnover occurred. However, to allow for the examination of party strength for all congressional seats, not just those that the same party held continually, if a member of a different party succeeded an incumbent, the party seat was split in two. An example illustrates the methodological approach. In 1928 when Senator James Reed, a Missouri Democrat, did not seek reelection, Roscoe Patterson, a Republican, succeeded him. Because Reed and Patterson belonged to different political parties, the seat was divided. If Patterson had been a Democrat, the voting record would have been treated as if no change had occurred. This methodology resulted in more than 96 Senate and 435 House seats being analyzed. The analysis of party seats is especially useful in testing the hypothesis that Norris led a few western Republicans in the fight for public power and reform in the 1920s.

Overcoming the problem of unequal voting records requires construction of an index for every party seat in each house of Congress to measure the degree of public power support on the roll call votes. In constructing the index, a pro–public power vote receives a score of one, while a vote against public power legislation scores zero. Dividing the number of votes cast by the total score of the votes creates an index with values ranging from 0.0 (always against public power legislation) to 1.0 (always supported public power legislation). If senators or representatives voted for public power legislation each time they voted, they score 1.0, regardless of the total number of times they voted. The number of votes cast does not matter, only the degree of support. The legislator who voted against the legislation each time scores 0.0. Those who voted for the legislation half the time score 0.5. Clearly, not all congressmen voted each time. The index, however, weights each seat equally to allow comparisons between 108 Senate party seats and 462 House party seats.[60]

The roll call analysis includes nine Senate votes: two votes to have the FTC conduct the utility investigation; an amendment to lease Muscle Shoals; four votes on either Senate bills or conference reports authorizing Muscle Shoals; the Senate's failed attempt to override President Hoover's veto of the 1931 Muscle Shoals legislation; and the Swing-Johnson conference report in late 1928. Five House votes are examined: a conference report vote to publicly develop Muscle Shoals; a vote to recommit Muscle Shoals legislation to committee; a vote on the Swing-Johnson conference report authorizing Boulder Dam; an amendment to lease Muscle Shoals; and another conference report vote to publicly develop Muscle Shoals.[61]

Information regarding the number of votes examined and the median and mean index score for the House and Senate is provided in Table 3.1. The mean and median index scores in both houses of Congress show a strong degree of support for public power legislation. In each house the mean index score surpassed .50: 35 senators voted for public power every time they voted, while in the House 158 seats always voted for public power. Large numbers of senators (23) and representatives (127) also opposed public power legislation on each vote. Clearly, many in Congress held strong views on the issue.

After determining the index for each party seat in the House and Senate, the influence of region and party can be tested. Multiple Classification Analysis (MCA) determines the influence of party and region on congressional voting. The U.S. Census Bureau's regional classifications are used to test regional influence.[62] MCA computes the grand mean for the dependent variable (the index score) for the entire unit of study, either House or Senate voting. The independent variables either add or subtract from the grand mean. The MCA coefficients for both the House and Senate are listed in Tables 3.2 and 3.3.

In the Senate, for example, the grand mean equals .57. For a senator from the Northeast, .32 is deducted from the grand mean, and if the senator was a Republican, an additional .16 is subtracted. Thus, a generalization can be made that for Republican senators from the Northeast the index score on the public power votes is .09 (.57–.32–.16). If a Northeast senator was a Democrat, only the regional value would be deducted. For a Democratic representative from the South, the predicted score is .74 (.55–.08+.27).

Several conclusions can be drawn from the data presented in Tables 3.2 and 3.3. In both houses, members who represented voters in the Northeast generally opposed the legislation, especially if they were Republican.

Table 3.1 Senate and House Public Power Index

Chamber	Years	Number of Votes	Index Mean	Index Median
Senate	1927–1931	9	.57	.75
House	1928–1931	5	.55	.60

Source: See note 60 for a methodological explanation and note 61 for vote citations.

Table 3.2 MCA Coefficients for Senate Votes, Region, and Party

Grand Mean	.57		
Region	N.	A.	b.
N.E.	20	-.32	
N.C.	29	.19	
South	37	-.04	
West	22	.11	.43
Party			
Demo.	51	.18	
GOP	57	-.16	.22
R²	.33		
Total	108		

Source: See Table 3.1.

To a far lesser degree the same held true for those representing the South. The major difference is that in the strongly Republican Northeast partisanship further lowered the index score. In the Democrat-controlled South, party affiliation more than negated the regional deduction. Individuals representing constituents in the North Central region and the West supported the public power legislation. Even after adding Republican party affiliation, when applicable, the index score is at the mean level for both houses in those regions. To briefly summarize, only the East consistently elected pro–private power senators and representatives, which is not surprising since many of the major fights over public power took place in the West, Midwest, and South.[63] The efforts of Senators Norris, La Follette, Johnson, and others from the West with progressive leaning should not be minimized, as they certainly provided the public power movement with strong leadership. The roll call analysis discloses, however, that support existed among more than a handful of individuals. Support, although stron-

Table 3.3 MCA Coefficients for House Votes, Region, and Party

Grand Mean	.55		
Region	N.	A.	b.
N.E.	126	-.14	
N.C.	155	.14	
South	146	-.08	
West	35	.23	.33
Party			
Demo.	195	.27	
GOP	267	-.20	.56
R²	.33		
Total	462		

Source: See Table 3.1.

gest in the West and North Central states, also existed in the South. Both Democrats and Republicans favored the public power legislation in those regions.

The identification of large blocs of senators and representatives voting for public power and related measures in the 1920s reveals even more than an intense political fight over electricity. It also shows a strong tie with the progressive reform tradition of the early twentieth century. Some of the leading proponents of public power in the 1920s had been long interested in reform. Senator Johnson led the reform crusade in California and was on the Bull Moose ticket in 1912. Senator La Follette was well versed in the reform tradition that his father started in Wisconsin. Senator Borah, who had voiced worry about water power site monopolization during Wilson's first administration, continued the fight into the twenties and thirties. Senator Walsh cut his political teeth fighting the mining companies in Montana. Senators Norris and Smith Brookhart (Progressive-Republican–Iowa) also were well versed in Midwest progressive politics.

To these senators and others, big business's dominance over American politics and its threat to the public good never seemed greater. The ever-widening use of electricity and the increasing concentration of corporate power in a handful of electrical utilities rekindled earlier questions about the state's role in the economic regulation of private enterprise. In the 1920s those supporting public development of Muscle Shoals and Boulder Dam viewed those projects as valuable tools in fighting the private utility industry. Although they clearly recognized that other benefits would be derived from such projects, construction of a Colorado River dam and development of the Tennessee River Valley presented public power advocates with an opportunity to confront private power. Public power developed into a major political controversy during the 1920s that reveals a tie with the Progressive Era among more than a handful of western senators who many scholars of American politics have traditionally argued maintained the progressive legacy after World War I.[64]

Instead of a few western Republican senators maintaining the progressive tradition during the 1920s, something quite different existed. A more accurate description of the Senate and House in the twenties is that strong progressive sentiment prevailed in all regions of the country except the Northeast. At the very least, the presence of progressive attitudes and behavior in Congress throughout the 1920s implies that progressivism did not decline after World War I to the extent some historians have maintained. Instead, strong progressive sentiment, focused on issues surrounding public power, existed throughout the 1920s and forged a link between pre–World War I reform and the reform ideal of Franklin Roosevelt's New Deal state.

In addition to testing for the influence of party and region, Multiple Classification Analysis can test the influence of other variables on congressional voting. In May 1931 in his letter to a Mississippi resident, Norris's secretary listed thirty-one senators whom he said held beliefs similar to Norris regarding private power.[65] Adding the presence or absence of a name on the list to the MCA tests the accuracy of that claim. If the senators that Norris's office listed did agree with the Nebraskan on power issues, it should appear in the MCA as a positive coefficient. If they opposed the legislation, the coefficient will be negative; if they were not predisposed one way or another, the coefficient will be near .00.

Adding a variable reflecting the degree of electrical modernization in a senator's home state provides a partial look at the influence of technology, or the lack of technology, on his voting behavior. Examining the percentage of American families that the Census Bureau identified with at least one radio in 1930 provides partial insight into the amount of electrical modernization in a state. Clustering on the percentage of homes in each state with at least one radio in 1930 revealed three groups: a group of thirty-one senators who represented fifteen states with less than 22 percent of all families having a radio; a second group of sixty-one senators from twenty-six states with between 22 and 51 percent of families having a radio; and a third group of sixteen senators representing seven states who had more than 51 percent of families owning at least one radio.[66]

Inclusion of the Norris letter and the percentage of families with radios brings the number of independent variables in the MCA to four: party, region, radios, and the Norris letter. The dependent variable continues to be the index score. The MCA coefficients for the important public power votes between 1927 and 1931 are reported in Table 3.4. The MCA reveals that the level of electrical modernization in a senator's home state, as measured by the number of families with at least one radio, influenced voting behavior. Senators from states with less than 22 percent of families having at least one radio showed a strong tendency to support efforts to establish public power projects and investigate private power. Conversely, those senators from the states with the highest percentage of families with radios opposed the public power legislation as did the middle group. Again, this result should not be surprising. The goal of public power advocates on the national level, and as will be shown on the local level, was to increase the level of energy used in American society. The underlying theory of the yardstick principle was to force down private rates through public competition to make electricity more accessible for widespread use. The coefficients for the percentage of families with radios suggest that local level political concerns influenced senatorial voting.

Multiple Classification Analysis also reveals that Norris's office knew well those who supported the Nebraskan senator on public power issues.

Table 3.4 MCA Coefficients for Senate Votes, Region, Party, Norris Letter, and Radios

	N.	A.	b.
Grand Mean	.57		
Region	N.	A.	b.
N.E.	20	−.13	
N.C.	29	.17	
South	37	−.11	
West	22	.08	.31
Party			
Demo.	51	.15	
GOP	57	−.13	.34
Norris letter			
Not on letter	77	−.13	
On letter	31	.33	.52
Radios			
1. < 22% with radios	31	.17	
2. 22%–51% with radios	61	−.07	
3. > 51% with radios	16	−.06	.27
R^2	.61		
Total	108		

Sources: See Table 3.1; Appendix 3.2 for the senators listed by Norris's office; and note 66 for radios.

The value of the coefficient for the letter equaled .33; the coefficient for those senators not on the letter equaled −.13. The senators that Norris's secretary listed strongly supported the public power legislation examined: the mean index score of the thirty-one senators equaled .97 and the median equaled 1.00. The statistical collaboration of the letter suggests that historians have underestimated the strength and breadth of public power attitudes. That nearly a third of the Senate identified by Norris's office and the roll call analysis voted as a bloc on the issues examined displays the strength of public power attitudes. Roll call analysis and archival evidence supports the conclusion that public power sentiment existed in the north central, southern, and western regions of the United States.[67]

An eclectic, and powerful, group of senators supported Norris on public power issues.[68] In the group were two past and two future vice presidential candidates. Hiram Johnson, Bull Moose candidate in 1912, and Burton K. Wheeler, Progressive Party candidate in 1924, represented ties to the progressive traditions of Theodore Roosevelt and Robert La Follette Sr. Charles McNary (Oreg.), Republican candidate in 1940, and Alben Barkley (D-Ky.), who served as Harry Truman's vice president from 1949 to 1953, later represented their party's national tickets. Other prominent individuals included Carter Glass (D-Va.), Woodrow Wilson's secretary of treasury from 1918 to 1920. Franklin Roosevelt later selected Thomas Walsh to be U.S. attorney general, although Walsh died before the new administration took office. Norris's office also considered Senators Smith Brookhart, who served as commissioner of the Agricultural Adjustment Administration from 1933 to 1935, "Cotton Ed" Smith (D-S.C.), who had headed the Southern Cotton Association before his election to the Senate, and the future Supreme Court justice Hugo Black as allies in the public power fight.

Political inexperience was not a common trait among the thirty-one pro–public power senators; instead most of them had extensive backgrounds in politics before entering the Senate. Nine had served in the House of Representatives, and seven more had served as governors. Two, Charles McNary and Sam Bratton (D-N.Mex.), served on their state supreme courts; Wheeler was U.S. district attorney in Butte, Montana, before entering politics. Nineteen of the thirty-one senators listed law as their primary occupation. Several others gave their occupation as newspaper publishers, editors, or reporters. The group also included one doctor, Henry Hatfield (R-W.Va.); one dentist, Henrick Shipstead (Farm-Labor–Minn.); a well driller, Peter Norbeck ("Roosevelt Republican"–S.Dak.); and one seemingly born politician, "Young Bob" La Follette.

The senators that Norris's office identified called both small towns and large cities home. Norris himself came from McCook, Nebraska (1930 population: 6,688), although his fellow Nebraska Republican senator, Robert Howell, had lived in Omaha since 1888 (population: 214,006). Hugo Black hailed from Birmingham, Alabama (population: 259,678), and Hiram Johnson came from San Francisco (population: 634,394). Both of Minnesota's senators, the Farm-Laborite Henrick Shipstead and Republican Thomas Schall, lived in Minneapolis (population: 464,356). At the other extreme, "Cotton Ed" Smith traveled to Washington from Lynchburg, South Carolina (population: 512), and Lynn Frazier lived on land outside Hoople, North Dakota (population: 325), that his parents had homesteaded in his youth.[69]

That senators from large cities and small towns were on the list from Norris's office suggests that neither a rural nor urban background predisposed voting behavior on public power. Adding a variable to test for such an influence in the entire Congress shows that the rural-urban split did not sway either Senate or House voting. According to the 1930 census, twenty-one states had a majority of their population living in urban areas.[70] Senators and representatives from rural states and districts did not vote differently from their urban counterparts. The lack of urban electrical modernization may be the reason that the urban-rural split did not influence voting. Those individuals representing more urban states and districts may have recognized the low levels of modernization among their constituents. Stated differently, the urban-rural split may have been a nonfactor since widespread electrical use did not occur in urban or rural America.

A variable that did influence House voting behavior was the presence or absence of state public utility district enabling laws. California enacted the first public utility district law designed primarily for electrical service in 1913, during Hiram Johnson's tenure as governor. During the Great Depression the *National Municipal Review* defined public utility districts as "political subdivisions, quasi-public corporations, of the state with territorial boundaries embracing an area wider than a single municipality, unincorporated as well as incorporated territory, within one or more counties for the generation, transmission and distribution of electricity."[71] The advantage for public power advocates in creating the districts was that they allowed municipalities and unincorporated areas to interconnect their electrical systems. Interconnection lessened problems of municipal debt limitations and allowed economies of scale to develop, at least partially. Those supporting public power recognized, as did private power officials, that larger units could more efficiently generate and distribute electrical energy. By the end of 1931 thirteen states had passed public utility district enabling laws.[72] The MCA coefficients for the House are reported in Table 3.5.

The influence of public utility district laws, as did the impact of electrical modernization as measured by radio ownership, suggests that local concerns over electricity affected congressional voting behavior. Another variable that can be used to test if local concerns influenced House voting is the presence or absence of towns with municipally owned power in a congressional district. Beginning in the late nineteenth century, towns and cities throughout the United States established municipally owned electrical generation or distribution systems (often both). Although more frequent in small towns, larger towns and cities such as Tacoma, Seattle, Los Angeles, and Cleveland also developed municipally owned power.

The traditional explanation for the development of municipal power is that either inadequate private finance capital existed to construct pri-

Table 3.5 MCA Coefficients for House Votes, Region, Party, and PUD Laws

	N.	A.	b.
Grand Mean	.55		
Region	N.	A.	b.
N.E.	126	–.10	
N.C.	155	.13	
South	146	–.08	
West	35	.10	.26
Party			
Demo.	195	.27	
GO	267	–.20	.57
State PUD Law			
State with law	78	.17	
State without law	384	–.03	.18
R²	.36		
Total	462		

Sources: See Table 3.1 and notes 70 and 71 for the public utility district citations.

vate plants or technological barriers prevented electrical transmission over long distances.[73] By the 1920s those arguments lacked substance. A large percentage of electricity used in the United States crossed state boundaries via long distance transmission lines that made the servicing of most communities technologically possible. These factors suggest that insufficient private capital or lack of technology did not motivate the decision to construct municipal systems. An alternate explanation of municipal power is rate setting and political control of service. After acquiring ownership of an electrical system, a town could determine its electrical rates.

Multiple Classification Analysis for the House excluded as an independent variable the presence or absence of a town with municipal power in a congressional district (the value of f. exceeded .05).[74] The reason for this exclusion was that party, region, and passage of state public utility laws were very tangible variables, while the presence or absence of municipal power was more problematic. A representative either did or did not represent a congressional district in the East and either was or was not a Republican. Municipal power, unfortunately, was not such a concise variable. The congressman representing one section of a major city had only one chance in one to have a town with public power in his district, but the lone congressman representing all of New Mexico was more likely to have a town with municipal power in his district simply because there were more towns. Excluding the region, party, and public utility district variables from the analysis of the relation of municipal power to congressional voting minimizes these problems.

Clustering the index scores for the House party seats revealed three analytically significant groups.[75] As reported in Table 3.6, a relationship existed between voting behavior on public power issues and the presence or absence of towns with municipal power in a congressional district. The absence of a town with municipal power appears to have been more of a negative influence on congressional voting than was the existence of a municipal power town a positive one. For all the House party seats examined on the votes between 1928 and 1931, about 72 percent of the towns had municipal power. Approximately 71 percent of the representatives voting strongly for public power represented districts with towns having public power. At the same time about 64 percent of the most anti–public power congressmen represented districts with municipal power towns. Taken together, as a measure of the influence of local-level issues on congressional voting, the analysis suggests that the presence of a town with municipal power in a congressional district had some influence on a representative's voting behavior.

The roll call analysis of Congress on the most important public power issues in the late 1920s and early 1930s reveals sizable blocs of pro–pub-

Table 3.6 Presence or Absence of Municipal Power by House Voting Groups According to
Congressional Districts

Voting Bloc	Districts with Municipal Power		Districts without Municipal Power		Total	
	N	Percent	N	Percent	N	Percent
Strongly Public Power	146	71.6	58	28.4	204	100.0
Moderate	87	85.3	15	14.7	102	100.0
Strongly Nonpublic Power	101	64.7	55	35.3	156	100.0
Total	334	72.3	128	27.7	462	100.0

$X^2 = 13.01, p. > .01., df. = 2$

Sources: See Table 3.1 and note 74 for information on determining congressional districts
with municipal power towns.

lic power senators and representatives. This finding is hardly surprising
for several reasons. The most important is that many Americans lacked
even basic levels of electrical modernization. At a time when congressmen often spent more time away from Washington than in the nation's
capital, constituent contact must have been greater. As the twenties
passed, the gap between those with electricity and those without in rural
and urban America widened, as did the growing awareness of the lack
of urban modernization and basic rural electrification. A strong concern
over electricity must have influenced congressional voting. Since early
in the century Congress had debated bills and resolutions addressing
electricity and electrical monopolies. Senators Borah, Norris, Johnson, and
others serving in Washington in the late 1920s had participated in those
debates. The findings of the Federal Trade Commission investigations
undoubtedly influenced congressional voting and the national outcry
against the private utility industry. FTC findings seemed to provide the
proof that public power advocates needed to convincingly make their case
against private power in front of the American people. All of these factors were a part of and contributed to the nationwide attention that the
fight over electricity received in the late 1920s.

The intensity of the public power debate made electricity a major national political issue in the years before the New Deal and forged a link
with the Progressive Era. Concern over electricity existed in rural and urban
American, in large cities and small towns, in Congress and local mayoral
elections, and among Democrats and Republicans. Congress attempted to
curb the private electrical industry's influence through establishment of
public power projects and utility industry investigations. Beyond Wash-

ington electricity entered the political debate in other ways. In small towns electricity became political during attempts to establish or maintain publicly owned systems. That debate also broke out in Seattle and Los Angeles. Despite very different histories, natural environments, and political traditions, public power battles with striking similarities occurred. The political debate over electricity permeated all levels of society.

CHAPTER FOUR

Small Town Motivation: The Quest for Inexpensive Electricity

Political controversy rocked the small Minnesota town of Lanesboro throughout 1928 as citizens debated the control of the decade's technological panacea: electricity. For twenty years a publicly owned generating and distribution system had furnished the town with electricity. Then, suddenly, opponents of municipal ownership questioned the need for continued public control and started to agitate for privatization of the system. Rate issues drove the political debate in Lanesboro, which had a population of about a thousand. In the end, those favoring public ownership of the town's generation and transmission system successfully beat back the privatization challenge.

The political debate over electricity was not unique to Lanesboro. What is significant, however, is the degree of awareness that existed in Lanesboro and other small midwestern towns regarding the promise that electricity held to ease the burdens of everyday life, improve daily living, and increase productivity for all Americans. Across the Midwest, people fought for cheaper electrical power with the same tenacity as did pro–public power senators, representatives, and governors nationwide. The size of the community meant little in the fight for inexpensive electricity. In the smallest villages many people believed that a "power trust" existed that prevented them from enjoying the fruits of modern technology. The daily or weekly newspaper kept them informed of the newest electrical convenience in advertisements featuring radios, refrigerators, washing machines, and stoves.

The discovery of a strong public power ideology in small town rural America gives a new perspective on the politics of the 1920s and 1930s. Although New Deal programs ultimately hastened the electrification and electrical modernization of rural and small town America, people had not waited passively for electricity.[1] Instead, they became politically active and fought for electrical power in the years preceding the 1932 election. That political activity reveals at least some basis for congressional support for public power in Washington. These findings further undermine the lack of capital and inadequate technology explanations of public ownership.[2]

A brief review of the demographics in the United States in the 1920s and early 1930s helps set the stage for studying the politics of electricity in small town America. In 1920 the Census Bureau revealed that a majority of the nation's population lived in urban areas. That revelation was tenuous at best because the bureau considered a town urban if its population exceeded 2,500. Accordingly, 51 percent of Americans lived in urban areas; by 1930 that figure grew to 56.2 percent. In 1930, 10,346 incorporated places had populations of fewer than 1,000, and 3,087 towns in the United States had populations between 1,000 and 2,500. Finally, 2,183 towns had populations between 5,000 and 10,000 people.[3] The importance of these numbers is that many Americans still lived in rural areas or small towns on the eve of the New Deal. Those people, to an even greater extent than their urban neighbors, lacked access to electrical energy and widespread electrical modernization. Accordingly, they fought hard to establish municipally owned electrical systems.

In October 1930 the Common Council of Bangor, Wisconsin, a small community of 665 people in La Crosse County, announced that they would hold a referendum to decide if the town should buy the private electric company that served it.[4] La Crosse County, bordered on the west by the Mississippi River, prospered agriculturally in the 1920s, with field crops and livestock products valued at more than $4.5 million, representing the region's agricultural mainstays. The debate over electric power began when local officials accused the private utility, owned by the Hussa Canning and Pickle Company, of overcharging for the electricity it provided. The election notice stated, "Shall the electric utility plant and equipment used and useful of the convenience of the public, known as Hussa Brothers Electric Power and Light Plant, owned by the Hussa Canning and Pickle Company be acquired by the Village of Bangor?"[5]

Private capital obviously existed since the Hussa Brothers had already built the plant with private funds. Control over rate setting was the issue in Bangor. Before the election a committee of the village board published a statement declaring seven reasons why they favored municipal ownership. The introduction to the declaration read: "[By] acquiring the electric utility property in the Village of Bangor and operating it under municipal ownership . . . cheaper electric rates can be obtained for the consumers of our village."[6] The first two reasons addressed the cost of electricity. Electrical customers in Bangor paid 15 cents per kilowatt hour for the first twenty hours of commercial power and the first ten hours of residential electricity, while people in nearby towns with municipal power paid on average between 9.5 and 11 cents per kilowatt hour. The implication for the citizens of Bangor clearly was that the Hussa Brothers overcharged for electricity. The statement then listed the rate per kilowatt hour for seven towns with municipal ownership as shown in Table 4.1.[7] For the seven towns the mean rate was 7.0 cents, the low rate was 5.0 cents, and the high rate was 9.75 cents.

The committee also proclaimed that municipal ownership would benefit the town in other ways. Public power would reduce the cost of municipal services such as street lighting and water pumping since electricity
would cost the town less. Private ownership sought to make a profit, but
the town would retain any profits made under public ownership. The statement attempted to dispel any notions that municipal ownership might be
radical in nature when it noted that thirty-nine other Wisconsin communities of comparable size and eighty-six towns and cities in the state owned
their electrical systems. The implication was obvious: municipal ownership was widespread and accepted. Finally, the committee said that no new
taxes would result. Mortgage certificates would finance the purchase of
the system after the state railroad commission set the price.[8]

Table 4.1 Rates of Several Small Wisconsin Towns (in cents per kilowatt hour)

Town	Population 1930	Step One	Step Two	Step Three	Step Four	Mean*
Kaukauna	6,581	11.6	8.7	5.8	2.9	7.25
Two Rivers	10,083	15.6	11.7	7.8	3.9	9.75
Sauk City	1,137	8.0				8.0
Reedsburg	2,967	6.5				6.5
Black River Falls	1,950	7.5				7.5
Lake Mills	2,007	7.0				7.0
Columbus	2,515	5.0				5.0
Mean Rate of seven surrounding towns with municipal power						7.0
Bangor (private)	665	15.0	11.0	7.0	3.5	9.125
Mean Wis. public rate, class b, c, d						7.0†
Mean Wis. private rate, class b, c, d						10.0†

Sources: Document distributed by the committee of citizens in Bangor, Wisconsin, in favor
of the municipal purchase of an electrical production and distribution system (mss UI, box
28, folder "Bangor, Wisconsin, Utilities Case, 1930," Loomis Papers); Bangor Independent,
October 30, 1930; and U.S. Department of Commerce, Bureau of the Census, Fifteenth
Census of the United States, Number and Distribution of Inhabitants. (Washington, DC,
1931), Table 5, "Population of Incorporated Places, 1930 and 1920," 1200–1203.
*For the cities of Kaukauna and Two Rivers, the document reported the step decrease of 2.9
cents. For the cities of Sauk City, Reedsburg, Black River Falls, Lake Mills, and Columbus, it
listed only the top rate; subsequent steps would have been lower. The mean rate for these
towns is thus strongly biased upward, but each town's mean rate was still lower than the
mean for Bangor.
†The document also contained these two figures. In Wisconsin, classes b, c, and d referred
to the population of the towns served; the only class a was Milwaukee.

Along with the village board's statement the *Independent* published a letter entitled "To the Citizens of Bangor" from the Hussa Canning and Pickle Company. The company argued that current rates followed the state utility commission's recommendations. The issue of electrical modernization entered the picture when the letter said that the purpose of lowering rates, as the company understood it, was to enable persons "to install household appliances such as refrigerators, vacuum cleaners, toasters, ranges . . . [so] these appliances could be operated economically."[9] Despite the contentions of the private power company, the town's electorate voted 250 to 57 to buy the power plant. The *Bangor Independent* reported that "the referendum on municipal ownership of the Hussa Bros. Light and Power Plant, drew an unusual large vote."[10]

The citizens of Bangor were very much aware of the possibilities of electrical modernization. During 1929 and 1930 the *Independent* carried many advertisements featuring electrical products. Radios headed the list of items advertised. In January 1929 an advertisement for an "Atwater Kent Radio" stressed that mass production made the radio's low cost possible.[11] Washing machines also were popular items. The Maytag Company's advertisement for the "Farm Maytag" is especially revealing. It featured both electrical and gas-driven models and stated that "this wonder washing Maytag is equally practical for farm homes with or without electricity."[12] Perhaps unknowingly, the advertisement specifically addressed the low degree of electrical modernization that existed in rural America. A Maytag advertisement the following week again featured the washing machine and contained a plug for the Maytag radio program that was broadcasted over more than fifty stations. The same advertisement offered a deferred payment plan.[13]

Advertisements for electric ranges and ovens that explicitly addressed electrical modernization also appeared in the Bangor paper. The top line of an advertisement for an "L&H Electric Rangette" read: "If it's electric, it's modern." The same advertisement also noted that the range required "no special wiring" since it plugged into any wall outlet, a reference to the problem of standardization that existed.[14] Another advertisement for an electric range equipped with a timer told readers that they could come home to a hot meal and consequently "enjoy more leisure hours."[15] The lack of electrical modernization again appeared when several advertisements for radios and washing machines stated that either battery-powered or gas-driven appliances were available for homes without electrical power.[16]

In 1930 fewer advertisements for washing machines, radios, and ranges appeared in the *Bangor Independent*.[17] In June an advertisement listing an electric iron and percolator did appear, and in August and October the paper contained an advertisement for a Speed Queen washer.[18] Several reasons might explain the decline in the number of advertisements that appeared in 1930. First, merchants may have saturated the market. Fewer advertisements existed because people stopped buying appliances. A second and more plausible explanation might be that people were beginning to feel the impact of the Depression and simply had less money to spend. The third and fourth possible explanations, somewhat related to the first two, were the lack of electrical modernization and high rates. Fewer people bought appliances in 1930 because they lived in homes without adequate wiring to operate such appliances. High rates are a corollary explanation. People could not afford the electricity needed to operate electric radios, washing machines, and ranges, so no incentive existed to buy such items. This premise is what Norris and other argued on the national level: only low-cost public power would facilitate wide-scale modernization. The impact of the Depression, coupled with the high cost of appliances, exacerbated this situation. The timing of the public power fight in Bangor suggests that by the fall of 1930 many town citizens had modernized partially and took action to lower the cost of operating electrical appliances.

Not only does the debate in Bangor allow a brief glimpse into local-level politics regarding the questions of public power and electrical modernization, but it also provides the opportunity to examine the relationship of local political behavior to congressional voting. Bangor was part of Wisconsin's Seventh Congressional District, where voters elected Merlin Hull, a Republican from Black River Falls, to Congress in 1928. Municipal power systems operated in fourteen towns in the district including Bangor and Black River Falls. Before going to Washington, Hull served as an elected official, first as a district attorney, then as a state representative, and finally as Wisconsin's secretary of state. Trained as a lawyer, Hull also farmed and published the *Jackson County Journal* (1904–1926) and the *Banner-Journal* (1926–1953). He voted against the Reece amendment to lease Muscle Shoals and voted for the conference report that called for the area's public development.

Additional evidence underscores Congressman Hull's commitment to public power. The *Bangor Independent* carried his editorial column where he often expressed his opinions about a variety of political issues. One of Hull's favorite topics was the FTC investigation of the electrical utility industry. In an October 1930 column, he discussed "the financing methods of the big holding companies which have so extensively gained monopolistic control over the public utilities of the country in the last decade."[19] To underscore his point, Hull wrote that FTC investigators had recently discovered that a North Carolina utility, through holding companies, had falsely increased the value of its stock from $39 million to $61 million. Another utility sold power to residential users at 7.0 cents per kilowatt hour but dropped the rate to 1.5 cents for commercial customers, all under the guise of state-level regulation. He condemned both practices as especially detrimental to hardworking, honest Americans. Hull's votes on public power and his views on the FTC investigation, when coupled with the attitudes of those he represented, suggest that a relationship existed between local politics and congressional attitudes.[20]

The number of towns with municipal power in the district and the publishing of articles about private power in the local paper indicate that public control of power was a pertinent local political issue. The area's congressman voted in a way that further underscores the argument that a relationship existed between the attitudes of the local electorate and the behavior of their elected officials on the national level. The implication is that local politics provided the foundation for support for public power and opposition to private utilities at the national level.

Three years after the people of Bangor voted for public ownership, the village of Pardeeville, Wisconsin, population 873, held a similar election. Situated thirty miles north of Madison in Columbia County, grain and hay dominated the area's economy, placing the county in seventh position among Wisconsin counties in the total value of field crops and twenty-eighth in the value of livestock products.[21] Issues similar to those that existed in Bangor came to the forefront in Pardeeville. Should the town buy the existing, privately owned power plant and distribution system? Agitation for municipal ownership began as early as March 1928. It was not until the winter of 1932–1933, however, that the debate became heated when the *Pardeeville-Wyocena Times* began publishing articles urging village leaders to explore ways of reducing electrical rates. The paper noted that other Wisconsin towns were contemplating similar moves.[22] Quickly, the debate in Pardeeville developed into a two-sided affair over who could provide the cheapest power and best service.

The *Times*, although it later supported municipal power, published a series of articles that J. W. Jamieson, the village council's president, wrote. His comments mirrored many that private power proponents made nationwide. Jamieson wrote that municipal ownership would result in less efficient management, and that "the high degree of service rendered by utilities today is due entirely to private initiative and could not have been obtained through municipal or government operation." He also claimed that the apparent lower rates that municipal systems charged could be attributed to different, less stringent accounting procedures. Finally, he stated that a smaller tax base would result since the private company paid taxes, but the proposed public system would be tax-exempt. A *Times* editorial, possibly written to refute claims of municipal mismanagement, stated that a method of reducing electrical rates must be found. The editor said that public ownership had accomplished that end elsewhere and the same might occur "with honest and economical operation."[23] In March the *Times* began carrying stories discussing the public power debates in other towns and comparing private and public rates in towns that had established municipal power.

A story in the March 9 issue, for example, reported that when the mayor of Lehigh, Pennsylvania, convinced the city council to order a diesel generator to light the city's streets, the Pennsylvania Light and Power Company offered to cut rates by 42 percent. According to the article the city still planned to buy the generator. The following week the paper reported that Hartford, Wisconsin, residents paid nine cents per kilowatt hour for municipal power. Revenue from the Hartford system financed a new city hall and community center. In the same issue the paper said that West Bend, Wisconsin, residents paid twelve cents for privately generated power.[24]

Another issue that emerged in Pardeeville involved taxation. Many small towns that generated and distributed their power produced enough revenue so residents did not pay any local property taxes. Jamieson challenged public power supporters on this point and admitted that although it held some merit there had been no local discussion of towns with failing public systems. He also charged that public power advocates made unfair rate comparisons with cities of much larger size such as Los Angeles, Seattle, Tacoma, Jacksonville, and Cleveland.[25] The success of public power in those cities had even become news in small Wisconsin villages.

The debate over public power intensified as village residents went to the polls to elect town officials. Voters elected Charles Smith Jr. as village president, and the paper quickly pointed out that his pro–public power stance had contributed to his victory. The *Times* stated that the paramount election issue had been public power, and the public power mayoral candidate had won because "the sentiment for reduced electrical rates had grown by leaps and bounds in the past few weeks."[26] Before the town voted to buy the private system the village's new president and board of trustees met with the owner of the private utility, Pardeeville Light Company, to try to persuade him to lower rates. The company's owner, Dr. Joseph Chandler, said he could only lower rates from 11.5 cents to 11 cents per kilowatt hour, claiming that revenue decreases the previous year prevented any further reduction. Village officials countered that documents on file with the state utility commission in Madison revealed a much different picture and that the past year had been quite profitable.[27]

Rates continued to drive the debate a week later when two members of the board of trustees returned from Stratford, Wisconsin. They reported that Stratford had voted to establish public power eight years earlier and had since enjoyed lower electric rates. In late July, Frank J. Curtin, Stratford's town clerk, visited Pardeeville and spoke in praise of municipal ownership. Curtin told Pardeeville residents what Stratford's citizens paid for electricity before and after the establishment of municipal power. The private rate for the first two hundred kilowatt hours was nine cents; the public rate was six cents. For the next two hundred hours Stratford's citizens paid the private company eight cents per kilowatt hour, but under municipal ownership they paid five cents for the next four hundred kilowatt hours.[28]

In June two hundred village citizens signed a petition calling for a referendum to decide if the town should buy the private power company. Late in the month the *Times* published a strong public power editorial demanding a vote. The editorial stressed four points. First, the village had approached the private company's owner, Dr. Chandler, in good faith about securing a rate reduction. Chandler said that a reduction could only occur if the Wisconsin Power Company, an Insull subsidiary, from which the Pardeeville company evidently bought supplemental power, also lowered its rates. Second, the village rates should be comparable to communities of similar size. On the third point the editorial echoed the words of Norris, Pinchot, and Roosevelt in calling into question the effectiveness of state regulation: "Electricity has become a practical necessity in the average American home, and the various states have established commissions to protect the rights of producer and consumer. . . . It is reasonable to assume that reports submitted to the commission by such corporations are always compiled with a view to obtaining larger dividends for its stockholders." The editorial's fourth point was a call for the village's citizens to take "a progressive step" and purchase the local utility.[29] The message was explicit and nearly identical to what public power advocates said on the national level in legislative fights over Muscle Shoals and Boulder Dam. Private power companies overcharged and were beyond the control of state regulators. Only one option existed for Americans to secure lower rates for electrical energy, public ownership. Just before the vote, the *Times* reported that a yes vote would equal lower electric rates. The referendum passed overwhelmingly 237 to 53.[30]

As had occurred in Bangor before the establishment of public power, the local paper in Pardeeville contained many announcements and advertisements relating to electricity. In the late 1920s the Wisconsin Power and Light Company ran many advertisements in the *Pardeeville-Wyocena Times* emphasizing good and expanding service.[31] Company officials also tried to defuse any notions that it fell under the control of the private utility industry. An announcement in June read: "We Are Owned, Patronized and Regulated by the People." The announcement continued that more than eleven thousand Wisconsin residents owned stock in the company and that state regulatory bodies controlled the company's rates and service. The following month the company addressed the issue of absentee ownership and stated that it did not operate on a "'here—today and gone—tomorrow' basis." Instead, it was part of the tax-paying community. Wisconsin Power and Light also stressed modernization and low rates in an advertisement that called electricity the "Untiring Servant at Wages All Can Afford." A December advertisement featured a sketch of a woman ironing and said that an electric flatiron cost only 5.5 cents per hour to operate.[32]

During the years before the establishment of municipal power, the *Times* featured many advertisements for electrical appliances. Advertisements for radios headed the list, although others for electric refrigerators also appeared.[33] In December 1929 a Pardeeville Electric Store advertisement urged people to give electrical Christmas gifts, listing lamps, toasters, percolators, corn poppers, waffle irons, vacuum cleaners, washing machines, portable heaters, and radios as possible choices.[34] Advertisements for electric or gas-powered Speed Queen washers similar to those that ran in the Bangor paper appeared in the *Times* in the fall of 1930.[35]

The number of advertisements declined in the early 1930s, just as had occurred in Bangor. Those that did appear featured smaller appliances such as irons and coffeepots.[36] As in Bangor, electrical modernization was very much on the minds of the citizens of Pardeeville. Private power interests also recognized the importance of electricity and stressed the fairness of rates and the quality of service to win support. Despite those assurances, citizens voted for public power in 1933 as had their congressman in Washington. In the 1926 general election, voters sent Republican Charles Kading to Washington. Kading practiced law and engaged in agricultural pursuits for a living. Before his election he had served in various local offices.[37] Kading voted for Boulder Dam in 1928. Each time he voted on Muscle Shoals he favored public development. As in Bangor, the district's congressman supported public power.

Besides the insight that the Pardeeville situation provides on the issues of private versus public rates and political control, it also enables the examination of two problems that could have developed when a town voted to buy an existing plant: the possibility of the private company filing lawsuits to invalidate the referendum and the difficulty of setting a fair purchase price. The private company that had served Pardeeville attempted to delay the purchase of its property through a series of legal maneuvers.[38] The inability of the involved parties to determine a just price delayed Pardeeville's purchase of the power plant. Under Wisconsin law it was the Public Service Commission's responsibility to set what it considered a fair price for the existing property. In Pardeeville the private company, the Pardeeville Electric Light Company, said that the because town officials made a mistake in filling out legal forms, the commission did not have the jurisdiction to set the price, thus invalidating any purchase. Company representatives considered the town's acquisition a "voluntary acquisition of utility property . . . rather than an adversary proceedings." The town claimed the acquisition was adverse. The difference was more than semantics; different sections of the legal code governed each type of acquisition.

The Public Service Commission believed that the town's takeover was by "adverse" means. If the company's claim that the acquisition had been voluntary was true, then the hearing would have been in error and ruled invalid. Company officials also argued that because mortgage bonds would finance the purchase of the plant, the sale by definition had to be voluntary. The assertion was that since people voted voluntarily, they freely decided to acquire the plant. The state supreme court ruled for Pardeeville.

Although Pardeeville won the initial ruling, the case remained in the state courts for several years. The court first ordered the commission to set the acquisition price in 1935. Because the court did not resolve the legal issues until July 1938, the commission, acting on the 1935 order, set the compensation price at $25,000. The company again sued, claiming that the commission had set that value based on property values as of December 31, 1935, not 1938, although fire destroyed some property in 1937. Between 1935 and 1938 the state supreme court ruled on the company's original suits and again ordered the commission to set the amount of compensation. The commission made an error when it did not appraise the property at a 1938 value even though that value probably had declined after the 1937 fire. In 1941 the state supreme court ruled in favor of the company on the issue of just compensation and ordered the Public Service Commission to decide the compensation.

It appears that the private company sought to delay the case and the takeover as long as possible. Despite the company's claims, the takeover was not voluntary. More revealing is the company's decision to have the compensation case reheard after fire destroyed part of its property. It is likely that the new amount would be less than $25,000 because of the fire damage. Despite the chance that it would take a loss on the property, the company willingly had the case heard in court to try to prevent the municipal takeover. The potential for profits was the most likely reason for the company's action, even at the risk of having to accept a lower compensation amount if the courts ruled against the company.

The people of Pardeeville's primary concern was lower rates; in other towns residents also expressed concern about profits from electrical sales leaving the community. Source material allows for the examination of both issues and their importance to the public power fight in southeast Missouri. In Sikeston, Missouri, population 5,676, the people voted to construct a municipal plant in April 1930. Before that time a private company furnished the city with electricity via a high-voltage transmission line. Whereas the citizens of Bangor and Pardeeville bought existing electrical systems, the people of Sikeston built their system. The primary reasons the citizens of Sikeston wanted to own their plant were lower rates and keeping profits made from electrical sales in the community instead of sending them to a private utility out of the area. Located in Scott County, the land around

Sikeston produced an abundance of grains and other field crops. Perhaps indicative of a lack of farm mechanization, the value of mules and mule colts in the county was among the highest in the state.[39]

Agitation for municipal power began in 1929, when a local paper, the *Sikeston Standard*, began gathering information calling attention to successfully operated municipal plants in Missouri and elsewhere.[40] In January 1930 the Missouri Utility Company's franchise agreement with the city expired, and the company sought a new, twenty-year agreement. The *Standard* opposed renewing the franchise agreement and stated so in several editorials. The editor said that Missouri Utility wanted a new lease because it returned a large profit on power sales in the town. A twenty-year lease would effectively squelch the municipal power debate for the length of the lease. A week later the paper's editor discussed rates and retaining profit as two reasons for supporting municipal power. Rates would remain the same until the public plant cleared itself of debt, but then they would decline. Under current conditions the private company made enough profit to pave more than a mile of city streets each year if the money stayed in the community.[41]

As had happened in Pardeeville, both sides made comparisons between the rates charged in Sikeston and other towns. The *Standard* published reports from several towns with municipal power—Shiner, Texas; Wakefield, Nebraska; and Slater, Missouri—all claiming that public ownership resulted in lower rates and usually lower taxes. A *Standard* editorial at the end of January again discussed rates and referenced the national debate. The editor said recently released findings of federal investigators regarding the private utility industry should remove any doubt about voting for public power.[42]

The town's other newspaper, the *Sikeston Herald*, also covered the debate over the municipal power proposal. In a January 23 article the *Herald* reported on the recent city council meeting where an outside engineering firm had presented a favorable report on the proposed plant. The *Herald* countered the *Standard*'s strong endorsement with more tempered reporting that detailed several residents' concerns regarding the report's accuracy. On the editorial page of the same issue, the *Herald* took a strong position against the project and called the engineering report "most unusual. . . . and more of an argument for a municipal power plant than an estimate of what one would cost." The paper criticized the report because it did not consider emergency costs, depreciation, and the amount of money allocated for routine maintenance. A news story also appeared on the editorial page discussing the problems that the people of Fredericktown, Missouri, had encountered with their municipal power plant after an ice and sleet storm.[43]

The *Herald*'s writers continued to question the wisdom of municipal power the following week when they published the current light rates and bills of thirteen Sikeston businesses and thirteen residential customers. The paper then listed what those bills would be if Sikeston's rates equaled those of the municipal power system in Forrest City, Arkansas. If those rates existed in Sikeston, the article maintained, the electrical bills of businesses and residents would increase 26 percent and 39 percent, respectively. An article that appeared in February reiterated the idea that public power would increase Sikeston's light rates when it compared the city's current rates with those charged in ten municipal power towns.[44]

To advance their cause, residents favoring municipal power in Sikeston organized the Citizens' Light and Power League. The league selected a president and secretary and distributed petitions calling for a vote to pass bonds to finance a public power plant. The *Standard* soon reported that more than two thousand people had signed the petitions.[45] Opponents of the proposed plant also organized a pressure group and held an inaugural meeting in early March.[46] Organizing political interest groups underscores the political importance that the town's citizens placed on establishing municipal power. The city council finally decided to place a $150,000 bond issue on the local ballot for citizens to vote on in early April. At the time the council authorized the vote, the Missouri Utility Company declared that it was cutting rates in Sikeston and about forty other communities in central and southeast Missouri. The *Standard* quickly linked the rate cut to the upcoming election and said the rate reduction was only in response to calls for municipal power.[47]

The *Standard*'s editors voiced strong support for the bond measure, while the *Herald*'s expressed equally strong opposition. The *Herald* questioned raising the city's indebtedness by $150,000 and stated that a small chance for success did not warrant such an expenditure. It urged those opposed to the plant to work for the defeat of the "white elephant."[48] As election day neared, municipal power opponents, now identifying themselves as the Citizens' Organization Opposing the City Light Plant, stepped up their campaign in a series of full-page political announcements in the *Herald*. One announcement focused on the prospect of higher rates if the bonds carried and listed, on a percentage basis, how much more residents in seven towns with municipal power paid in comparison with Sikeston. The announcement called the bonds liens against private property and claimed that "the argument that the light plant will pay all this [the bonds] and save our property is speculation, highly experimental and risky."[49]

After three months of intense debate the voters of Sikeston approved the bond initiative by a 1,240 to 517 vote (70.5 percent) on April 1, 1930. A small controversy followed, since a few people did not vote on the power bonds but did vote on other ballot issues. Missouri law required a two-thirds vote to pass bond measures. If election officials had included the number of blank bond ballots in the total count, the percentage of yea votes would have been less than the two-thirds needed for passage. Following some debate, state officials excluded the blank ballots from the total count thus validating the vote.[50] The city then awarded contracts for construction of the plant and system that featured two 448-kilowatt diesel generators. A board of public works, which the mayor appointed and the city council approved, supervised the plant's operation.

The Sikeston plant began operation on May 31, 1931. By January 1932 it furnished power for 1,050 of the town's 1,250 customers, while the remaining customers continued to buy power from the Missouri Utilities Company. The plant in its first six months of operation turned a net profit of $6,070. Local authorities calculated that when the plant operated at full capacity for an entire year, the resulting net profits would be approximately $26,950 per year.[51]

In Sikeston electrical modernization and cheaper rates entered the public power debate. Similar to what had occurred in Bangor and Pardeeville, the newspapers in Sikeston contained many advertisements and announcements encouraging the purchase and use of electrical appliances. Before the establishment of municipal power the Missouri Utilities Company often ran newspaper advertisements featuring the latest electrical innovations. The quest for home modernization became a political goal of the community in the spring of 1930 when the town's mayor proclaimed the "modernization of the homes of the city is a most important step."[52] An editorial in the *Standard* called modernization essential to civic improvement and progress and the foundation of the community. The paper reported that the program itself followed President Hoover's lead in seeking the return of prosperity through home modernization.[53] For twenty-six weeks the *Sikeston Standard* printed a series of articles addressing some aspect of modernization. An Iowa newspaper had compiled the material, and Congressman F. Dickinson Letts (R-Iowa) had presented it to President Hoover's secretary. In March, articles that addressed the electrical aspects of modernization appeared, urging readers to install plenty of electrical features and outlets in order to use electrical energy fully.[54]

Electrical modernization also found its way into advertising in the *Sikeston Standard*. An advertisement placed by a private company read: "Use Electric Power to Make Home Work Easier." Invoking themes similar to those that Pinchot, Norris, and others articulated, the advertisement continued: "Electric power for doing home work has become an accepted factor by women everywhere. It not only lightens duties that were arduous, but it releases for pleasure the many hours hitherto spent in housework. The cost of wiring your home is not great."[55] Missouri Utilities Company spokesmen also pushed electrical modernization in advertisements that invoked such phrases as "Modernize Your Home," "Let Electricity Work for You," and "Electricity Is Cheap in Sikeston."[56] Many merchant-sponsored advertisements for radios, refrigerators, ranges, coffeepots, flatirons, waffle irons, and other appliances appeared in both the *Sikeston Standard* and the *Sikeston Herald* in 1930 and 1931.[57]

Viewed together, the emphasis on home modernization, lower rates, and the desire to keep profits within the city treasury shows the high degree of concern felt by Sikeston's residents regarding electricity and public power. That concern, similar to what existed in the other small towns examined and in Congress, involved creating a better future using electricity. Explicit in that belief was the idea that the private corporation that previously had provided power overcharged customers and drained money from the local economy. As in Bangor and Pardeeville, political control of electricity for economic reasons, not insufficient capital or technology, drove the decision to develop municipal power. In response to a survey that Ely's Institute for Research in Land Economics conducted, the superintendent of the town's board of public works noted that the plant provided the only source of revenue except local taxes. The superintendent said the plant had "proven to be the 'goose that lays the Golden Eggs' to us."[58]

Sikeston was part of Missouri's Fourteenth Congressional District. Two different legislators represented Sikeston between 1928 and 1931. Voters sent Democrat James F. Fulbright to Congress in 1922, 1926, and 1930, although he lost reelection campaigns in 1924, 1928, and 1932. Fulbright had served in the Missouri Assembly from 1913 to 1919, the last two years as speaker pro tempore. His career in state politics followed a six-year career as the prosecuting attorney in Ripley County, Missouri, and in 1919 he began a two-year term as mayor of Doniphan.[59] While in office from 1927 to 1929, Fulbright voted for public development of Muscle Shoals and Boulder Dam.

Dewey Short defeated Fulbright in the 1928 general election. Educated as both an intellectual and a minister, Short graduated from Baker University in Baldwin, Kansas, in 1919 and from Boston University in 1922. He also attended Harvard University, Heidelberg University, the University of Berlin, and Oxford University. As a professor at Southwestern University, he taught ethics, psychology, and political philosophy. Short ran successfully as a Republican for Congress in 1928, although he lost his reelection attempt in 1930. He returned to Congress in 1935 and served until 1955. In 1957 he became assistant secretary of the army during Eisenhower's second administration.[60] While in the House, Short initially favored leasing Muscle Shoals as indicated when he was paired in favor of the Reece amendment. Although he did not vote on the 1930 Muscle Shoals bill, he showed his support in a pair and voted for the conference report that called for public development.

In Missouri's Fourteenth Congressional District, seven towns either publicly produced or bought their electrical energy. As in Wisconsin it appears that local politics influenced the voting behavior of the district's congressional representatives. On the local level the importance of political party affiliation somewhat mirrored that found in Congress. The Democrat Fulbright usually supported the public power legislation, whereas the Republican Short sometimes opposed it.

As part of its growing interest in public utilities in the United States, the Institute for Research in Land Economics that Richard Ely founded in the early 1920s undertook a study of municipal power. Part of the information came from government agencies such as the Census Bureau or from private organizations like NELA. The staff did, however, engage in an extensive mailing campaign to make the data as complete and accurate as possible. The institute sent a form letter to towns that had appeared in other sources, asking if a municipal plant existed, the date of its origin, and the type of generator used.[61]

The responses Ely received further reveal the political nature of the debate regarding electricity. Another Missouri town cited reasons for wanting public power similar to those of Sikeston. In his reply, the city clerk of Sullivan, Missouri, population 2,013, responded that they wanted to build a municipal plant, but the Missouri Electric Power Company had filed a suit that delayed construction. The clerk claimed that the power company was "playing for time" and called its suit groundless. It appears that rate control and money leaving the community motivated the town's decision to build the plant. In his response, the clerk wrote that "they [the power company] get around $7,500 per month out of our city."[62] It was not apparent from the clerk's response if the $7,500 was in profits, but evidently money was the issue. The clerk did not make clear what electric services such as heating, lighting, and cooking were available in Sullivan. As in the other towns studied, agriculture dominated the area around Sullivan, and Franklin County ranked high in the value of dairy products and field crops.[63]

Clarence Cannon, a Democrat, represented the people of Sullivan and the rest of Missouri's Ninth Congressional District. Two other towns in Missouri's ninth district either produced or distributed electricity publicly. Trained as a lawyer, Cannon's career in politics began in 1915 when he became the parliamentarian for the U.S. House of Representatives. First elected to Congress in 1922, he served for more than forty years until his death in 1964.[64] Cannon cast yea votes each time he voted on a public power issue. He did not vote on the Reece amendment but was paired against it. Again, the implication is that a relationship existed between local-level politics and congressional voting behavior.

The town clerk of Whalan, Minnesota, population 155, responded to the institute's questionnaire in October 1930. Whalan once owned a small plant for street lighting but since November 1928 had bought power from Lanesboro, Minnesota, a town about three miles away, and distributed it publicly. Whalan financed the distribution system through bond sales that required voter approval, suggesting that voters knew about the issues confronting the town regarding electricity and voted to abolish its private control.[65]

Lanesboro municipally produced its electricity and the power that it sold to Whalan. In responding to the questionnaire, Whalan's clerk stated, "The current is purchased from Lanesboro at a reduced price and distributed again at a fair gain for the municipality."[66] The city clerk mentioned bond sales, reduced rates, and fair gain. The reduced rates may have been in comparison with the rates a private company charged the community before 1928, since the village only produced municipal power for street lighting before that time. Fair gain suggests that the citizens of Whalan believed that the private company overcharged them for electricity. Both phrases hint at the idea that the townspeople believed the private company had treated them unfairly.

Lanesboro had established its municipal power plant in 1908. In 1928, however, some of the town's citizens began to question the need to continue public ownership. Public power supporters quickly organized and silenced the calls for privatization. Lanesboro's local newspaper, *LeVang's Weekly,* supported public power and carried many articles that discussed public power issues locally and from across the nation. In January 1928 the paper carried a story about Muscle Shoals and called the area a "priceless natural resource." The article quoted Norris extensively about the political activities of the private utility industry in both the Muscle Shoals and Boulder Dam controversies.[67]

In March 1928 *LeVang's Weekly* published an article by Dr. A. P. Lommen, a commissioner on the town's recently created utility board. Lommen squarely addressed what he believed to be the advantages of municipal power—even if additional generating capacity became necessary—and why the town should retain public power instead of "hooking up with the High Line or Power Trust." He first cited the rate issue. Lommen said that Lanesboro's rates were less than half of what other villages in the area paid for private service. Second, if the village switched to private service, it would lose a large source of revenue.[68]

The importance of public power came to the political forefront as Minnesota began considering senatorial candidates in 1928. *LeVang's Weekly* reprinted an article that first appeared in the *St. Paul Pioneer Press* that contained a list of questions directed to Senate candidates. The second question was "What about the encroachment of private interests on power rights at Muscle Shoals and Boulder Dam?"[69] The question directly addressed the major public power issues that Congress debated and revealed that Muscle Shoals, Boulder Dam, and the activities of private power were issues of political importance in Minnesota.

Public power questions also entered the local mayoral contest in Lanesboro in the spring of 1928. The eventual winner, G. B. Ellestad, broadcasted a statement denying charges that he was less than supportive of municipal power. He denounced allegations that he favored a flat electric rate and opposed power sales to other towns (such as Whalan). Finally, he denied that his son worked for a power company or that he owned utility stock.[70]

Rates and taxes continued to be subjects of articles in *LeVang's Weekly* in the spring of 1928. An article in April reported that Lanesboro had the second lowest rates in the Northwest: only Tacoma, Washington, had lower rates. The same article claimed that municipal power paid part of the town's general expenses, resulting in some of the lowest taxes in the region for Lanesboro's residents. The following month the paper ran a story about private power entitled "Greatest Lobby Ever Organized" that reported the degree of corporate control of the electrical industry nationwide.[71] As did the *Pardeeville-Wyocena Times* and the *Sikeston Standard*, *LeVang's Weekly* published articles about the success of public power elsewhere. Stories about Colby, Kansas, and Jackson, Minnesota, appeared in June and July. In August the paper ran an article that Norris had written entitled "Politics and Your Electricity Bills." Norris repeated many themes that appeared in other speeches and writings. He discussed concentration and corruption in the utility industry, called for hydroelectric development, and outlined the success of public power in Tacoma, Seattle, and Ontario.[72]

At the same time that *LeVang's Weekly* featured articles about the private utility industry, it also carried many advertisements for electrical appliances. As in Bangor, Pardeeville, and Sikeston, the emphasis was on using electricity. Advertisements for radios appeared in numerous issues. Several advertisements stressed the advantages of electricity to the poultry farmer in the form of electrically powered incubators and other equipment.[73] Smiling female operators were featured in advertisements for electric washers touted as "simple, safe, efficient, and economical" and available on terms. An announcement in May told the public to keep an eye out for the new line of Frigidaire refrigerators.[74] In the fall of 1928 several advertisements featuring radios appeared, and one stressed the importance of having a radio to keep up with national events, politics, and football scores.[75] In October a washing machine, available with a gas motor for homes without electricity, appeared in an advertisement. The following month a General Electric vacuum cleaner appeared.[76] The articles and advertisements published in *LeVang's Weekly* show that despite its small population (1,014), important issues in Lanesboro were electrical rates, revenue, and modernization. Stories about national politics also reveal that the town's citizens were aware of the utility industry, Muscle Shoals, Boulder Dam, and municipal power in other towns and cities. Printing Norris's article again shows his national stature as a public power spokesman and the town's awareness of national political events.

Minnesota's First Congressional District encompassed both Whalan and Lanesboro. Seventeen other towns in the district had municipal power. Both towns are located in Fillmore County, a region rich in agriculture output. The value of livestock, livestock products, and crops in the county all ranked near the top in Minnesota in 1930.[77] Allen Furlow, a Republican, represented the district from 1925 to 1929. Furlow, a graduate of George Washington University law school, practiced law and served in the statehouse before his election to Congress.[78] While in Congress, he voted for Muscle Shoals and Boulder Dam on the key votes. In 1928 Furlow lost in his reelection bid to Victor Christgau. Educated as an agriculturist, Christgau also served in the state senate from 1927 to 1929, when he resigned to take his House seat.[79] He also voted for public control of Muscle Shoals. On the five major power votes in the House between 1928 and 1931, the congressmen from Minnesota's first district voted for public power each time. It again appears that a strong relationship existed between local politics and congressional voting behavior.

Some towns, instead of building a power plant, contracted with a private company to buy electricity wholesale and then distribute it publicly. Such was the case in Stark, Kansas, where the city clerk also returned the institute's survey. In Stark, a town of 197 people, a group of private citizens built the first electric system in 1920 and sold power for street and residential lighting. The city bought the distribution system in 1928 and strung four miles of high-voltage cable to connect with the Kansas Utility Company's system at Salsburg. The high line furnished power for all of the town's lighting and electrical needs. Adequate private capital appears to have existed in Stark, since a group of private citizens built the first system in 1920. By 1928 sufficient technology existed to make the high-voltage transmission link possible, and Stark's residents chose to buy power and distribute it publicly.[80]

Stark, located in Neosho County in southeast Kansas, was part of the state's Third Congressional District, an area where a variety of agricultural enterprises existed including dairy farming, cattle, and field crops. Unlike the other towns thus far examined, Stark's congressional representative usually opposed public development of Muscle Shoals and the Boulder Dam legislation. William Sproul, a graduate of Kansas State University Law School, represented the third district. Before his congressional election he served as mayor of Sedan, Kansas (1921–1923). When not involved in politics, the Republican congressman raised cattle and engaged in the oil and gas business. Sproul opposed public control of Muscle Shoals and construction of Boulder Dam in 1928. He initially favored leasing Muscle Shoals in

1930. When that failed, he voted for public development as contained in the conference report.[81]

Townspeople in Yoakum, Texas, population 5,656, decided to construct a publicly owned generation and distribution system after the franchise for the town expired on December 31, 1931. At first, the town wanted to purchase the existing plant and distribution system, but the private utility company refused to sell. Instead of instigating a legal suit and condemning the private company's property, Yoakum's citizens decided to construct a publicly owned generation and distribution system consisting of three 420-horsepower diesel engines that would produce almost 940 kilowatts of electricity.[82] Adequate technology and capital apparently existed in Yoakum, since a private plant already operated. Yet, the townspeople decided to fund and built a municipal plant instead of continuing the private service of an existing one. The most logical explanation was rate control. The actual generation and distribution system must have been adequate, because the town initially wanted to buy it; quality of service does not appear to have been an issue.

Positioned approximately halfway between Austin and the Gulf Coast, cattle and field crops dominated the local agricultural economy with a combined value of more than $6 million.[83] Joseph Mansfield represented Yoakum and the Ninth Congressional District in the House of Representatives. Mansfield was Horatio Alger in disguise. As a young man he worked as a farm and nursery laborer. Later he was a baggage master and freight clerk for the Southern Pacific Railroad. After studying law he became a member of the Texas bar in 1886. Before his election to Congress he held several public positions including district attorney, school superintendent, and county judge.[84] A Democrat, Mansfield did not vote on the Boulder Dam conference report or the Reece amendment. He did, however, support public power the three times he voted. Two other towns besides Yoakum had public power in the ninth district. As in most of the other towns, it appears that a relationship existed between local politics and congressional voting.

The local political debate that existed in each of these small towns supports the thesis that politics drove the decision to establish public power. Examining aggregate level data provides yet another method for exploring the issues surrounding the decision to produce or distribute electricity publicly. Looking at the number of towns that opted for public distribution of power gives insight into this issue. In the 1920s adequate technology existed to enable a town to buy power wholesale and transmit it over long-distance transmission lines, such as in Stark, Kansas. Distribution would occur over a municipally owned system. Two reasons existed to explain this purchase and distribution procedure. Buying electricity wholesale allowed a town to get the best price possible. The publicly owned distribution system meant that the town could decide how much profit to make, within legal limits. Public distribution also meant that any resulting revenue would remain in the local economy, a concern expressed in Sikeston, Missouri, and Sullivan, Kansas.

In 1925 slightly over half the communities with public power in the United States purchased electricity wholesale and distributed it publicly.[85] In 1932 that percentage rose to almost 60 percent. This information contains several implications important for understanding municipal power. The fact that by the mid-1920s half the communities bought power breaks down the technological explanation of public power.[86] Technology made the municipal purchase and distribution of power possible. Without transmission lines it would have been difficult for a community to buy power wholesale. Public money financed the construction and maintenance of the distribution system, which included the placement of power poles, the stringing of lines, meter installation, and the establishment of an agency to oversee operation, billing, and maintenance. Public money also would have financed right-of-way privilege costs for transmission lines and line construction. A composite view of the eight municipalities examined is represented in Table 4.2. Several features of the table merit comment. The first is size. The towns' populations varied from 155 people in Stark to 5,676 people in Sikeston. By nearly any definition Stark was a small town. The reason for establishing a public distribution system, as Stark's city clerk reported, was revenue control, not lack of technology or capital. Despite a population of only 155, the town voted to buy the existing privately built and owned distribution system and build the high-voltage line. Sikeston

Table 4.2 Composite Table of Towns with Municipal Power

Town	Population 1930	Reason for Mun. Power	Congressional District	Towns with Mun. Power
Bangor	665	rates	WI 7	13
Lanesboro	1,014	rates/ revenue	MN 1	19
Pardeeville	873	rates	WI 2	13
Sikeston	5,676	rates/ revenue	MO 14	7
Stark	197	revenue	KS 3	18
Sullivan	2,013	rates	MO 9	2
Whalan	155	rates/ revenue	MN 1	19
Yoakum	5,656	rates	TX 9	3

Source: For population figures see U.S. Department of Commerce, Bureau of the Census, *Fifteenth Census of the United States, Number and Distribution of Inhabitants* (Washington, DC, 1931), Table 5, "Population of Incorporated Places, 1930 and 1920," 426, 573, 576, 627, 1091, 1200, and 1202.

also bought the existing system and built the high-voltage line necessary to buy power wholesale. In both municipalities, technological advancement contributed to the establishment of municipal power. In Sikeston the necessary bond measure passed after an intense political debate over electrical rates played out in the town's newspapers.

The other six towns' populations ranged from 197 to 5,656. In these towns the citizens believed that private utilities treated them unfairly. Each town responded to this perception when it decided to produce, distribute, or buy and distribute electricity publicly. Several generalizations are possible after examining these towns. One, population, within the range of the towns studied, did not appear to influence a town's decision to enact public power legislation. Two, politics, not capital or technological problems, motivated the development of public power. Additionally, all the towns were in agriculturally prosperous counties in their respective states.

The data contained in Table 4.3 allow for another generalization involving the political attitudes and actions of the congressional representatives of the towns. In the seven congressional districts studied, Republicans controlled four, Democrats controlled two, and one district split between the two parties. The nine men who represented the seven districts between 1928 and 1931 cast a total of twenty-seven votes on public power issues. Twenty-three times the votes favored public power legislation—more than 85 percent of the time. Only Congressman Sproul representing Kansas's third district voted against the legislation. The qualitative evidence discussed supports the quantitative analysis that a relationship existed between municipal power in a congressman's district and his voting behavior.

Although most of the men who represented the eight districts held law degrees, they came from diverse backgrounds. One worked for a railroad, another was a professor and minister, and several farmed. Still, for the most part, consistency in voting was the norm. Thus, it appears that these people voted out of deeply ingrained convictions and believed that government could be a positive influence in everyday life. Muscle Shoals, Boulder Dam, and the private utility industry may not have been the paramount issues in the local congressional campaign, but they did appear to be issues nonetheless. The consistency in congressional voting behavior over time rules out vote swapping. In at least some towns, people were well aware of national political issues. In local politics individuals voted to create municipal power systems to battle the private companies. On the national level their congressmen responded to the private utility industry when they voted for Muscle Shoals and Boulder Dam.

The implication of small town municipal power and the voting records of the congressmen who represented these towns in the 1920s and early 1930s should not be underestimated. Although the towns may appear as isolated cases, they represent an aspect of American political history that

Table 4.3 Voting Records of Congressmen Representing Small Towns

Congressman	Town	Dist.	Party	Mpt.*	Vote One	Vote Two	Vote Three	Vote Four	Vote Five
Sproul, William	Stark	KS-3	R	18	N	Y	N	Y	Y
Furlow, Allen/ Christgau, Victor	Whalan/ Lanesboro	MN-1	R	19	Y	N	Y	N	Y
Cannon, Clarence	Sullivan	MO-9	D	2	Y	N	Y	—	Y
Fulbright, James/ Short, Dewey	Sikeston	MO-14	D/R	7	Y	N	—	—	Y
Mansfield, Joseph	Yoakum	TX-9	D	3	Y	N	—	—	Y
Kading, Charles	Pardeeville	WI-2	R	13	Y	N	Y	N	Y
Hull, Merlin	Bangor	WI-7	R	14	—	—	—	N	Y

Notes: *Mpt represents the number of towns in the district with municipal power. Vote One: Pass S.J. Res. 46 conference report: to develop publicly Muscle Shoals (y = 211, n = 147, May 25, 1928, Congressional Record [C.R.] 69, p. 9957). Vote Two: Douglas motion to recommit H.R. 5773: to construct Boulder Dam (opposed by those favoring the project, y = 137, n = 219, May 25, 1928, C.R. 69, p. 9989). Vote Three: Agree to Boulder Dam conference report, H.R. 5773 (y = 167, n = 122, December 18, 1928, C.R. 70, p. 837). Vote Four: Reece amendment to S.J. Res. 49: to lease Muscle Shoals area (opposed by those favoring public control, y = 186, n = 135, May 28, 1930, C.R. 72, p. 9766). Vote Five: Pass conference report on S.J. Res. 49: to construct Muscle Shoals, without Reece amendment, y = 216, n = 153, February 20, 1931, C.R. 74, p. 5570).

most historians have long considered dead and is largely ignored in the historiography of the 1920s. The decision to build and finance municipal power was a political decision that individuals made to correct either perceived or real evils in society. All eight towns were in the West or Midwest. Despite their relative size and geographic isolation, municipalities developed public power for political reasons. The monthly electrical bill served as a constant reminder of the power of private utility companies. That reminder not only existed in small rural towns but also motivated people in larger towns and cities to fight for public power.

CHAPTER FIVE

Seattle and Washington State:
Focal Points of the Public Power Fight

Nearly everyone in the public power fight in Seattle agreed that the city deserved the title of the "Best Lighted City," but they agreed on little else. Nowhere in the United States did the debate between public and private power reverberate louder than in the Pacific Northwest, particularly in Seattle and across Washington State. Seattle City Light, the publicly owned utility established by voters early in the century, competed directly with the predecessor of Puget Sound Power and Light (PSP&L), the private electrical company that served the area.[1] The fight intensified throughout the 1910s and reached a vicious pitch by the late 1920s, leading to charges of socialism, communism, and political recall.

Seattle and Washington State provide unique settings to examine the political debates over electricity in the years before the New Deal. Unlike many other towns and cities in the United States, residents of Seattle and much of the state had access to an abundance of undeveloped and developed hydroelectricity. Great amounts of potential hydroelectric power existed in the region, made possible by the heavy snowfall that fed nearby mountain rivers. The abundance of hydroelectricity contributed to the long and difficult contest between public and private power interests. Each side not only competed for present and future customers but also for undeveloped hydroelectric sites in the Cascade Mountains. As City Light grew, its continued existence depended on securing additional sources of electrical energy. Both City Light and PSP&L officials believed that the area's vast hydroelectric potential would hasten the region's industrial and commercial development.

Seattle is unique not only for the great amounts of potential electricity found nearby but also for the high degree of labor activity and unionization that has characterized the city's history. Unlike Los Angeles, where public ownership also developed, Seattle's history is full of episodes of labor organizations and unrest. The most famous was the Seattle general strike in January 1919 that touched off a nationwide wave of fear and contributed to the Red Scare. Historian Carlos Schwantes notes that "organized labor played a more prominent role in Washington and British Columbia than perhaps any other frontier region in North America." Union membership of nonagricultural workers in Washington often was among the highest in the United States.[2] A brief review of Seattle's history sets the stage for studying the power fight that engulfed the city.

Seattle developed late in comparison with other Northwest cities, particularly Portland. Although part of Oregon Country, most early settlers who made the overland trip west preferred to turn south toward the riches of Oregon's Willamette Valley instead of north toward Puget Sound. That slow beginning started to change in 1851, when Arthur Denny led a group of settlers to Elliot Bay establishing what grew into Seattle. Northwestern historian Gordon Dodds notes that even in 1865 Seattle had yet to distinguish itself from the other communities that lined Puget Sound's shoreline. The discovery of coal east of Seattle foretold its future as a city economically oriented to commerce and trade and, in time, industry. Because of its central location, Seattle grew into the center of economic activity for the area's growing lumber and coal camps.[3]

Still, the growth of Seattle and the Washington territory remained slow. In 1890, a year after Washington gained statehood, the Census Bureau reported Seattle's population as 42,837. Two events soon caused Seattle's population to explode: the completion of the Great Northern Railroad in 1893 and the Alaskan gold rush in 1897. The town's population in 1900 surpassed 80,000.[4] As Seattle enlarged its commercial base to fasten ties with Alaska, California, the East, and beyond, its population increased, and it soon surpassed Portland as the jewel of the Pacific Northwest: "In money, population, political influence, and cultural accomplishments, Seattle . . . reigned supreme."[5]

As Seattle's and the entire region's population expanded, so did the commercial activity that anchored the economy. Throughout the region the extractive-based industries consolidated themselves and became ever more dependent on outside investors. The expansion of the extractive industries and, in time, the accompanying transportation networks increased the region's laboring population, especially migrant laborers who often lacked work.[6] The increasing size of the area's labor force did not mean a quick move to unionization. Instead, the Knights of Labor and the American Federation of Labor (AFL) encountered many roadblocks, including "geographic isolation, the attitudes of workers in the region, the nature of the labor market, and the political and cultural framework within which unions operated." This situation did not mean that there was no labor movement, but it lacked strong ties with national organizations. Throughout the 1890s the AFL failed to make significant headway in the Pacific Northwest.[7]

Labor organizers finally started to make serious inroads in Washington State and Seattle as the nineteenth century came to a close. In October 1898 Social Democratic party organizers formed a local branch in Seattle. Eighteen months later the various locals founded the state organization that held its first convention in Seattle in July 1900. At that meeting delegates called for the "collective ownership of the means of production and distribution . . . [and] for immediate reforms as direct legislation and municipal ownership." The Social Democrats also pledged their support to the area's growing trade unions.[8] Schwantes notes that formation of the International Workers of the World (IWW) in 1905 pushed labor radicalism in the Pacific Northwest into a new era. Despite calls for worker unity, internal divisions soon racked the Wobblies, although the IWW did gain supporters in the region's wood products industry. Notwithstanding the Wobblies' activities, the AFL gained control of labor in Washington State by the time World War I broke out.[9]

World War I profoundly impacted Seattle. In 1914, historian Dana Frank writes, the city continued to serve as a transportation center for the resource-rich region. What manufacturing occurred involved natural resources from the area, especially lumber but also grain, fruit, and fish. The handful of manufacturing firms that did exist catered to the local economy. The war changed much of that as huge federally funded shipbuilding works developed to meet the needs of American businesses suddenly cut off from the European merchant marine. Frank estimates that at war's end 20 percent of the city's workers belonged to the AFL. That number included 20,000 recently organized workers and another 35,000 metal workers who moved to Seattle during the war.[10]

World War I proved a boom to Seattle's economy, as it did for the entire nation. Ten federally financed shipyards turning out both steel and wooden ships drove the economic expansion of nearly all sectors of the economy. Economic expansion was so great that a labor shortage soon developed, resulting in a massive migration to Seattle. Between 1910 and 1920 the city's population grew by nearly a third. The labor shortage gave unprecedented bargaining power to Seattle's workers, while the line between the AFL and the IWW became blurred as "wartime union fever" swept through the city. In early 1919, between 60,000 and 65,000 Seattle workers belonged to unions, up from 9,000 in 1915 and 40,000 in 1917. Frank writes: "Nineteen-eighteen Seattle was one of those moments like 1886 or 1968 when activism and consciousness erupt[ed]."[11]

The stage was set for the Seattle general strike of February 1919. With the war winding down in the fall of 1918, federal ship orders declined and the wartime advantages that shipyard workers enjoyed vanished. In October 1918 the shipyards granted only small wage increases to skilled workers and none to unskilled laborers. After the new year the wooden shipyards started to close, and owners realized they could wait out any labor stoppage. Finally, in late January 1919, 35,000 shipyard workers walked off their jobs. At stake were not just shipyard wages, but the entire future of the city's labor movement. The Seattle AFL responded by calling a general strike that quickly gained the support of the city's union members. In early February at least 65,000 Seattle workers struck and remained off the job for up to five days in peaceful protest.[12]

Many in Seattle, including the pro–public power mayor Ole Hanson, reacted swiftly and vocally to the general strike. Unfortunately for labor, the strike occurred on the heels of the Bolshevik revolution in Russia. Some in the United States, including Hanson, saw the Seattle general strike as merely the first wave of revolutionary upheaval that would soon engulf the entire country. Hanson called the general strike "an attempted revolution which they expected to spread all over the United States" (he himself profited from the labor unrest when he resigned his office to take to the lecture circuit).[13] Throughout 1919, labor unrest exploded across the United States, including major strikes in steel and coal. Calvin Coolidge's handling of the Boston police strike helped propel him to the vice presidency.[14] Labor took a beating, sometimes literally, in the United States in 1919 and during the 1920s. In Seattle, riding a wave of enthusiasm, the AFL initially emerged intact after the general strike. Nevertheless, even in Seattle, labor was much weaker at the end of the 1920s than at the time of the general strike. In her study of Seattle labor during the 1920s, Frank notes a paradox in the fact that although union membership surpassed prewar figures, it lacked the militancy of the earlier years.[15]

Against this background of rapid population growth, economic expansion, and labor activism, the fight for public power played itself out in Seattle. The situation seemed ideal for public ownership, a city with a liberal if not radical labor tradition that might welcome municipal ownership. As in many American cities progressive reform had also had its heyday in Seattle. During its many battles with PSP&L, City Light could count on the support of the *Seattle Union Record,* the newspaper that the Central Labor Council owned. City Light usually did well when it asked voters to approve power bonds, and the superintendent of City Light also enjoyed widespread public support. When Seattle mayor Frank Edwards fired City Light's superintendent, J. D. Ross, in 1931, voters quickly recalled the mayor; his replacement rehired Ross.

The Seattle public power fight is also significant in that the contest took place within the city limits. Although public power advocates from across the nation decried the wastefulness of duplicate systems, such systems did exist. Public power backers did not easily give ground to private power. Photographs of Seattle in the interwar years show two sets of power lines—one public, the other private—running down the city's streets. During the 1920s Seattle often found itself in the center of the national debate over municipal power as opponents of private power nationwide pointed to the success of City Light. Private utility spokesmen also expressed concern about City Light and attempted to undermine its popularity.

The public power fight extended across the entire state. Several times public power supporters attempted to pass laws to hasten the development of public power statewide. Initial attempts in the early 1920s failed, although the voters approved a 1930 referendum allowing for the establishment of public utility districts.[16] Besides the debate over enabling laws, a controversy over private utility rates developed in the mid-1920s in Walla Walla and surrounding communities in southeast and central Washington. That debate allows for the examination of several issues discussed by public power spokesmen on the national level.

The power fight in Seattle and across the state brought to the public eye James D. Ross. Popularly known as J. D. Ross, he started his service with City Light as an engineer in 1902 and served as superintendent from 1911 to 1935. After serving on the Securities and Exchange Commission, President Franklin Roosevelt appointed him the first director of the Bonneville Power Administration in 1937. Ross became a political symbol not only of City Light but of public power nationwide.[17] Throughout his career he offered strong support for public power and equally strong contempt for private power. His rising stature was evident, as he frequently served as an "expert witness" on issues related to public power, including the Walla Walla rate case.[18] Ross, City Light, attempts at statewide referendums, and the Walla Walla rate case were all part of the public power story in the 1920s. Their interrelatedness precludes studying them as separate historical events. Public power forces outside Seattle often cited the city's cheap electrical rates as a reason for public power. Attempts to establish a statewide system carried consequences for City Light as well.

Politics provides the unifying theme in all the chapters of the public power fight in Seattle and Washington State in the years before the New Deal. Debates over rates, the securing of future power supplies, the right of cities and towns to sell electricity beyond their municipal limits, and the extension of public power into unincorporated areas all required the making of political decisions, and all transcended the issue of electricity. Each side believed that it was fighting for a higher purpose. Private utility proponents argued that nothing less than the future of free market capitalism was at stake; the establishment of public power would lead to socialism. Public power advocates also saw the debate on an equally grand scale. Who would control electricity, the energy source essential to modern society, they asked? Who would be involved in day-to-day decisions: private monopolies with absentee owners who sought only profit at nearly any cost or individuals on the local level? Public power supporters denied charges of socialism and any hidden agenda to socialize all industry. Instead, they believed, as did Pinchot, Norris, La Follette, and others nationally, that the public should control natural resources for development. The creation of municipal power systems, even if not accomplished statewide, would expose and ultimately force down unnecessarily high private rates. That articulation of the yardstick principle was identical to the views of public power spokesmen in Congress and in small town America.

The issue of electrical modernization was an underlying theme in the public power debate. Ross and other supporters of public power constantly called for increases in the domestic consumption of electricity. As early as 1915 the *Seattle Star* wrote of Ross: "He talks of the time not far in the distant, when all the homes of Seattle not only will be lighted by electricity, but all Seattle housewives will be cooking the family meals on electric ranges."[19] At the end of the 1920s local papers reported that Seattle led the nation in the use of electrical ranges and linked the use of electricity to health. "The modernization of Seattle houses through general and generous use of electricity for cooking and the scores of other household requirements may logically have more than a little to do with the fact that Seattle is the healthiest city in America, with the lowest death rate, thinks J.D. Ross."[20] In its 1930 annual report, City Light stated that Seattle had more electric ranges than any city in the United States.[21] Such a claim, however, did not mean that every resident lived in an electrically modernized dwelling. Returning to the "electric hearth," the radio, as an indicator of electrical modernization shows that more than 52 percent of Seattle's 100,996 families had at least one radio in 1930. Among the ninety-three American cities with populations of 100,000 or more in 1930, Seattle ranked thirty-sixth in the percentage of families with radios.[22] This statistic underscores the continuing importance placed on securing low-cost electrical energy in Seattle and Washington State, despite the seeming abundance of developed power.

City Light and PSP&L did agree on the importance of electricity to Seattle and the state not only for household use but for industrial development as well. Inexpensive power, many thought, might attract new industries and businesses. The abundance of cheap hydroelectric power in the state put the public power debate in the national spotlight, and that spotlight shone brightest on Seattle. The dual generating and electrical systems that existed for more than forty-five years in the city meant that the battle was usually intense and continually before the public eye. Despite Seattle's large population and the abundance of electricity, the basic political issues over rates remained identical to those in many small towns throughout the United States.[23] Technology did not play a large role in the Seattle electric fight because of the closeness of hydroelectric sites. Both City Light and PSP&L relied on nearby hydroelectric sites for energy. During the formative years of City Light, transmission lines carried current less than fifty miles to the city.

Electricity had a fragmented beginning in many cities as small companies fought for resources, territory, and customers; Seattle was no different.

A group of Seattle businessmen founded the Seattle Electric Company in 1900 and sought advice from the Boston-based Stone and Webster engineering and consulting firm. Stone and Webster officials served as general managers of the Seattle Electric Company and supervised the consolidation of the city's streetcar lines and lighting companies. In the first decades of the twentieth century, the company began to develop hydroelectric sites on the Snoqualmie, Puyallup, and White Rivers in western Washington and built two steam plants in Seattle.[24] The Seattle Electric Company became part of the Puget Sound Traction, Light, and Power Company when the latter organized in 1912, first under Maine and then later, Massachusetts laws. Besides the Seattle Electric Company, Puget Sound Traction, Light, and Power also acquired the Seattle-Tacoma Power Company, the Pacific Coast Power Company, the Puget Sound Power Company, and the Whatcom County Railway and Light Company. The consolidation of the five companies occurred through stock exchanges followed by liquidation of the former companies.[25] The new name more accurately reflected PSP&L's scope of operation that included much of western Washington. In 1919 the company dropped "traction" from its name when it sold its railway holding in Seattle to the city.

Charles Stone and Edwin Webster, classmates at Massachusetts Institute of Technology, founded the Boston-based company bearing their names in 1889. By 1929 the firm's assets exceed $100 million. Besides providing engineering and management services to utility companies, Stone and Webster also served as an investment house. In 1930 the firm reportedly had built 10 percent of the central electric stations in the United States and controlled sixty public utility companies.[26] Stone and Webster provided technical and operating services for PSP&L until 1955.[27]

The origins of Seattle City Light date to the development of Seattle's municipal water system in the late nineteenth century. The city established a municipal water system and drew water from the Cedar River, approximately forty miles east of Seattle. R. H. Thompson, city engineer, supervised the water system's construction and began calling for the establishment of municipal power in 1893. He finally succeeded in 1902 when the city's residents approved a $590,000 bond issue to construct a 2,400-kilowatt powerhouse on the Cedar River. The plant went on-line in 1905 and began illuminating the city's streets after City Light took over the lines of the Seattle Light Company. A second bond measure to construct a public distribution system passed in 1905, and City Light soon began serving private homes.[28] Escalating demand forced the city to expand the generating capacity at the Cedar River site to 8,000 kilowatts, but not even the larger turbines could meet Seattle's rapidly growing need for power.

Nearly before the cement had dried at the Cedar River powerhouse the private versus public power debate over rates emerged in Seattle. Before the development of public power in Seattle, PSP&L charged twenty cents per kilowatt hour. *Northwest Magazine* reported in 1913 that after the public plant began operating, rates had fallen dramatically. In his history of Seattle, Richard Berner noted that the threat of public competition forced the private company to lower rates from twenty to twelve cents per kilowatt hour in October 1904, three months before City Light began selling energy for street lighting in January 1905.[29] Others also have commented on the lower rates charged in Seattle and Tacoma after each town established public power. Electrical rates per kilowatt hour for twenty-seven Oregon and Washington municipalities in 1912 as reported by the Northwest Electric Light and Power Association are contained in Table 5.1, which demonstrates that towns with municipal power had significantly lower rates. The rate of twenty cents per kilowatt hour that existed in Seattle before City Light went on-line was extremely high. Even if PSP&L charged Seattle customers the average private rate of 12.6 cents, the rate that City Light charged still would have been much lower.

City building, specifically the issue of using electricity to attract new business and industry to Seattle, emerged as part of the public utility debate. *Northwest Magazine* called power "the fulcrum on which rests the factories of the city" and said that the lower rates would attract new industries and jobs to Seattle.[30] PSP&L also believed that low-cost power would attract new industry to the Puget Sound region. In 1914 the company ran an advertisement in a construction journal in which it took credit for Seattle's industrial growth, made possible by the company's generation of cheap and abundant electrical power.[31]

Table 5.1 Private and Public Utility Rates in Kilowatt Hours for Twenty-Seven Northwest Cities in 1912 (in cents)

Town	Rate	Town	Rate	Town	Rate
Aberdeen	9.0	Albany	9.9	Arlington	15.0
Anacortes	13.5	Bellingham	10.0	Chehalis	11.4
Clarkston	9.0	Colfax	14.0	Everett	13.5
Grandview	13.0	Kelso	12.0	Kennerick	13.0
Medical Lake	15.0	Montesano	11.25	North Yakima	12.0
Olympia	18.0	Pasco	13.0	Port Townsend	14.4
Portland	14.25	Richland	13.0	Seattle*	7.0
Spokane	10.0	Tacoma*	6.25	Walla Walla	12.0
Waitsburg	12.0	Wapato	14.85	Wenatchee	13.5

*Towns with public ownership
$\bar{X}$ = 12.7 cents for towns with private power
$\bar{X}$ = 6.63 cents for towns with public power
Source: *Proceedings of the Northwest Electric Light and Power Association* (Seattle, 1912), 62, contained in Dick, "Visions of Abundance," 249.

In 1917 the *San Francisco Examiner* did a special feature on Seattle that focused in part on private versus public power rates. City Light initially charged eight and one-half cents for the first twenty kilowatt hours, with the rate dropping to four and one-half cents for every kilowatt hour in excess of sixty. The *Examiner* reported that the private company matched City Light's rates wherever direct competition existed. At the time of the article, public rates in Seattle were six cents for the first sixty kilowatt hours and four cents for every additional hour. The paper concluded that despite private utility attacks on City Light the reduction from twenty cents to six cents per kilowatt hour in seven years underscored the success of municipal power in Seattle.[32]

Private power interests acknowledged that Seattle enjoyed low rates and deserved the "Best Lighted City" title, but with reservations. In commenting on City Light's fiscal report for 1911–1912, *Electric World* tried to downplay City Light's success, probably to prevent it from gaining national attention. An editorial argued that water power produced at a "nominal cost" had to be considered when studying City Light and that without cheap energy the public plant could not have developed as it did.[33] The editorial implied that without cheap hydropower City Light's low rates could not exist, but it did not discuss the differences between the city's and PSP&L's rates.

Seattle City Light received attention from beyond the West Coast. In 1913 the *Milwaukee Leader* ran a story entitled "Seattle Breaks Grip of Light Trust and Reaps Big Profit on City Plant." The article reported that City Light returned $200,000 to the city each year from "its war with the local light and power trust" and quoted City Light management as saying that "the fight for municipal power has not cost the city of Seattle one cent . . . and everything possible is done to hamper us [City Light]." The newspaper also cited the decline in rates since the establishment of City Light and admonished Milwaukee's residents to pick up the public power banner.[34]

Throughout the debate PSP&L took issue with how much profit City Light reported. The main issue was that City Light did not pay taxes because it was a public entity. In newspaper advertisements in 1914, PSP&L charged City Light with mismanagement and borrowing from other public funds to finance power projects. PSP&L further claimed that taxpayers financed misguided improvements but received little benefit because City Light did not pay any taxes. Two such advertisements appeared in the *Seattle Post-Intelligencer* on January 30 and 31, 1914, with titles that read "Municipal Ownership: A Burden on the Taxpayer" and "Municipal Ownership Cheats the Taxpayer."[35] City Light officials dismissed such charges and said that any profit went back into the city budget or for system improvements. Taxes continued to be an issue in the fight over public power in Seattle and across the state well into the 1920s. In 1924, during a rate debate in eastern Washington, J. D. Ross, head of City Light, claimed that private utilities raised the tax issue to avoid the real problem of high rates. He stated, "If a power company pays eight percent in taxes and charges you three times as much for your power where do you get off?"[36] The only reason private utilities raised the tax issue, Ross believed, was to divert public attention away from high electric rates.

From the beginning Ross viewed PSP&L as an evil component of the "power trust" that wanted to crush City Light because it charged lower rates. City Light soon faced the problem of securing additional sources of electrical energy that brought it into direct competition with PSP&L. Installing a hydroelectric dam on the Cedar River was relatively easy because the city already owned the dam site. When demand exceeded the river's generating capacity, city engineers had to look elsewhere for power. Writing in 1935, Ross recalled that private power interests prevented City Light from securing additional hydroelectric sources in the 1910s. Unable to develop more hydropower Ross pushed for, and City Light built, a steam plant on Lake Union not far from city center. He later said that during those years the greatest threat to City Light was not private power, but a lack of electricity.[37]

Seattle's population explosion during World War I coupled with the war economy created new electrical demands in the Puget Sound region. Contemporary observers estimated that Seattle's population increased by 75,000 in 1918 alone. The number of customers that City Light served and its operating budget also expanded. The city's mayor at the time, Ole Hanson, stated that City Light served 57,000 customers and maintained an operating budget of $1.75 million. That growth took place despite "strong competition [and] is but another proof to the unprejudiced observer that all public utilities should and must be operated by the people themselves."[38] After the war Ross reported that City Light had to refuse contracts equaling 3,000 horsepower (2,238 kilowatts), and he urged the development of hydroelectricity on the Skagit River northeast of Seattle.[39]

The fight over hydroelectric power on the Skagit River became an often repeated story in the struggle between City Light and PSP&L. In 1932 the *Nation* recounted the culminating events leading to City Light securing an adequate hydroelectric supply. In 1917 city engineers surveyed potential dam sites within 125 miles of Seattle and located three areas suitable for the city's power needs. A few days before the deadline to submit bids, City Light discovered that Stone and Webster interests had obtained the rights to the three areas the city wanted. City Light had not earlier considered the Skagit River because Stone and Webster already held a temporary permit. That permit, however, expired shortly after Seattle lost out on the three original sites: the White River, Sunset Falls on the Skyomish River, and Lake Cushman. Frustrated in its efforts to secure rights to the areas already surveyed, the city decided to go after the Skagit River. Ross personally went to Washington, D.C., and filed the required papers with the secretary of agriculture, who would make the final decision. Stone and Webster representatives argued that the time and money already invested under the temporary permit for the Skagit River should entitle them to power permits for the river. Ross successfully countered that Stone and Webster's securing the permits showed the company's intent to develop power elsewhere. He also argued that no construction had occurred on the Skagit. Secretary of Agriculture David Houston ruled in favor of City Light in December 1917 and stated that PSP&L had withheld the Skagit site from development.[40] Ross maintained that private power interests offered Seattle's pro–City Light mayor at the time, Hiram C. Gill, $15,000 in cash and $9,000 more to pay off his home mortgage if he resigned.[41] After a debate that lasted most of 1918 and involved PSP&L and the War Department regarding issues related to Seattle's wartime power demands, City Light finally submitted a power survey in 1919.[42] The first Skagit River dam went on-line in 1924.

Although the Skagit River guaranteed Seattle's power needs for the immediate future, city residents welcomed the passage of the Federal Water Act in 1920 as a means of helping the development of Seattle, the state, and the entire West Coast. A *Seattle Post-Intelligencer* editorial said that the act "should make this [Seattle] the leading manufacturing section of the Pacific Coast." The two most important elements in attracting new industries, the editorial continued, were cheap energy and good transportation. Development of the state's hydroelectric sources would supply the energy, and Seattle's deepwater harbor provided worldwide shipping possibilities. Waxing eloquent, the editorial declared: "Men of vision predict that water power will cause Seattle to become the greatest manufacturing center of the nation in the years to come, and that a large part of the nation's population will one day be found in Western Washington."[43] Many thought that making it legal for cities to sell power to unincorporated areas would speed the economic development envisioned in the *Seattle Post-Intelligencer*.

The issue of municipalities selling power to customers beyond their city limits or to other cities became a statewide political concern starting in the early twenties. The drive to permit such sales culminated with voter approval of a referendum in 1930 allowing for the creation of public utility districts. Controversy first developed not on a statewide scale, but instead involving Seattle's and Tacoma's municipal systems. The controversy began in 1921 when PSP&L denied Tacoma Light and Power supplementary electricity despite the existence of a contract to provide such power.[44] In an attempt to avoid a similar situation in the future and to plan for unforeseen electrical shortages, a transmission line interconnected the two cities' municipal systems in 1922. The thought behind the line was that in a time of shortage one city could supply the other with supplemental power, if available.[45] That seemingly innocuous project touched off a minor furor in the public versus private power debate in the Puget Sound region.

Both cities approved the $150,000 project in the spring of 1922, and PSP&L officials said nothing. In late July, though, the company claimed that it already had contracted with Tacoma to supply emergency power if the municipal plant could not meet the city's needs. Company president A. W. Leonard maintained that PSP&L would restrict the use of the proposed line until 1930 because of the existing contract. Ross believed ulterior motives influenced PSP&L's decision to wait until July to announce publicly the existence of the contract. He said that the company had purposely waited until the cities had approved the line and awarded contracts.[46] Ross's statement suggested that PSP&L had delayed announcing its opposition to the power line to embarrass or financially damage the municipal systems. Preventing Seattle and Tacoma from linking their electrical systems would mean that each city might not have enough electricity to meet emergency demands until the completion of new plants. Shortly after the PSP&L announcement, the Seattle City Utility Council unanimously voted to reject the PSP&L offer to use existing lines. The cities then built the Tacoma-Seattle transmission line.[47]

The debate over connecting Seattle's and Tacoma's electrical systems foreshadowed the legislative debate over interconnection on the state level in early 1923. State legislators in Olympia introduced several bills to allow municipal power systems to sell electricity beyond their boundaries. One bill, known as the Davis bill, would have allowed municipal sales, but with a 5 percent tax. A second bill, which Homer T. Bone of Tacoma submitted, called for tax-free municipal sales. Bone, at the time a member of the Farm-Laborite party, soon became one of Washington's leading public power advocates. In 1933, after his election to the U.S. Senate as a Democrat the previous fall, he testified in favor of the Muscle Shoals development before the House Military Affairs Committee.[48]

Stone and Webster concerns zealously opposed any legislation allowing municipalities to sell power beyond their boundaries. Friends of private power believed that PSP&L was especially vulnerable, because with the near completion of Seattle's first Skagit River project and Tacoma's Cushman Dam, both cities potentially would have excess power to sell. The speaker of the Washington State House, Mark Reed, who favored municipal power, accused PSP&L lobbyists of trying to delete the 5 percent tax from the Davis bill to make it unpassable. He believed that because most legislators favored the tax the legislation would never pass without it, which explains PSP&L's goal of trying to delete the tax provision. Other opponents of the bill charged that Seattle was trying to dominate the entire state and labeled municipal power as socialistic. An attorney for the Washington Power Company of Spokane, a subsidiary of the Electric Bond and Share

Company, called the bill "nothing more than a socialistic move."[49] Underlying PSP&L's opposition was the fear that municipal power systems sold power at lower rates than private utilities.

Reed introduced a third power bill in early February 1923 to allow municipal sales, but with a 5 percent tax on all sales both within and outside a city's boundaries. The law would have required adding the tax each time a municipality sold power. Thus, if Seattle sold power to another town, a 5 percent tax would be added; when the second town sold the power to a customer, the tax would be imposed again. On February 15, 1923, the Washington legislature considered all three power bills. After several readings the House approved the Reed bill, although it ultimately failed to pass the state legislature and appeared on the November 1924 ballot as an initiative.[50] Legislators never conducted a vote on the Davis bill and postponed it indefinitely.[51] After two hours of debate the House defeated the Bone bill; following its defeat, supporters successfully worked to have the Bone bill placed on the November 1924 ballot.[52]

The initial setback that supporters of the Bone bill suffered in early 1923 did not signify a decline in the intensity of the public power debate. Although the bill did not come to a popular vote until November 1924, other issues began to develop. In April 1923 City Light announced another rate cut and abolished the one dollar fee to open new accounts. The city broadened the superintendent's power to allow the authorization of fixed contracts for electric water heaters and ranges with a guaranteed rate for three years. The following month PSP&L claimed that overall its rates were lower than City Light's.[53] In June of the same year, Oliver Erickson, who chaired the city's utility committee, announced plans to work for the establishment of a statewide public power system that would interconnect all publicly owned electrical plants. The *Post-Intelligencer* supported Erickson's plan for such a system and declared that the state should reserve its resources for all the people.[54]

At the sixteenth annual convention of the Northwest Electric Light and Power Association, held in Seattle in June 1923, utility executives defended their enterprises. W. H. McGrath, a PSP&L vice president, denied that a few individuals controlled utility companies and instead argued that thousands of small stockholders owned public utilities. He blamed a "radical press" for the distorted view that only a few individuals or groups of individuals dominated the utility industry.[55] Association spokesmen at the convention attacked City Light's Skagit River projects as unnecessary and criticized city officials for beginning them without making a power survey. The private interests further argued that the project blindly used public credit.[56] A *Seattle Times* editorial criticized City Light in late July along the same themes, maintaining that the project would generate more power than Seattle could ever use. The paper linked the perceived excess Skagit power to the Bone bill. Public power advocates in Seattle and throughout the state, according to the editorial, privately realized the blunder of the Skagit project and through the Bone bill sought new markets for the surplus power to cut their losses. The *Times* concluded that public ownership, like the direct primary, had failed and should be abolished.[57]

The political debates over the Bone power bill, between PSP&L and City Light in Seattle, and between the proponents and opponents of municipal sales across the state continued to simmer in the fall and winter of 1923. In 1924 the fight intensified as a November vote on the Bone power bill approached. In eastern Washington, citizens in Walla Walla led a group of communities that sued Pacific Power and Light, a private utility, over rate issues. As the general election approached, public and private power advocates debated the merits of public and private ownership across the state.

On January 18, 1924, PSP&L ran an advertisement in the *Post-Intelligencer*, a pro–public power paper, and in the *Seattle Times*, claiming that Portland, Oregon, had private rates comparable to those that City Light charged. The advertisement also stated that in 1905 the highest private rate in Seattle was not twenty cents per kilowatt hour, as public power advocates claimed, but ten cents per kilowatt hour. Besides charging "exactly the same rates charged by the politically operated plant," PSP&L paid $8.24 in taxes out of every $100 of gross revenue. Finally, the advertisement said that the state did not need more tax-exempt property, but more taxable property. Five days later a *Post-Intelligencer* editorial responded that cheap power, not low taxes, was the magnet that attracted new industries to a city.[58]

The issues of utility taxes and rates and the various power bills dominated the general campaign in Washington in 1924. Washington's Democratic party endorsed the Bone power bill in its platform at the state convention in May. A *Post-Intelligencer* headline referred to the bill when it read: "McAdoo, Dry, Bone Bill Forces in Control of Party Platform Never More Progressive."[59] Advertisements that the Northwest Electric Light and Power Association sponsored attacked the Bone bill. The association argued that the bill's intent was not to allow municipal sales of power but to permit the confiscation of private property and place it under "political management." The bill's tax-free provision would result in local and state governments having smaller tax bases, causing a need for increased taxes.[60]

Each side accused the other of unfair campaign methods during the fight over the power bill. The bill's supporters complained to the police that private utility representatives harassed potential petition signers. PSP&L spokesmen countered that they had obtained police permission to distribute literature at the same location where Bone bill supporters gathered signatures. Two days after the alleged harassment occurred, the Northwest Electric Light and Power Association ran an advertisement claiming that supporters "of the Bone bill caused the arrest of two disabled war

veterans" who were only admonishing people to read the bill before sign-
ing the petition. The advertisement reiterated that millions of dollars of tax
money would be lost if the bill passed.[61]

Stories in the *Seattle Post-Intelligencer* noted a change in the private
power advocates' tactics. Where earlier in the campaign private power
interests accused Bone bill supporters of wanting to "unload" excess water
power, they now charged that public power proponents wanted to "grab"
property from private power companies. The newspaper contended that
instead of removing property from the tax rolls, cheap public power would
attract new industries, resulting in enlarged tax rolls. The paper acknowledged that the Bone bill contained a condemnation clause but said that its
only purpose was to condemn small distribution systems in order to bring
inexpensive power to more municipalities.[62] In mid-June, speakers at a Bone
bill rally sponsored by the King County Democratic Club repeated that
theme, arguing that residents in Seattle's Ballard district paid 25 to 50 percent more for electricity before the city annexed the district. Although
PSP&L continued to operate in Ballard, the company lowered its rates to
the same level as City Light. Passage of the Bone bill would result in similar developments in other cities, even before the construction of publicly
owned lines.[63] Speakers at the rally articulated on the local political level
the yardstick principle of public power that was part of the argument for
Boulder Dam, Muscle Shoals, and other public power projects. Public
power did not have to serve every resident of a city; the presence of even
a small number of customers would reveal the high rates that private utilities charged and force down those rates.

When discussing the rate issue, public power advocates often cited the
ratio of capital debt to generated horsepower to underscore what they
believed was private power's overcharging of customers. High debt forced
private utilities to charge higher rates to meet greater financial obligations.
Critics of private utilities believed that debt accumulated because of holding company stock purchases, stock watering, and overcapitalization. Supporters of the Bone bill reported that City Light owed $131.24 for every
horsepower of electricity produced, while the Stone and Webster Company
debt equaled $318.77 for every horsepower of electricity generated.[64] Pri-
vate companies passed on the debt to customers through higher rates. Data
contained in a paid advertisement that appeared in a community newspaper in October 1924 a few weeks before the general election are reported
in Table 5.2.

The Washington State Federation of Labor Executive Board favored
both the Bone power bill and the La Follette–Wheeler Progressive party
presidential ticket. At the Labor Temple in Seattle in late October, Homer
Bone and Norwood Brockett of PSP&L debated the power bill. Brockett
repeated the ideas that the bill would allow for mass condemnation of

Table 5.2 Amount of Debt per Horsepower of
Electricity Generated in 1924

Company or Town	Debt per Generated Horsepower
Stone and Webster (PSP&L)	$318.77
Washington Power & Light Co.	$273.07
Pacific Power & Light Co.	$550.38
Private Average	$380.74
Ellensburg	$136.80
Seattle	$131.24
Tacoma	$22.70
Centralia	$0.00
Public Average	$72.69

Source: *Lake Shore News*, October 16, 1924, J. D.
Ross, comp., *J. D. Ross Scrapbooks* (Suzzallo Library;
Seattle: University of Washington, microfilm), vol. 10.

private utilities throughout the state. Bone charged the private utilities with
distorting the facts and using questionable tactics, including attempts to
"forge, steal, and destroy" petitions in attempts to sway public opinion.[65]

The Bone bill lost in the November general election, although people
continued to discuss power issues throughout the state.[66] Public power
advocates persisted in fighting for the right of municipalities to sell power
beyond their boundaries. In the late 1920s the Federal Trade Commission
utility investigation estimated that private power forces spent $175,000 to
defeat the Bone bill in 1924. Some newspaper people told Bone that private power spent $1 million to defeat the initiative. Public power advo-
cates reportedly spent much less, although Bone borrowed $6,000 against
the value of his house to help finance the effort.[67] As Washingtonians debated the Bone bill in 1924, people in eastern Washington began to question the rates charged by the private utility that served the area.

The rate controversy in eastern Washington in 1924 underscores several points in the nationwide public power debate and the growing stature of J. D. Ross. The first was the issue of rates; the second was the method
that private utilities used to calculate capitalization values. Determining
capitalization was important because setting electrical rates involved what
constituted a fair return on capital investment. The controversy began when
public officials in Walla Walla started examining the rates charged by
Pacific Power and Light (PP&L). American Power and Light was the holding company that controlled PP&L. As of December 31, 1929, American
Power and Light owned all but 15 of PP&L's 57,550 common stock shares.
The Electric Bond and Share Company organized American Power and Light

in 1909 and provided all of its operation and management functions. American Power and Light lacked operating personnel; except for one person, the officers for each company were the same individuals.[68]

City officials in Walla Walla and twenty-six surrounding communities believed that PP&L overcharged for electricity and included obsolete and overvalued property when determining the area's rate structure. Community officials also wanted a refund for excessive rates paid since 1913.[69] Walla Walla's mayor said that the area paid more for electricity than any similar region in the country despite the availability of cheap water power. Sounding city building themes, the mayor said he hoped that a new rate schedule would help attract additional commerce and speed the region's development.[70] In the spring of 1924 the Walla Walla City Council authorized the chamber of commerce to appoint a special committee to investigate the rate situation. The committee found that power cost twice as much in Walla Walla as in Spokane and four times the amount charged in Tacoma; it demanded "substantial relief" from either PP&L or "other sources." The committee believed that the company had deliberately inflated property values to justify higher rates to the state Public Works Commission. Pacific Power and Light officials countered that the higher rates resulted from the region's sparse population.[71]

In a speech to the Walla Walla Chamber of Commerce in April 1924, Ross claimed that PP&L overcharged area customers, adding that the private company should be given the chance to lower its rates. If the company did not do so, the city should find other sources of electricity or develop a municipal power supply. Probably not by coincidence, while Ross was telling area businesspeople that PP&L overcharged, company officials announced a rate cut for Walla Walla. The *Walla Walla Union* reported both Ross's chamber of commerce speech and PP&L's rate reduction announcement on the front page of the same issue.[72] In its next issue the newspaper accused PP&L of lowering rates in an attempt to stop the city's lawsuit and commented that the company's announcement "has only given the rate committee determination to go ahead."[73]

Officials of the state's public works department began hearings in August 1925. The cities' major complaint against PP&L was that it based its rates on a falsified rate structure. Specifically, the rate structure included overvalued or unused property, property in Oregon, and incorrect depreciation and maintenance calculations. Pacific Power and Light defended the inclusion of the unused plants when it declared them necessary backup plants. The cities also charged that they paid much higher rates than towns with municipal power and that the company received a net return of greater than 8 percent, the legal allowable amount.[74] Under examination the chief engineer for the Washington Department of Public Works said that he thought PP&L included property in Oregon when the company determined the valuation of the Walla Walla–Yakima district. The Oregon property's value was $873,922, or 18.5 percent of the district's $4.7 million valuation.[75]

Witnesses delivered more damaging testimony when they revealed that PP&L bonds and stock prorated to the Walla Walla–Yakima district far exceeded the value of the company's property in the district. Besides the property in Oregon, the company included unused plants in eight Washington communities and overvalued a transmission line that ran between Pasco and Lind in determining the area's rate base. The communities charged that the total worth of the unused plants and overvalued property equaled $1.17 million. Inclusion of the unused plants and inflating the value of the transmission line resulted in two things. First, it increased the electrical rate for Walla Walla–Yakima district customers. Second, it resulted in stock watering, which was the inflating of property values to allow for increased security sales.[76] The complaint further charged that the company included water rights as depreciable property and figured depreciation at rates higher than 3 percent, the amount the state allowed. Because the state commission regulated the securities that a company could sell, based on a company's net worth and operating expenses, including obsolete property artificially increased that value and allowed for greater securities sales.

The power company also included the amount it paid the federal government in income tax and water right fees as operating expenses. Including those expenses enabled the company to increase how much money it reported as necessary for doing business, which in turn resulted in the company setting higher rates to cover the costs. State regulations, however, allowed neither form of expense. The *Walla Walla Daily Bulletin* reported that PP&L sold nearly $9 million of securities based on the area's rate structure of only $6 million. Including obsolete plants and unallowable payments inflated the rate schedule enough to pay dividends on the company's securities.[77] Before the hearings concluded, testimony revealed that the company's return was 12.31 percent instead of 11 percent; the 11 percent included an 8 percent return and depreciation costs. The company thus overcharged the district's customers nearly $600,000 from 1913 to 1923 and overvalued property in the area by more than $5 million (47 percent).[78]

Walla Walla and the surrounding communities won their battle for reduced electrical rates. In late December 1925 the Washington State Board of Public Works reduced PP&L's valuation for the area by 15 percent, which the company passed on to its customers. The board agreed with the plaintiffs regarding the Oregon properties when it ruled that PP&L improperly included them in the district's rate schedule. The board also ruled that PP&L could not include three power plants in the Yakima–Walla Walla district when calculating the district's valuation. Finally, the board set the allowable deprecation rate at 3.5 percent annually.[79]

The charges that Walla Walla and the other communities made are important in understanding public power in Washington State. The claim of high rates in Walla Walla and surrounding communities showed the growing concern over electrical costs in regions other than Puget Sound. Citizens believed that private companies overcharged and so hampered economic growth. Walla Walla's mayor and other politicians nationwide realized that inexpensive energy attracted new businesses. The statewide debate over public power in Washington remained alive throughout the twenties and resulted, in part, in the passage of the public utility district law in 1930.

The Walla Walla committee's accusations against PP&L mirrored the charges public power advocates made nationwide. On the surface the complaint was overcharging, but public examination of the company's records revealed how and why overcharging occurred. Most notable was the inflation of property values, bookkeeping manipulation, and stock watering. Including obsolete plants or plants in other states inflated a company's rate base, as did including payments to the federal government. Depreciation also became an issue. Critics charged that power companies artificially raised the depreciation rate, which meant a company could charge more to meet future needs. The quicker property depreciated, the faster the company needed to raise money to replace it. Together those practices produced higher rates and stock watering, both important to holding companies. Inflated values resulted in paper stock because nothing tangible backed the stock. The inflated operating companies' profits, such as PP&L, generated profits for holding companies, here American Power and Light and Electric Bond and Share. Of course, when values began to drop, as when the economy contracted after October 1929, many utility company securities became worthless.

Although state regulators resolved the Walla Walla area rate case in 1925, the situation in Seattle remained politically volatile. Several episodes in Seattle politics underscore the political nature of the city's public power fight. In 1923 proponents of reform began to argue for the passage of a new city charter that would establish a city manager form of municipal government. One reason for concern was the persistent delays in completion of the first Skagit project. Supporters of the plan thought that the inefficiency of the existing form of government had contributed to unnecessary delays in completing the project. The first attempt to revise the city charter through a voter-approved amendment failed in the spring of 1924. Undaunted, proponents of revision decided to put the issue before voters in March 1926.[80]

J. D. Ross opposed the establishment of a city manager form of government, fearing that private power supporters backed the plan in an attempt to destroy City Light, so he founded the City Light Patrons Club to work for the plan's defeat.[81] The city's legal counsel, Thomas Kennedy, dealt the plan's supporters a blow when he ruled that the proposed charter did not specifically allow the city to sell utility bonds without voter approval. That omission would seriously hamper not only City Light but all city-operated public utilities. Voters defeated the charter by a three to two margin, although only 40 percent of those eligible to vote did so. The defeat of the charter represented a victory for Ross and City Light, who led the opposition to and "shared the responsibility for the defeat of the measure."[82] In 1931, when City Light attempted to create an engineering group, that effort also turned into a highly politicized affair, and Ross and City Light again became embroiled in city politics.

City Light had relied on the city's engineering department for engineering work since its establishment. An independent firm concluded in 1929 that City Light might operate better if it had engineers trained specifically in electrical engineering. The enactment of that recommendation required amending the city's charter. Both the *Post-Intelligencer* and the *Times* opposed the amendment, as did the business community, because of the cost. Just days before the vote, it appeared that the revision would fail. Seattle's mayor at the time, Frank Edwards, took action that paradoxically ensured the amendment's passage. After friends teased the mayor at an election eve party that Ross enjoyed greater popularity than Edwards, he fired Ross. Edwards later said that he dismissed Ross for inefficient management of City Light. The following day 52 percent of the voters endorsed the amendment.[83] Ross and his supporters believed that the private utility industry controlled the mayor, while Edwards charged that Ross and his defenders belonged to a "communist conspiracy." Voters vindicated Ross in July 1931 when they voted 35,659 to 21,839 to recall Edwards. The city council then elected an interim mayor whose first action was to reappoint Ross. Ross's firing and reappointment "represented a triumph for municipal ownership and J. D. Ross. Because the recall battle . . . had been fought as a struggle between the 'Power Trust' and municipal ownership."[84]

The 1926 debate over a new city charter and the 1931 controversy over the engineering amendment reveal several things about City Light and public power. In 1926 voters rejected the new charter, in part because its passage would have prevented utility bond sales and because of the perceived threat to Ross and City Light. The inability to sell bonds would have hurt all utilities but especially City Light, which depended on bonds for project construction. Bond sales, for example, funded the Skagit River projects. In 1931 voters again saw a risk to City Light when the mayor fired Ross.

Even before his dismissal, however, people had organized the Citizens' Municipal Utilities Protective League in the winter of 1931 to support the engineering amendment. League members also came to Ross's defense after his termination. Although Ross wanted the amendment, the league's organization and support showed that people in Seattle favored public power to the extent of forming political pressure groups. On the surface Ross's dismissal seemed the result of personality clashes, but much more may have been involved. Edwards attempted to paint Ross and other public power supporters as communists, and a probusiness Seattle newspaper said Ross plotted to "sovietize America."[85]

Even more revealing is Edwards's relationship with PSP&L officials, which might have included payoffs from the company. Proof of payoffs was never forthcoming, although FTC investigators discovered correspondences between PSP&L president A. W. Leonard and Stone and Webster officials in Boston regarding Edwards. In February 1930 Leonard wrote to a Mr. Clifford, a Stone and Webster official: "I hope you had a chance to meet Mayor Edwards while he was in Boston. . . . I understand that he had a very pleasant time while in Boston and was very much pleased with the attention paid him while there." In March 1930, after the city election, Leonard again wrote Clifford: "Mayor Edwards was elected by a large majority, and two of the old members of the city council were defeated by two better men from our standpoint. I hope now that Mayor Edwards will feel that he is justified in carrying out some of the suggestions he has previously made relative to personnel, etc., of the lighting department." After Ross's firing, Clifford wrote Leonard: "It is extremely unfortunate that Ross is now in a position to play the role of a martyr. . . . As you know, the Seattle situation has been my real worry."[86]

It appears that Ross's dismissal was much more than a question of a personal animosity between Ross and Edwards. Instead, his firing appears to have represented an attempt by Edwards and PSP&L's holding company, Stone and Webster, to undermine City Light and may have included company payments to Edwards. The Municipal Utilities Protective viewed Edwards's recall as a fight between private and public power. In preparing recall petitions the league's president said that the petitions would "present to the people a clear-cut issue between City Light and the Power Trust."[87] Clearly, Ross had become the symbol of the success of Seattle City Light for both public power supporters and opponents.

Stone and Webster officials had good reason to worry about "the Seattle situation." Seattle City Light and Ross had achieved national prominence by the 1920s. Throughout the decade municipalities from across the country asked Ross to speak in support of public power projects or to provide testimony regarding public power. Individuals nationwide wrote to Seattle officials asking for information about City Light's rates, often asking if they were as low as reported. Several examples illustrate Ross's and City Light's national prominence.

When people in Colorado Springs, Colorado, began debating the public power issue in 1925, Ross traveled there to campaign for the establishment of municipal power. While in Colorado Springs, he reported to the city council on the possibilities of developing water power in the Pike's Peak area. Ross stated in his report that they could build a new system for $550,000, or about half the amount that the city's private utility company thought it would cost. Ross told a Kiwanis gathering that the competitive system was the only good system. He also said that utility executives lacked interest in local affairs because they lived elsewhere.[88] The citizens of Colorado Springs ultimately voted first to buy the private plant and system and then to build a new power plant and distribution system.[89]

Individuals and local government officials from all parts of the country made inquiries requesting information or advice regarding municipally owned power. The town clerk of West Point, Mississippi, wrote Seattle's mayor soliciting his opinion about municipally owned water and electric plants. The clerk complained that "paid agents" had arrived in town "to work up sentiment" to sell the public plant to private interests. The purpose of the clerk's inquiry was to learn about the experiences that cities with public power had had with the electrical utilities.[90] The mayor of Jackson, Mississippi, also wrote Mayor Edwards requesting an electric rate schedule and other information regarding Seattle's public power plant. At that time Jackson was considering a proposal to build a municipal plant "as a means of securing more advantageous rates."[91]

A resident of Muskogee, Oklahoma, wrote to ask about a magazine article entitled "The Low Electric Rates in Seattle." The article claimed that the average rate in Seattle was less than two cents per kilowatt hour, that City Light had a net balance of more than $1 million, and that more Seattle residents used electric ranges than did residents in any other city in the world. The letter writer wondered how all those things came into being.[92] A Watsonville, California, resident wrote a similar letter asking about the income and expenses of the city's plant. The letter's author claimed that his town's citizens believed that they were paying double the reasonable amount for power and were considering building a public plant.[93]

City Light's stature continued to grow in the late 1920s. Besides letters from individuals and small towns, City Light and Ross responded to other inquiries. In 1928 the Wisconsin legislature appointed an interim committee to conduct hearings on municipal ownership of electrical utilities. The committee sent a questionnaire to City Light in an attempt to gather information on municipal power. Ross's responses reveal much about his views on public power. He stated that municipalities should have eminent domain to interconnect and sell power beyond their boundaries. When asked about the incentive for economical management of municipal facilities, Ross stated that a greater incentive existed than in private operations: "No watered stock. No aunts and uncles employed, and all under public eye." In reply to another question, he said municipal power offered better service. City Light served 93,000 customers, while PSP&L had only 30,000. In response to the important question of rates, Ross answered that a house within the city limits that City Light served paid $10.00 for power, while a house "just across the 60 ft. street at City limits" paid $21.30. He added a note to the questionnaire in which he addressed the relationship of debt to electricity produced. City Light owed $171 per horsepower of electricity generated, while PSP&L owed $473.[94]

It was that type of nationwide attention that caused so much consternation among private power officials. Stone and Webster officials' apparent meddling in the 1930 mayoral campaign was one of several attempts that private power representatives made to discredit or destroy City Light. PSP&L president A. W. Leonard publicly declared in 1927 that he had formulated a five-year plan to take over City Light. He assailed Ross for questionable financial tactics and asserted that City Light would sink in a sea of red ink. Leonard argued that leasing the city's power, light, and railway property represented the only solution to the problem.[95] Homer Bone quickly pledged his support to City Light in any takeover fight. He said: "We will be prepared to ladle out to that gentleman and his outfit enough concentrated hell to the square inch to furnish him food for reflection for the balance of his life." The primary weapon Bone planned to use would be how much capital debt per horsepower that PSP&L generated, which he believed exceeded $400 per horsepower of electricity. With the completion and expansion of several Skagit and Cedar River projects, City Light's capital debt would drop to $109 per generated horsepower. Bone vowed to use that information to its fullest advantage. He linked municipal power in Seattle with municipal power in Tacoma when he stated that an attack on one city's system represented an attack on the municipal plant of the other city.[96]

The National Electric Light Association had already planned to discredit City Light before Leonard made his intentions public. In January 1927 Seattle's pro–public power newspapers, the *Star* and the *Post-Intelligencer*, published articles discussing the Voters' Information League. Founded in the early 1920s the league had undertaken an investigation into City Light's finances. The *Star* called on the league to reveal its source of financing. League officials, however, refused to reveal the names of its contributors, although the league's secretary did say that local businessmen, league members, and homeowners contributed money to the league. The *Post-Intelligencer* reported that the league would soon reveal the findings of its study.[97]

Puget Sound Power and Light provided partial funding for the Voters' Information League. In June 1927 the NELA Public Policy Committee, meeting in Atlantic City, appointed a special committee to investigate the "Seattle municipal ownership situation." Released in 1928 the committee's report included the following excerpt:

The Seattle situation is of national importance. Seattle has the second largest municipally owned plant in the country. Its rates are continually cited as lower than those charged by privately owned plants. It has been particularly prominent in spreading misleading propaganda as to its success throughout the country. At a time when active proposals are being made to extend the activities of Government in business in other localities, the claim of successful results of such a policy in Seattle is dangerous and requires refutation. Although not in the same measure, the situation in the neighboring city of Tacoma and that in Los Angeles and in Cleveland are for the same reason of importance to the entire industry.[98]

The report continued that PSP&L had allocated $150,000 to expose damaging information regarding City Light. PSP&L would publicly contribute the money to the Voters' Information League under the pretense that it wanted the investigation made public as a taxpayer and to protect its property. League members asked NELA to contribute an additional $25,000 per year for three years to help publicize the findings nationally.

The Voters' Information League mailed unsigned statements regarding City Light's transmission and distribution systems to a Los Angeles attorney who forwarded the statements to the Los Angeles Bureau of Power and Light. The bureau's chief electrical engineer, E. F. Scattergood, then wrote Ross asking about the nature of the Voters' Information League. Scattergood noted that the statements were "neither frank or truthful." The Los Angeles department also received an inquiry from P. C. Stoess, president of the Voters' Information League, seeking information about power sold, number of employees, and the average amount of power sold per employee. Scattergood thought that conditions differed so much between Seattle and Los Angeles that Stoess's inquiry served little purpose.

Scattergood saw through the guise of the letters. In responding to the unsigned engineering report, he called the Seattle system economical, satisfactory, and well suited to the particular situation found in that city. He called the outside engineering statement an apparent "attack on the Municipal Lighting Department," also noting that the report contained many unsubstantiated statements in an attempt to discredit City Light.[99] Ross also received a letter of support from Judson King, chairman of the National Popular Government League. King called Ross "one of the men that the country cannot afford to lose at this important post of progress." King told Ross that if he needed any help Ross should send him "the dope," and he would write an article for *Labor*.[100]

Stoess sent several letters directly to City Light requesting information about the number of kilowatt hours generated and delivered to customers between 1905 and 1927. Ross responded to Stoess and took issue with the activities of the league, specifically complaining that Stoess had hired a consultant predisposed against municipal power. Ross asserted that Stone and Webster funded, at least partially, the Voters' Information League despite assertions that it was a public institution. Ross continued, "You have placed yourself in the peculiar position of attacking City Light with an insidious statement to leave the public mind up in the air at the same time you are apparently subsidized by Stone and Webster."[101]

City Light's 1928 annual report contained the same themes: "A heavily subsidized press is deliberately spreading libelous propaganda throughout the nation against the Seattle power system in hope of destroying its financial credit and to fool the people of the nation and hide the real facts. . . . They spend this money in the fear that a long suffering public may learn the true facts."[102] Ross and City Light replied to the league's attack in a pamphlet entitled "Debunking the League of Misinformation." Ross used the findings of the FTC utility investigation in his defense of City Light.[103] In 1928 the league issued a public report that acknowledged that PSP&L provided financial assistance for its activities.[104]

The resolution of the Seattle public power fight most likely would occur only if either City Light or PSP&L sold its holdings to its adversary. Leonard, of course, had threatened to take over City Light, but that never happened. The first call for the city to buy PSP&L's property came in 1916, when city engineer R. H. Thompson proposed a $10 million bond to finance the acquisition. Periodically throughout the 1920s Ross suggested that City Light should buy PSP&L's property within the city.[105] While PSP&L was conducting its campaign against City Light, the city renewed efforts to buy PSP&L's property in Seattle. The city council thought that the duplication of services cost Seattle too much revenue. Ross believed that the additional revenue created by new customers would pay for the acquisition of PSP&L's property.[106] The following year an ordinance was introduced authorizing a study to learn the cost to City Light if it acquired PSP&L's distribution system and several generating plants.[107]

In 1929 Ross and Norwood Brockett debated the question at a King County Democratic Club meeting. The *Post-Intelligencer* reported that each speaker blamed the other for raising the issue, and both stated that the situation could not continue. Ross repeated that public power provided competition that drove down private rates and cited data from Florida, Texas, and Virginia as examples. Brockett countered that both Spokane and Portland had lower private rates than those charged by City Light. Ross challenged the validity of Brockett's statement.[108] The scope of the debate broadened when Brockett accused public power advocates of wanting "government operation of all industry." Ross denied that statement and claimed that the policy of NELA was not "to argue municipal ownership [but to] call them socialists."[109]

As the 1920s drew to a close, public power forces in Seattle and across the state enjoyed new popularity. Information made public by the Federal Trade Commission regarding the utility investigation damaged the electrical utility industry nationwide. It was a triumphant year for public power advocates in 1930 when Washington voters approved an initiative allowing for the establishment of public utility districts. A public utility district, popularly known as a PUD, allowed for a county or part of a county to organize itself, regardless of municipal boundaries, for producing, buying, and selling electricity. In Washington the establishment of the PUD law fulfilled many dreams for those who worked for the passage of the Bone initiative in 1924.

The establishment of a public utility district benefited citizens in unincorporated areas the most. Farmers especially gained because they would be able to purchase electricity from public and private enterprises. Before the passage of the PUD bill, a farmer, because he did not live in a municipality, did not have the option of voting for the establishment of a municipal power plant or system. In his study of Ross and public power, historian Wesley Dick wrote, "In effect, the PUD combined rural electrification and municipal ownership." With that thought in mind it is not surprising that the Grange was the main sponsor of the PUD referendum in Washington.[110] Passage of the initiative also allowed cities to sell power beyond their municipal borders, which was beneficial to Seattle, Tacoma, and any other town with municipally owned power.

The legislation did not become law without a long and acrimonious battle between public and private power forces. Advocates of the PUD law filed petitions with the state in January 1929. The first option was to have the legislature enact the law, but failing that, supporters placed the bill on the general ballot in November 1930. A *Seattle Times* headline during legislative hearings on the law read: "Same Old Faces, Same Old Tune, at Power Bill Fight."[111] A. S. Goss, the master of the state Grange, told legislators that the bill would solve the "real farm problem" by bringing electricity to rural areas so farmers could receive the same benefits as "city dwellers." Before the referendum passed, less than half of Washington's farmers used electricity (47 percent), and those that did paid "exorbitant rates."[112] A witness from Tacoma told listeners that the private companies overcharged their customers and that they would save $4 million if the entire state had rates equal to those in Tacoma. An attorney for the Washington Water Power Company countered that statement when he told the hearing's audience that the bill was socialistic.[113]

An editorial in the *Seattle Star* strongly supported the PUD initiative and cited lower rates as the proposed law's greatest benefit. The bill would serve as an "equalizing measure" that would grant residents outside municipal limits the right to either construct public plants or purchase power from cities with municipal power and therefore receive the advantages of "cheap municipal power and light."[114] The state senate defeated the PUD bill by three votes. Opponents of the bill attempted to defeat the measure without a roll call vote; supporters, however, successfully pushed for the recorded vote. The *Star* reported the names of the senators voting for and against the bill under the headline "Cut This Out for Your Scrapbook." Below the headline were two columns: one read, "These voted for cheap power," the other, "These voted against cheap power." The defeat of the bill in the legislature automatically placed it on the general election ballot.[115]

Leonard announced that PSP&L and other private power companies in the state would not make an organized effort to oppose the district power bill. He did say that the private companies had signed a statement opposing the bill, and that taxpayers might want to think about the provision of the bill that allowed for a tax levy on public utility districts.[116] Despite Leonard's announcement that PSP&L would not make an organized effort to oppose the district power bill, FTC hearings in 1934 revealed that the company quietly spent $124,000 to defeat the initiative.[117] In many ways the findings of the FTC hearings had tied the hands of the private utilities against actively opposing the district power bill, as they had done in 1924 against the Bone bill. By 1929 the private utilities' heavy financing of public power opponents and the utilities' attempts to influence public opinion were public knowledge. The Grange effectively used the FTC findings regarding stock watering in the campaign for the bill.[118] An editorial in the *Post-Intelligencer* attacked the financing of "canned propaganda" and "citizens committees." The editorial charged that PSP&L provided 89 percent of the funding for the Voters' Information League and had contributed $175,000 to defeat the Bone bill in 1924. The most significant point the editorial argued was that the consumer had financed all those undertakings through higher rates.[119]

During the campaign the Grange pushed hard for the district power bill: "A nation cannot long exist half slave and half free." Abraham Lincoln's words appeared in a *Grange News* article discussing the bill, as the writer asked why half the state should have the right to cheap power and not the other half: "Is this not a measure of freedom for the cities and slavery, under the domination of the power trust, for the country?" The bill would end that injustice. The private power companies opposed the district power bill because they feared competition. One need not look beyond Seattle to see the impact that competition had on private rates. The article used the example of two houses on either side of a street. The house on the city limits side paid the private company 5.5 cents per kilowatt hour, while the house on the other side of the street, outside the city limits, paid 7.5 cents per kilowatt hour.[120] Voters approved the Grange bill allowing for the establishment of public utility districts in the November 1930 election by a vote of 152,000 to 131,000.[121] Public utility laws had already passed in California in 1913 and in Arizona, Nebraska, and Montana in 1915. Between 1927 and 1936 ten other states passed laws allowing for the creation of public utility districts, and in 1930 numerous states elected pro–public power governors.[122]

As the 1920s came to a close, public power in Seattle and Washington State had clearly become a major political issue. Just as had occurred elsewhere, rates and electrical modernization drove the intense political battle over public power that raged in Seattle between City Light and PSP&L and across Washington State during the 1920s and early 1930s. The presence and size of competing electrical systems in Seattle helped put it in the national spotlight, as supporters and opponents of public power kept an especially close eye on the city's power fight. Those favoring public power considered Seattle a shining microcosm of what could happen nationwide if public power prevailed. The private utility industry looked to Seattle with a great amount of trepidation, constantly worrying about the amount of national publicity that shone on the success of City Light. Private power so feared City Light's success that it actively tried to destroy it. Although the intensely political debate occurred in a city with access to an abundance of power and a liberal, if not radical, labor tradition, a similar battle developed in resource-scarce and politically conservative Southern California.

Los Angeles, California: The Triumph of Public Power in a Conservative and Arid Setting

Public power forces in Los Angeles won a long and acrimonious battle that matched the intensity of the public power fight nationwide. The Los Angeles municipal power debate mirrored the Seattle controversy in several ways. As in Seattle, private companies continued to operate in Los Angeles after the establishment of public power. Opponents of the city's municipal power system claimed that public power resulted in lower tax revenues and was socialistic in nature. The development of a municipal water system in Los Angeles also preceded the establishment of public power, and all parties recognized that electricity was essential to economic growth and industrial development. As had happened in small towns, in Seattle, and across the nation, the issue of electrical modernization entered the debate. Despite these similarities, a crucial difference distinguished Los Angeles from Seattle: an abundance of cheap hydroelectric power did not naturally exist close to the city. Instead, the public generation of hydroelectricity resulted from the city's successful attempt to import water from the Owens Valley in the eastern Sierras. By 1928, when Congress passed the Boulder Dam legislation, city officials believed electricity to be as important as water for building the dam.

In Seattle, the general strike represented a milestone in the town's history and labor movement. In Southern California the dynamiting of the *Los Angeles Times* building in October 1910 and its aftermath stand out as a defining moment in the city's early-twentieth-century history. Stark differences existed between Los Angeles and Seattle not only in terms of climate, geography, and access to cheap hydroelectricity but also in the overall political climate and history. Whereas Seattle at the beginning of the twentieth century still depended on its resource-rich hinterland for its economic livelihood, in Los Angeles a cycle of real estate–driven boom and bust had already occurred. People looking for work migrated to Seattle, while in Los Angeles fears developed that without new forms of industry the area might not develop into anything more than a tourist mecca. Despite the boom of the late nineteenth century, the City of Angels had humble beginnings.

Spaniards expressed the first European interest in Southern California. Overlooking picturesque San Diego Bay is the statue of Juan Rodríquez Cabrillo, whose ships explored the California shoreline in the early 1540s.[1] Spanish settlement would wait another two hundred years. In 1769 a group of Spanish explorers and missionaries traveled north from San Diego and camped in the area that eventually became Los Angeles. The establishment of the first Spanish mission in California occurred two years later. Then, in 1781, the founding of Los Angeles took place—only the second Spanish town in all of California at the time.[2] Not much happened in Los Angeles for the first eighty years of its existence. Cattle ranching and farming dominated the region's economic base and provided a livelihood for the 1,500 people who lived in the town at mid-nineteenth century. Life began to change after the United States took control of California following the Mexican-American War. Whereas in 1850 Hispanics composed three-quarters of the population, thirty years later whites represented 80 percent of the town's 11,200 residents.[3] Migration to Los Angeles and Southern California continued unabated into the twentieth century.

Social commentator and writer Carey McWilliams noted that the nature of the American immigrant to Los Angeles differed greatly from those Americans who migrated to other parts of the United States. They were, McWilliams wrote, "fairly well-to-do people. . . . unlike the usual frontier influx."[4] More recently, historian Carol O'Connor pointed out that the people who moved to Los Angeles made a conscious decision to do so that resulted in a desire to make "the city 'the choicest part of the earth.'" From that desire emerged a strong booster spirit dedicated to making Los Angeles second to none.[5]

Los Angeles boosters knew no limits. A combination of private interests and public money helped make up for the area's inadequacies. For much of its history Los Angeles was California's second city behind San Francisco, a situation that was unlikely to change until an adequate transportation system developed. A railroad link to the east was critical. The first connection occurred in 1876, when the Southern Pacific Railroad ran a line from San Francisco to Los Angeles. Ten years later the completion of the Santa Fe Railroad gave the city its second eastern tie. Ironically, San Francisco boosters favored Los Angeles over San Diego as the Santa Fe's western terminus because they feared that the shipping possibilities of a railroad tie to San Diego's natural port might diminish the importance of San Francisco Bay. Los Angeles lacked a decent harbor, but that too changed within a few years. By the turn of the century Congress had allocated money for the dredging of San Pedro Bay and the construction of a protective seawall. Within only a few decades Los Angeles had obtained not only two railroads but also a world-class deepwater port.

Shipping and trade soon became two of the mainstays of Los Angeles's regional economy. In the 1920s Los Angeles boosters could claim that their city had the leading port on the West Coast. Completion of the Santa Fe in 1886, which resulted in a rate war with the Southern Pacific, set off the first wave of real estate speculation in Los Angeles and in the process swelled the city's population. In an eighteen-month period beginning in January 1887, people planned for more than sixty new towns in Southern California. From 1880 to 1890 the city's population increased by nearly 40,000 and Southern California's by 135,000.[6] The land boom of the eighties came to a halt, but within a few years oil gushed from the Los Angeles plain. Another oil boom hit the region in 1920. Hollywood, another important element of the developing economy that would help mold the image of Southern California in subsequent years, emerged in the 1910s.[7] "This new and unique American city," historian Kevin Starr writes, "was based on oil, maritime trade and shipping, industrial manufacture, agriculture, banking, movie-making, and tourism."[8]

The tremendous growth of Los Angeles and Southern California did not happen without significant controversy, most noticeably the long-running battle to make the city an open shop town. Boosters believed that maintaining an open shop, if not the complete elimination of organized labor, would serve as an enticement to eastern banking and manufacturing interests.[9] The fight over the open shop and organized labor eventually became known as the Forty Year War, prompting one writer to call the city the "bloodiest arena in the Western world for Capital and Labor."[10] McWilliams wrote that from 1907 to 1910 a state of industrial warfare threatened to tear Los Angeles apart, culminating in a number of strikes in the spring of 1910. A harsh antipicketing measure soon became law, and the arrest of strikers caused an even greater increase in union activity. The number of labor and socialist publications grew, as did membership in the Socialist party, whose mayoral candidate Job Harriman received 58,000 votes in the 1911 primary. The explosion at the *Times* building in 1910 ultimately shattered the labor movement, which the newspaper quickly blamed for the incident. A few days before the final mayoral election in December 1912, the paper's publisher, General Harrison Gray Otis, and the defendants in the case, the McNamara brothers, struck a deal—the defendants pleaded guilty in exchange for jail time. That plea undermined the Socialist ticket and spelled the end of Harriman's mayoral aspirations. McWilliams noted that the bombing and the guilty plea set back union organization in Los Angeles, already retarded, another twenty years.[11]

The end of the forty-year labor fight in favor of antiunion forces was not the only manifestation of the conservative political climate that existed in Los Angeles. Although frequently perceived both in the past and present as situated on the cultural and social fringe, Los Angeles politics often have been conservative. That fact was never truer than in the 1920s. The *Los*

Angeles Times, the city's leading newspaper, remained conservative not only through the twenties but also until the early 1960s.[12] Another equally important indication of Los Angeles's political conservatism is that the city charter required a two-thirds approval of bond issues. A simple majority was not sufficient to approve bond sales for municipal projects, and bond issues failed several times for that reason. California law also required a two-thirds vote for a municipality to acquire the property of a private utility if the municipality would incur a debt in the process. The law cut both ways; a city needed approval from two-thirds of the voters before it could sell a publicly owned utility to a private company. The state enacted that provision to protect citizens against "unsuspecting or corrupt city councils." If a bond issue failed to receive a two-thirds vote, six months had to pass before the city could hold another vote.[13] Change at the ballot box did not always come easily. Although a simple majority could not pass the necessary bonds required for public power, the fact that power bonds often passed by more than a two-thirds vote shows the widespread support that Los Angeles voters gave to municipal power.[14]

By the 1920s the booster-engineered Los Angeles infrastructure was in place; the city began to emerge as the leading urban center in the West, and California as the most influential state in the region.[15] Public and private officials in Los Angeles had foreseen the role that the city could play in the state's, region's, and nation's future and took steps to fulfill its potential. Although people today recognize the dominance of Los Angeles and California after World War II, it was in the twenties that city officials and private interests continued to create the foundation for that dominance. As the 1920s ended, officials had successfully pushed for construction of Boulder Dam, ensuring the supply of cheap, publicly controlled electricity and water that they believed essential to continued economic growth. Southern California Edison officials also recognized the importance of electrical power to the area's continued growth. People needed water to live, but without electricity Southern Californians would be jobless. An adequate water supply also was essential for agriculture and business. The emerging airplane and motion picture industries, for example, required huge amounts of electricity.

Besides its economic importance and cultural leadership, national political leadership also began to emerge from California. Not only did Californians lead the effort to build Boulder Dam, but individuals who would play significant roles in twentieth-century American politics also began their careers in the state. During the 1920s Richard Nixon spent the later years of his youth in Southern California and attended Whittier College before going to Duke University Law School. In the 1930s Ronald Reagan launched his public life in Hollywood before entering politics. During the 1940s one of the more controversial Supreme Court justices in the country's history, Earl Warren, served as governor before his appointment as the high court's chief justice. California's large population, and accompanying electoral votes, has made it a factor in nearly every presidential election since World War II. In seven of the thirteen presidential elections between 1948 and 1996, a Californian was on the Republican ticket, and that ticket won six times. The political leadership in power before the New Deal set the stage for the state's influence after World War II.[16]

In Seattle, technology did not play a large role in the public power debate because of the short distances from the generation sites to the city. A different situation existed in Southern California, where the projects required high-voltage transmission lines to transmit to Los Angeles power generated on either the Owens Valley Aqueduct or at Boulder Dam. The projects also required the city to transmit power to pumping stations to bring the water to Los Angeles. California, and the entire West, had been an early leader in long-distance transmission. Before World War I California had more high-voltage transmission systems than any other region in the world; within the United States it was second only to New York in how much power could be generated by either hydroelectric or steam-fueled central stations.[17] The high degree of hydroelectric development and long-distance transmission in California makes it difficult to explain the Los Angeles municipal power situation from a lack of technology perspective. By the 1910s engineers had surmounted the barriers to transmitting electricity over long distances. In fact, technological advances in part made possible and later contributed to the development, consolidation, and survival of municipal power in Los Angeles. If technological barriers to electrical transmission had still existed, the Los Angeles municipal power system would not have developed as it did.

In Seattle, City Light and PSP&L debated rates where an abundance of electricity existed. If supply determines price, as classical economic theory postulates, the low rates in Seattle should not have been surprising. Cheap and plentiful water power, it seems, guaranteed low rates. That, of course, is not how the situation developed in Seattle and Washington State: public competition, not supply, drove rates down. The Los Angeles public power debate allows for the study of rate issues where an abundance of cheap electricity did not exist. Examination of the development of public power in Los Angeles reveals that even in a resource-scarce region, rate debates over private power remained important issues. As occurred in Seattle and elsewhere, the rates that the public utility charged forced down private rates. Again, the yardstick principle of public power became a factor in the fight over electrical rates. In small towns and in larger cities with or without resources, rate setting was the most important point of contention in the political fight over public power.

Despite the conservative political atmosphere that existed in Los Angeles, public officials realized the steps they had to take to guarantee the city's future. Lacking natural resources, city officials successfully pushed for public funding and ownership of water and electrical systems. To understand this situation fully, remembering the climatic conditions and geographical location of the Los Angeles basin is important. The title of Carey McWilliams's book, *Southern California: An Island on the Land,* best describes the region. Isolated by mountains and desert to the north and east, Mexico to the south, and the Pacific Ocean to the west, the Los Angeles basin sits on a semiarid plain. Until the beginning of the twentieth century, area residents drew water from the Los Angeles River. Following a decade of tremendous population growth in the 1890s, civic leaders realized that the city's continued expansion depended on finding additional water sources.[18] In what became the first of several major efforts to import water, politicians and engineers turned to the Owens Valley on the eastern side of the Sierras, 250 miles from Los Angeles, as the source to supplement the city's water supply. Hardly a decade had passed before the city began looking to the Colorado River for more water and for electricity. The political fight over municipal ownership of electricity was a major political issue in Los Angeles through the 1920s and brought together supporters of municipal power on both the sides of the political spectrum.[19]

During the debate over the Owens Valley project, water was the primary objective, although the electrical potential of the plan quickly became apparent. Engineers realized that the elevation drop between the valley and the city meant that the aqueduct could generate a tremendous amount of power. Los Angeles's interest in the Colorado River revolved around both electricity and water. Additionally, the power that the river could generate would enable the city to establish a complete electrical monopoly. The long-distance transmission of electricity made both projects feasible. High-voltage transmission lines sent Boulder Dam power over several hundred miles of rough terrain to Los Angeles. Adequate private capital existed in Los Angeles to establish privately owned utility companies. In fact, three different electrical utilities operated in Los Angeles before the city constructed its own distribution system. Neither technological limitations nor the lack of private finance capital adequately explains the development of municipal power in Los Angeles; rate setting and political control of electricity drove the public power debate. The same issues that existed in Seattle and in the small rural towns already studied came to the forefront in Los Angeles.

Historians, journalists, and novelists have often told the story of diverting water from the Owens Valley to the city of Los Angeles, which became the basis for the Hollywood movie *Chinatown.* Early commentators such as Morrow Mayo put forth the idea of a conspiracy: a land syndicate purchased most of the available agricultural acreage in the San Fernando Valley and then convinced, or manipulated, the city to build the aqueduct. The aqueduct's terminus was in the valley, and according to the conspiracy theory the value of the syndicate's property skyrocketed when the aqueduct guaranteed an adequate water supply. Authors writing since World War II have downplayed the conspiracy theory and generally recognize that several reasons exist to explain the project's construction.[20]

Because city leaders initially believed that the future of Los Angeles depended on finding additional sources of water, historians have paid less attention to the importance of electrical power in the debate over the construction of the Owens Valley Aqueduct. William Mulholland, the first engineer and manager of the city's water department, succinctly summed up the project's importance to the city when he noted, "If we don't get the water, we won't need it."[21] The *Los Angeles Times* broke the story of the proposed aqueduct project in 1905 and emphasized the importance of water with little mention of power. Within a week, however, the press began discussing the project's power potential. A *Times* editorial invoked city building themes when it said that cheap power would light the city's streets and provide power for industrial development, "transforming Los Angeles into one of the most important manufacturing cities in the country." In his study of the Owens Valley controversy, historian Abraham Hoffman refers to the aqueduct's hydroelectric potential as an "added blessing . . . [that] held the promise of modernizing the city at an inexpensive price."[22]

Most people realized that selling the electricity generated by the project would help finance the aqueduct's construction. Various engineering reports stated that the aqueduct could generate between 36,000 and 70,000 kilowatts of electricity. The city's Board of Water Commissioners estimated potential aqueduct generation to be about 60,000 kilowatts; an amount so great that after supplying municipal needs, enough power would remain for sale to offset "a substantial part of the indebtedness to be incurred by the city in completing this project." The city's press and civic officials estimated that annual revenues from the sale of aqueduct power would be between $1 million and $2 million.[23]

In order for construction to begin, several issues needed resolution. The most important were whether public or private interests would build and control the project and who would market the electricity that the aqueduct generated. In Los Angeles the press accused private power interests of attempting to gain control of the project or, failing that, trying to block the entire project. Mulholland claimed that only Southern California Edison opposed the project, although Edison officials denied charges of interference. The point of contention was electrical rates. As the *Times* pointed out, whoever controlled the aqueduct's electricity could "fix the price of power in Los Angeles."[24]

Ultimately, President Theodore Roosevelt decided that public agencies would construct and control the project. Officials in Washington, D.C., became involved because the developer needed to buy land for the proposed aqueduct route from the federal government. Bureau of Reclamation proposals to establish a reclamation project in the Owens River Valley further complicated the issue. By 1905 the lines were clearly drawn between local residents in the valley and the city of Los Angeles over control and use of the river's water. In Los Angeles people debated who would develop the project if the city gained rights to the water. In June 1906 Roosevelt, at the urging of Pinchot and Senator Frank Flint (R-Calif.), decided that the river's water would best serve Los Angeles. The water would be publicly owned, and an amendment attached to the bill at Roosevelt's request prohibited the sale of excess water to private interests.[25]

Roosevelt's decision reflected his growing belief in a conservationist ideology: diverting the Owens River's water to Los Angeles would serve the greatest public good. Roosevelt did not deny that the valley's residents held genuine interests, only that building the aqueduct could better serve the interests of Los Angeles and the nation. In making his decision the president declared, "It is a hundred or thousand fold more important to state that this [water] is more valuable to the people as a whole if used by a city than if used by the people of the Owens Valley."[26]

Financing the Owens Valley project required voter approval of bond measures. In August 1905, even before the federal government approved the project, Los Angeles voters passed a $1.5 million bond to purchase necessary right-of-ways, land, and water rights. Two years later voters approved by a ten to one ratio a $23 million bond to finance building the aqueduct. Yet, neither bond initiative contained provisions to develop the aqueduct's hydroelectric potential.

Distribution of aqueduct power emerged as a major political issue in 1910, when the mayor, George Alexander, and the city council placed a $3.5 million bond measure on the ballot to finance construction of aqueduct power plants for municipal power. Voters approved bonds by a seven to one margin.[27] Authorizing construction of the power plants led to the question of what to do with the power generated. Public power advocates of course wanted public distribution, although private power interests offered to buy the electricity.[28] Then, in 1911, voters decided ten to one in favor of a public distribution system.[29] Four considerations influenced the vote on the power bonds. One, the sale of power would help finance aqueduct construction. Two, the promise of inexpensive electricity would attract new industries to the city. Three, a delay in construction of power facilities until the project's completion would result in additional costs because of the need to divert water. Four, the inseparability of power and water; since its inception people always considered power a part of the project, and failure to generate electricity would suggest the project's incompleteness.[30]

In his work on the Los Angeles public power fight, historian Nelson Van Valen also posed the question of why the city decided to construct the power system in the first place, and he identified two reasons. First, reform elements in the city in the first decade of the century wanted to bring public utilities under control; among those targeted were the private electrical utilities that served the city. City officials had grown dissatisfied with "poor service, high rates, and interference in the city's governance." Second, Van Valen believed that the city's Spanish heritage gave people a "tradition of municipal ownership and distribution of water of the Los Angeles River."[31] Others historians also have argued that the decision to establish municipal ownership of water, and then electricity and gas, in Los Angeles was not a result of radical political agitation, despite the high degree of labor unrest at the time. Instead, it developed from the demand for good service at lower rates, a fundamental demand of the public power movement everywhere.[32] The subsequent fights over rates and public ownership that developed in Los Angeles suggest that cost and municipal control of electricity represented the most important reason for public ownership.

Receiving the federal government's support for the project and securing voter approval of the necessary bonds marked the conclusion of the first chapter of the municipal power story in Los Angeles. Most local business concerns and newspapers strongly supported construction of the aqueduct, although that backing weakened in subsequent years after the project's completion. The broad consensus that developed for a public entity building the aqueduct broke down over the issue of who should distribute the electricity produced at the aqueduct's generation sites. Political debates that originated over distributing aqueduct power in the 1910s continued into the 1930s and did not completely end until Los Angeles began to receive power generated at Boulder Dam.

After Los Angeles citizens voted to develop the aqueduct's electrical generation capabilities, they needed to decide how to distribute the power. At the time, three private companies served the Los Angeles power market, any of which could have purchased aqueduct power for resale if permitted. The Los Angeles Gas and Electric Corporation distributed 87 percent of its power for domestic lighting and provided additional current for street lighting. Pacific Light and Power Company, which Henry Huntington gained control of in 1913, sold most of its power to streetcar companies and provided all the energy used by another Huntington business interest, the Los Angeles Railway. Southern California Edison sold 75 percent of its electricity to industrial or business customers but also served about half the city's domestic users. In 1917 SCE purchased Pacific Light and Power, a move that created the fifth largest operating company in the United States, with an authorized capitalization equaling $100 million.[33]

The question city leaders and voters faced in the 1910s was whether to sell aqueduct power wholesale to private companies for distribution or to build a distribution system to market the power. E. F. Scattergood, who had made initial estimates of aqueduct power for the city and subsequently became chief electrical engineer for the municipal power system, believed from the outset that the city should sell the power to the public at the lowest rate possible. He recommended that the city sell aqueduct electricity at seven cents per kilowatt hour, two cents lower than the private rate. The proposed rate dropped to six and one-half cents before the bond vote and later fell to six cents. Although private utilities in the city offered to pay $1 million per year for aqueduct power, Scattergood believed that the city could make more money through direct sales.[34]

Scattergood was not alone in calling for public control of the aqueduct's electricity. From the beginning, reformer and physician John Randolph Haynes was one of the most articulate proponents of municipal ownership in Los Angeles. In 1905 he urged the sale of aqueduct power for municipal purposes and said that private interests were trying to gain control of any potential electricity. Haynes found an ally in the *Los Angeles Examiner*, a Hearst newspaper that strongly supported municipal ownership. Haynes and Henry Loewenthal, the paper's editor, soon became political mates. In the resulting thirty-year battle over public ownership, "Haynes usually could count on the support of the *Examiner*."[35] He served on the Los Angeles Board of Water and Power Commissioners from 1921 to 1937.

Funds raised through bond sales would fund the construction of the distribution system. Los Angeles voters first went to the polls in April 1913 to vote on distribution bonds. Although 60 percent of the electorate voted for the bonds, the measure lacked the necessary two-thirds vote needed to pass. The following year the city again asked voters to finance construction of the distribution system. In his discussion of the 1914 bond vote, Van Valen argues that the private versus public power controversy played a much larger role than in 1913. The *Times* reported that confiscating private utility property was only the beginning, and soon other businesses such as hotels, stores, and city railways would be confiscated: "The Socialistic war on business and against private ownership is an insidious attack on all business and property."[36] Despite the newspaper's claims of impending socialism and statements similar to charges made in Seattle and Washington State and elsewhere by private power officials, more than 70 percent of the nearly 80,000 voters approved the sale of bonds to finance the public distribution system.[37] If Van Valen's assertion is correct, the bond approval was a public power victory and a private power defeat.

In his history of Los Angeles, Boyle Workman, who served on the city council from 1919 to 1927, wrote that in July 1914 private utilities charged five and one-half cents per kilowatt hour for electricity in the city. That rate was three and one-half cents less than they charged when Scattergood first proposed public sale of aqueduct power. Workman attributed the private rate reduction to potential city competition when he wrote, "Without generating or selling one penny's worth of power, the city as a potential competitor, had forced the electric rate down to 5.5 cents a kilowatt hour." Within a few years customers in Garvanza, East Los Angeles, and part of Hollywood began using public power at a rate lower than the private companies.[38] Apparently unknowingly, Workman enunciated the yardstick principle. Even before municipal distribution began, the threat of public power forced down private rates. Some estimates suggest that where the Bureau of Water and Power built transmission lines in direct competition with private companies, the private companies lost about 70 percent of their customers to the city.[39]

Critics of municipal power might counter Workman's argument by saying that private rates dropped not because of potential competition, but because of improved technology that made the generation, transmission, and distribution of electricity cheaper. In 1913, for example, Pacific Light and Power transmitted electricity 241 miles to Los Angeles, and SCE received power from a 117-mile transmission line.[40] The issue represents the essence of the power fight: did private rates drop in Los Angeles because of municipal power or improved technology? The private companies serving the city operated in distinct geographical regions and did not compete directly with one another. Even if Pacific Light and Power or SCE suddenly could sell power cheaper, no compelling reason existed for them to do so other than municipal power. Timing also suggests that competition drove down private rates. The private companies' long-distance lines had been serving the city for over a year. According to the technological explanation, rates should have dropped soon after the transmission lines began operation. Private companies began lowering rates before the votes on the bond initiatives but not immediately after the long-distance transmission lines went into operation. They also might have lowered rates to sway the vote against municipal power, since bond supporters argued that the city could provide power at rates lower than the private utilities.

After the completion of the distribution system, the city competed directly with the private utilities serving Los Angeles. Because of duplicate systems, if the private companies charged a higher rate they risked losing customers to the city. Although the private utilities had lost their monopoly of electrical service in Los Angeles, they retained their monopoly in other areas in Southern California. Arthur Kemp's letter in 1917 to a prospective stockholder, in which he stated that SCE enjoyed a virtual monopoly in the rapidly expanding Los Angeles power market, illustrated that the company was well aware of that monopoly and the profit it could render.[41]

Contemporary observers sympathetic to public ownership, such as Workman, Haynes, and Scattergood, believed that rates represented the main issue between the private utilities and the public power system in Los Angeles. Other people and organizations also thought rate setting was the primary concern. In 1917 the City Club of Los Angeles prepared a report on municipal ownership of utilities in which it argued that lower rates were the principal benefit. The report concluded that water rates had dropped by nearly one-third since municipal ownership of the city's water system began and contended that private utility interests were responsible for delaying aqueduct water power distribution. Municipal ownership of utilities would result in a general savings of at least 10 percent. The report attributed the higher rates of private utilities to their "profitable nature."[42]

Southern California Edison officials seemed to recognize the company's tenuous situation; soon after construction of the municipal distribution system began, they initiated negotiations with city officials to sell SCE property within the city. In his 1953 study of Los Angeles politics, Vincent Ostrom concluded that SCE showed a willingness to negotiate after the city started selling power in direct competition with the private company. The parties completed a purchase and operating agreement in April 1917. At the same time the city agreed to increase the aqueduct's generating capacity and sell the excess power to SCE. Ostrom concluded that two usually antagonistic groups contested expanding the aqueduct's generation capacity when the required bonds came up for voter approval.

Traditional opponents of municipal power were against the idea because of their general hostility to public power. Voters who usually supported municipal power joined the traditional opponents because they opposed the sale of any municipally generated electricity to private utilities. The combination of those forces defeated the bond measure, as only 42 percent of the voters supported the sale of the bonds. In 1919 the bond initiative to buy SCE property, without the provision to sell excess aqueduct power, received more than 68 percent of the vote. That 26 percent more people voted for the second measure than the first supports Ostrom's conclusion that the intent to sell power to SCE was the major reason the first measure failed. That conclusion, in turn, suggests the support for retaining public control over all aqueduct power and how much distrust Los Angeles voters held toward private utilities. Los Angeles Gas and Electric, evidently in an attempt to prevent municipal power from expanding in the city, unsuccessfully sued to block the agreement, although the suit impeded the enactment of the agreement until 1922.[43]

During the years when the Los Angeles Water and Power Bureau and Southern California Edison negotiated their agreement, the growing importance of electricity became apparent to the city's civic and business leaders as they began focusing increasing attention on the Colorado River as the next source of electricity and water. Whereas water was the first objective and electricity a secondary factor in the Owens Valley, the importance of getting power from the proposed Boulder Dam was as important, if not more so, than water. Haynes and other supporters of municipal power quickly realized the advantages that Los Angeles would receive if the city gained control of electricity generated at the dam.[44]

By the 1920s electricity had become the focus of the Los Angeles business community. Beginning in 1922, the Los Angeles Chamber of Commerce began publishing the monthly periodical *Southern California Business*. Throughout the 1920s magazine articles tied the continued growth of Los Angeles and the entire Southwest to the construction of Boulder Dam. Commenting on the Colorado River Compact signed in 1922, one article said, "Few of us hoped for agreement between these seven great states whose future growth and expansion are intimately connected with and totally dependent upon the development of the Colorado river, both in hydroelectric power and waters for irrigation." An accompanying map showed nine potential power markets in Nevada, Arizona, and California.[45]

Los Angeles's attempt to secure any power generated at the proposed dam represented attempts to modernize on a grand scale. The very future of the city rested on successful efforts to import more electricity. Private enterprise also recognized both the increased demand for and benefits of electricity as revealed in advertisements and articles that appeared in *Southern California Business* in the 1920s. In 1923 a lighting firm's advertisement said that "increased efficiency" resulted from better lighting that electricity made possible.[46] An article entitled "The Cradle of Electric Energy" also appeared that year, and in January 1925 the magazine published an article called "Industries Make Huge Power Demand." The following month R. H. Ballard, vice president and general manager of Southern California Edison, penned "Getting in Ahead of Power Needs" for the magazine. The benefits of electrical usage were not limited to industry; in 1928 a story appeared with the title "Southern California Leads in Farm Electrification." Included in the article was a discussion of San Fernando Valley farmers who owned "300 electric ranges, 200 electric water heaters and as many electric refrigerators. . . . Countless electric irons, vacuum cleaners, toasters, percolators, washing machines, waffle irons, curling irons, fans, warming pads and a host of other appliances" existed in the farmhouses in the valley.[47]

Southern California Edison also discussed electrical modernization and associated reduced rates with expanded usage. In a 1927 rate reduction announcement, the company said that twenty years earlier only one in ten women used an electrical iron, but that SCE customers currently used

312,000 electric irons. An accompanying advertisement stated: "Electricity is your most economical servant—USE MORE OF IT."[48] The Department of Water and Power also advertised in *Southern California Business* and stressed that lower rates equated savings for customers and greater profit for businesses. In the same advertisement the department stated that low rates were attracting eastern businesses to the city.[49]

In the fall of 1925 the magazine featured articles that discussed the proposed Boulder Dam site. "The truly important fact is this . . . Boulder Dam will guarantee adequate water and cheap power to the cities of Los Angeles, Pasadena, Glendale, and Riverside—and to the entire Colorado River Basin."[50] Municipal power enterprises served the four cities listed. R. W. Pridham, the chamber of commerce's president, issued a statement presenting the chamber's views on Boulder Dam. The organization favored a high dam to prevent flooding, provide water, and "make available a large volume of hydroelectric energy, an important necessity for agricultural, industrial and community development in the Southwest."[51]

Other articles in the magazine in the mid-twenties emphasized the importance to the city of industrial electrical energy. A city employee wrote an article in 1925 and concluded that nearly every industry and business in Los Angeles used electricity. The city's total industrial load approached 142,000 kilowatts of which municipal power supplied 90 percent. The writer estimated that an additional 30,000 kilowatts would need to come on-line in the following year to meet the growing demand for energy, an increase of more than 20 percent. By 1927 he figured that the city's industrial consumption would surpass 246,000 kilowatts. To meet the growing demand, the Los Angeles Bureau of Water and Power planned to spend $7 million to improve its distribution system.[52]

Private utility officials also realized that the city's continued growth required increasing amounts of electrical energy. R. H. Ballard, of SCE, wrote an article that emphasized the same themes as the city employee. Primarily, he stressed that electricity provided the basis for continued industrial expansion. California's growth required electrical utilities to expand and develop to meet future power needs. SCE, he said, spent $143 million between 1918 and 1925 for new power plants and transmission projects, which included $25 million in 1925 alone. California led the world in electrical generation, Ballard stated, and anyone contemplating a move to the state could be sure that ample power existed and would continue to exist in the future.[53]

Both SCE and the Los Angeles Bureau of Water and Power used *Southern California Business* to reach the business community for advertising purposes. SCE's advertisements emphasized "abundant" and "dependable" power. The company also stressed its low rates and in 1927 announced a rate reduction from 6.5 cents to 5.6 cents that it hoped would encourage the use of electrical appliances.[54] A March 1926 Bureau of Water and Power advertisement focused on day-to-day living when it claimed that cheap and dependable power enabled Los Angeles grocery stores to provide "superior service" by using modern appliances. Another advertisement emphasized the importance of building Boulder Dam to secure a permanent source of cheap electricity for the city.[55]

In 1927 the Los Angeles Chamber of Commerce, Southern California Edison, and the Bureau of Water and Power joined forces in an attempt to attract new businesses and industries to Los Angeles. The three organizations sponsored advertisements that appeared in national magazines such as *Scientific American, Atlantic Monthly,* and *Time.* The advertisements discussed the size and spending power of the city's population, market size, abundance of labor and raw materials, and cheap, abundant, and dependable electrical energy. An advertisement that the Bureau of Water and Power sponsored told the reader to compare Los Angeles's electrical rates with rates in other industrial cities.[56]

In the mid-1920s all eyes looked east to the Colorado River and the proposed Boulder Dam as the city's next great source of electrical energy. The importance of electrical generation at the proposed dam and public power supporters' belief that the dam would serve as a powerful weapon in fighting the electrical utility industry has been well established. Although most people viewed Boulder Dam as a multipurpose dam, electricity was the primary point of contention in the legislative and public debates over the project's authorization. Advocates of both private and public power knew that without Boulder Dam electricity, Los Angeles would not continue to prosper.[57]

Even before the Swing-Johnson legislation authorizing Boulder Dam construction passed in December 1928, residents voted on several bond issues in Los Angeles to contract with the federal government for the generation or purchase of power from the proposed dam. A May 1924 proposal, in which the city would have contracted with the federal government to generate power at Boulder Dam, lacked the necessary two-thirds majority by only 2,500 out of the almost 160,000 votes cast.[58] In August of that year, voters overwhelmingly approved a $16 million bond to improve the municipal power system by a margin of more than 100,000 votes.[59] Public power supporters found electoral success in 1925 as well. Voters approved a $2 million bond issue for "preliminary surveys for the Colorado River Aqueduct," although congressional approval of the Colorado River Compact, allowing for the division of the river's waters, had not yet occurred.[60] As the city continued to push for a Colorado River dam, debates over municipal power continued in Los Angeles.

As in Seattle and elsewhere, city politics became enmeshed with the Los Angeles municipal power debate in the 1920s. George E. Cryer, the mayor in the mid-1920s, was a strong supporter of public power and favored public control of Boulder Dam. Cryer helped establish the Los Angeles Water and Power Protective League that worked for the election of pro–municipal power candidates to public office. In 1925 the league supported Cryer's successful reelection bid as well as twelve city council candidates using the campaign slogan "Protect Your Water and Power." The election represented "an overwhelming victory for the public ownership ticket," as did the passage of water and power bonds in 1926 that totaled $21 million.[61] Using the phrase "Protect Your Water and Power" shows the attitudes that existed among pro–municipal ownership forces in Los Angeles. The league used the word "protect" in the same context as did public power advocates nationwide: protect the municipal power system from private powers' assaults. The use of "your" referred to the public; water and power were municipal entities that they believed the public rightfully owned.

Other public interest groups also had become active in the municipal power debate in Los Angeles during the twenties. In 1921 the Public Power League organized itself to push for the public development of Boulder Canyon. An added purpose of the league was to "defend public power against the private power corporation's . . . 'malicious propaganda' which they had launched against Los Angeles in the interior counties."[62] The mayors of Pasadena and Riverside, two cities with municipal power, both belonged to the league. Shortly after the Public Power League organized, municipal power opponents founded the People's Economy League, which consisted of civic and business leaders who opposed city development of the Colorado River.[63]

In a sense, Southern California Edison created a de facto public interest group through its efforts to promote stock sales to area residents. The company wanted the number of stockholders to exceed 100,000, although most only owned a few shares and a handful of individuals owned the vast majority of voting stock.[64] In 1917 SCE began selling stock publicly, and a letter to department heads and district agents outlined some advantages of public sales: "Consumers who are stockholders will be boosters for the company and in many ways of great benefit."[65] A report presented at the 1920 National Electric Light Association Convention addressed customer stock ownership, stating that selling securities to customers would help a utility receive "a fairer public opinion."[66] Company officials instructed SCE security salespeople to be selective in whom they approached about stock purchases. One salesperson suggested to his colleagues that they contact a prominent life insurance company to find out who had just received benefits. The same person said that lists of teachers in a town could be obtained from the school superintendent. Another salesman told a sales meeting that a Pasadena bank manager had given him a list of prominent individuals.

A third salesperson thought it wise to check local newspapers for names of individuals who recently bought or sold property and therefore might have money to invest.[67] SCE management told sales personnel not to make sales to "Mexicans or illiterate foreigners" if they attempted to sell stock to factory employees.[68]

Clearly, SCE wanted to target as its stockholders prominent individuals in a community: people whom the bank manager might know, or individuals acquainted with people with enough money to purchase life insurance. Although not particularly wealthy, schoolteachers often maintained a prominent role in community affairs. It would not hurt private power to have stockholders in the classroom during debates about bond issues and the role of government in day-to-day life. The people approached about stock purchases appeared of at least middle-class status and were publicly active—the type of individual likely to vote in local elections. SCE, in a prepared stock questionnaire, denied any political purposes in its stock sales program. In response to a hypothetical question that read, "Does company want to sell stock in order to get votes and put through legislation contrary to the will of the people?" the scripted reply was: "Emphatically no. . . . The company's interest is the development of California and the prosperity of its people, for only through their prosperity can we prosper."[69] Despite SCE's public position, internal memos and minutes and the NELA report reveal that the company knew the political advantages of widespread stock sales. Mass ownership would bolster the public image of SCE and private power.

In his study of the Los Angeles municipal power fight, Van Valen also examined the relationship between stock ownership and voting. Contemporary observers in the late 1920s estimated that about one-half of the "100,000 Club" stockholders were registered to vote in Los Angeles. In 1926 the total individual investment of two-thirds of Edison stockholders was less than $300, and "approximately 70,000 of the company's approximately 90,000 stockholders" invested less than $500. On the other end of the spectrum, one-third of the stock was owned "by one-half of one percent . . . and approximately one-half of the stock was held by approximately two percent of the shareholders."[70] A 1928 advertisement announcing a rate cut reiterated the idea in the phrase "owned by those it serves" that appeared at the bottom of the page.[71]

The organization into interest groups of proponents and opponents of municipal power in Los Angeles in the 1920s underscores the significance of electricity to the city and the region. Los Angeles residents recognized that importance and established political pressure groups to work for the enactment of their political agendas. None of the groups organized against new power projects overall or Boulder Dam specifically; each group, including SCE stockholders, knew they would soon need additional power sources. As had happened during the planning and construction of the Owens Valley project, few, if any, denied the importance of electricity to the continued growth of Los Angeles. Instead, the debate was over who should build the proposed Boulder Dam and the accompanying transmission lines. The technological impediments to long-distance transmission had been eliminated, and no technological debate existed in Los Angeles. Public power advocates believed municipal power to be cheaper and more efficient than private power and an effective method of attracting new business and industry to the city. Private power partisans judged municipal power wasteful and politically dangerous. Creation of political interest groups reflected the intense political debate over municipal power in Los Angeles.

As the 1920s came to a close, the power situation in Los Angeles remained complex. Although the agreement signed between the city and SCE in 1919 resulted in the city acquiring the private company's distribution system, the Bureau of Water and Power could not generate enough power to serve all its customers. To make up for the shortage, the city bought power from SCE. The Los Angeles Gas and Electric Corporation also still operated in the city. Despite widespread support among citizens and officials alike and strong showings on bond issues, the Los Angeles Bureau of Water and Power had not yet established an electrical monopoly, and three electrical enterprises continued to hold vested interests in the fight over municipal power.

The city took the first steps toward establishing a monopoly in April 1930, when it signed a contract with the federal government to purchase electricity generated at Boulder Dam. Although six years would pass before the dam started generating current, the contract meant that in the foreseeable future the city would not have to buy power from SCE.[72] After voters approved a charter revision that made it legal for the city to borrow money from the federal government, the city received a $23 million Reconstruction Finance Corporation loan in 1933 to build the necessary transmission lines from Boulder Dam to Los Angeles. Voters later approved a bond measure to refinance the loan.[73]

City officials started the slow process of acquiring the Los Angeles Gas and Electric Corporation electrical distribution system in the late 1920s. In 1927 a bond issue to purchase the company's electrical distribution system lost at the polls. Shortly after the bond's defeat the city sued the company, charging that the company had violated its 1911 franchise agreement. Specifically, the suit claimed that the company, among other things, was selling power for nonlighting uses and operating in areas that Los Angeles annexed since 1911, which were not covered by the franchise agreement.[74] Although it took several years, the city won the suit, and the company sought a new franchise to operate within Los Angeles.[75] Voters twice rejected initiatives to grant the corporation a new franchise. In late 1936, voters authorized officials to purchase Los Angeles Gas and Electric's electrical distribution system.[76] In October of that year, Boulder Dam, then known by its current name of Hoover Dam, began generating electricity. On January 1, 1937, the city terminated its purchasing agreement with SCE, and the Bureau of Water and Power established a monopoly in Los Angeles.[77]

The importance of electricity in the development of Los Angeles cannot be overstated. Kevin Starr writes that electricity literally made the city: "Nighttime Los Angeles had become a wonderland of light. From atop Mount Lowe one beheld Los Angeles, Pasadena, and fifty-six contiguous cities and suburbs spread out in a vast sea of illumination. In sheer extent, the horizontal equivalent of vertical New York, there was no other spectacle like it in the United States."[78] The long-distance transmission of electricity from distant generation sites made possible that "spectacle" and the establishment, growth, and eventual monopoly of public power. Technology was an issue only so far as it made municipal power possible in Los Angeles. Private finance capital never became a factor in the Los Angeles public power debate. Even before power from the Owens Valley aqueduct went on-line, the controversy between public and private power advocates revolved around rates. Public power proponents in Los Angeles believed that lower public rates forced down private rates. That attitude matched the belief that had emerged in Seattle, Washington State, and across the nation and was another example of the yardstick principle of public power. In Los Angeles, proponents and opponents of public power organized themselves into political interest groups to further their political views. Despite the relative conservatism and animosity of the *Los Angeles Times*, power bond measures usually passed in Los Angeles. Through their support of bond measures, Los Angeles residents showed their willingness to use local government to secure lower electric rates and fight private power companies. From Congress to small towns to the growing metropolis of Los Angeles, the debate over municipal power revolved around rates and political control of electrical systems.

CHAPTER SEVEN

Politics, Electricity, and the New Deal

Public power forces had enjoyed considerable success in the 1930 elections. Voters in numerous states had approved referendums allowing for the formation of public utility districts. Several pro–public power governors had been elected, including New York governor Franklin D. Roosevelt. The ongoing Federal Trade Commission investigation of the electrical utility industry remained front-page news in the early 1930s, ultimately resulting in a ninety-five-volume report. In the Senate, George Norris did not actively push for Muscle Shoals legislation in 1932, undoubtedly waiting for a president more friendly toward public development to occupy the White House. Senator Walsh, Norris's fellow public power advocate, led the successful effort to recall the chairman of the Federal Power Commission, Otis Smith, who was considered too friendly toward private power. Although the Supreme Court ultimately ruled against the recall, the public power movement had flexed its muscle.

In March 1932 Judson King published *Power Records of the Presidential Candidates,* a pamphlet that discussed the leading presidential contenders' views on private and public power, detailing those who had been too supportive of private power. A few months later, with his empire crumbling around him, Samuel Insull finally relinquished control of his far-reaching utility holdings; criminal charges soon followed. Finally, in September 1932, Democratic presidential nominee Franklin Roosevelt called for federal power development on the Columbia, Colorado, and St. Lawrence Rivers and in the Tennessee Valley in his public power speech in Portland, Oregon. On the local level in Seattle, Los Angeles, and numerous small towns, public power experienced continued success in the early 1930s. It had clearly come of age as the 1932 general election approached. Although the country's economic collapse added urgency to the fight for electricity, it was not a flash-in-the-pan political issue. Instead, it had been developing since before the turn of the century, gaining intensity as each year passed. In the 1920s and early 1930s, electricity was headline news.[1]

The story of electricity in the years before the New Deal was in essence a political one. Decisions regarding efforts to build public power projects, the push for electrical modernization, and the private utility industry's attempts to sway public opinion merged in the political arena, whether in the village council or in Congress. Since early in the century, when engineers had solved the technological impediments to long-distance transmission,

143

people had realized the potential impact of electricity on their lives and society. By the 1920s most people deemed electricity an essential part of modern society. The identification of a politically oriented public power ideology before the New Deal in local, state, and national politics has important implications for the study of American political history. Four factors make the political story of electricity in the 1920s historically compelling.

The first major element is that electrification and electrical modernization were not apolitical processes. Instead, people actively worked to acquire better electrical service at lower rates. This approach had occurred from the earliest days when towns first electrified their lighting and transportation systems. People challenged private power to provide less expensive electricity; if private power failed to respond, public ownership sometimes resulted. Those supporting public power used the political process to raise fundamental concerns about the development of the new technological wonder, electricity. They wanted to enact legislation that would allow as many people as possible to benefit from electrical modernization, but they did not seek to nationalize the private utility industry. The local and national press constantly reminded the public of electricity's modernizing potential.

The political contest occurred in small midwestern towns, in larger cities, and in Congress, as citizens and politicians debated the development and use of electrical energy. People who believed in the desirability of public power organized themselves into political interest groups to advance their agenda. Opponents of public power influenced the debate through organizations such as the National Electric Light Association or local organizations opposed to public ownership. Despite the presence of political debates, recent historians have largely ignored them and instead focused on the technological aspect of electrical power or electricity's social impact. The social and technological histories of electricity are certainly important and worthy of the attention given to them. Concentrating only on those aspects, however, obscures the importance of the political aspects of electrification, electrical modernization, and technology. The history of public power in cities as diverse as Seattle and Los Angeles demonstrated to many the political possibilities and technological success of locally controlled electrical generating and distribution systems. In those cities and in small towns, people made the political decision to publicly control electrical technology.

The second major point of historical importance is that people showed a willingness, if not a preference, for government involvement to achieve their goals. Similar to earlier critics of unfettered private enterprise, the public power movement in the twenties thought government could and should be a positive social and political influence on the local, state, and federal levels. Not only did people show an inclination for government involvement, but available evidence shows that they often elected congressmen who favored public power.

When Americans looked to the government for assistance in the 1930s, it was not without precedent. In the 1920s people had turned to the government for help in achieving a better standard of living that they believed electricity could provide and that private power was subverting. In the 1930s many again looked to their political leaders for relief from the Great Depression. Certainly, the Depression represented a different and more drastic set of circumstances and challenges for every level of government in the United States than did the quest for less expensive electricity in the 1920s, but in both instances people saw government as a positive social agent.

The active role that individuals took to secure inexpensive electricity in the 1920s demonstrates the importance of examining local-level politics. Although studying mass behavior often has been associated with the new social history, the history of public power shows the appropriateness of such an examination of political history. Regardless of the relative decline of partisan politics in the twentieth century, people still engaged themselves in the political process. In participating in the political debates over electricity, individuals in the 1920s exhibited a forward-looking view by believing that the widespread use of electricity would significantly improve their living standard.

The combination of these first two factors—the quest for modernization and a positive statist role—that became manifest in the political process provided a partial, yet crucial basis for the New Deal's resource development, electrical modernization, and utility reform programs, which compose the third historically compelling aspect of the public power fight. A Congress well versed on the power controversy welcomed FDR to Washington in March 1933. Roosevelt's election in the dreary days of 1932 is often considered a dramatic departure from politics as usual in the United States. Many historians and political scientists argue that a realignment of American politics began in 1928 when the Democratic party received urban electoral support. Roosevelt's victory in 1932 completed the realignment process and marked the beginning of the fifth electoral system.[2] Although FDR's sweeping victory indicated that an electoral shift had occurred, the strong public power attitudes that reflected a positive statist position suggest that the election of 1932 did not represent a complete political break with the past. Instead, strong political sentiment for government action to prevent economic abuses and modernize the country had existed several decades before the New Deal. Despite the widely accepted belief that the New Deal was a dramatic break from past politics, it also represented the partial culmination, not the beginning, of the public power movement in the United States.

Franklin Roosevelt held many of the same ideological beliefs that individuals in the public power movement articulated in the years and decades before 1932. Roosevelt himself expressed concern about conservation during his tenure as a New York State senator. As governor of New York he pushed for the New York Power Authority and public development of electricity on the Saint Lawrence River. His Portland power speech further reflected those beliefs. FDR carried those ideological concerns into the White House, bringing a vision and energy regarding natural resources not seen since the Republican Roosevelt occupied the Oval Office. Despite the enthusiasm that Roosevelt and the New Dealers displayed in their attempts to formulate water power and conservationist policies, they did not enter a political arena hostile to such ideas. Instead, in the spring of 1933 FDR and his advisers found large blocs of senators and representatives who had long been fighting for public power. When Congress passed the Muscle Shoals legislation that spring, for example, veteran legislators cast the majority of yea votes in each chamber.[3]

Roosevelt built on the bipartisan public power tradition that existed in Congress during the 1920s and early 1930s. That tradition existed in nearly every region of the country and was particularly strong in the West. Qualitative and quantitative evidence reveals the strong degree of public power activism in Congress. FDR provided the public power movement with the most important things that it lacked in the 1920s: White House support and a presidential signature. The goal of the public power movement and of New Deal reform legislation was to improve the nation's standard of living. In the 1920s this goal became most evident in the fight for public power projects and the investigations of the private utility industry. Lowering private rates through construction of public power projects would allow more people to use electricity and hasten the country's move to a modernized future. That thought, reflected in the yardstick principle, existed on the local, state, and national level. Roosevelt shared those goals and ideas regarding electrical modernization. During the First One Hundred Days, legislation creating the Tennessee Valley Authority, with strong White House support, sailed through Congress. The protracted fight over Muscle Shoals legislation during the 1920s, the swiftness with which Congress established the TVA in 1933, and its success in modernizing the region make it perhaps the most famous New Deal power project. Nearly as famous was the Rural Electrification Administration that finally brought electricity to rural America.

The Public Utility Holding Company Act restricted the size and influence of holding companies, although it did not deal them a death blow. The legislation prohibited many private utility practices that public power spokesmen had previously targeted and that the FTC investigations had made front-page news. Title Two of the Federal Housing Administration law provided low-cost, government-backed financing to enable people to modernize their homes. In the 1930s in the Pacific Northwest, the federal government oversaw the construction of Bonneville and Grand Coulee Dams on the Columbia River and the establishment of the Bonneville Power Administration. Nearly all of those New Deal programs contained aspects of the public power movement's agenda dating from the beginning of the century.

Not only did a strong degree of continuity exist between the 1920s and early 1930s and the New Deal, but identification of the political fight for electricity that began at the turn of the century and grew in intensity through the early 1930s also reveals a link with the reform traditions of the Progressive Era. The growth of private power systems raised anew the antitrust debates that characterized progressive concerns at the beginning of the twentieth century. Public power advocates in the twenties articulated some of Theodore Roosevelt's New Nationalism ideas. Norris, Pinchot, and others recognized the desirability of large-scale systems; it was the intention of the systems' owners that caused concern. Those supporting public power in the 1920s parted with turn-of-the-century reformers in one important way: they did not believe regulation and antitrust action could effectively control private power. Some power systems needed public ownership because only public ownership could serve as the yardstick to reveal the industry's overcharging. The yardstick principle, public power advocates believed, would act as the shield against economic abuses that the private utility industry perpetuated. The tie between the Progressive Era and the New Deal represents the fourth major point of importance of the public power fight in the 1920s. The connection to Progressive Era reform manifested itself in several ways.

The most important of these was the concern felt by public power proponents about the concentration of corporate power. From the earliest years of the twentieth century into the 1930s, when discussing private power they often referred to the "power trust," which many of them thought paled in comparison to the corporate power of the railroads and other large-scale business enterprises that emerged in the late nineteenth century. Their criticisms of the "power trust" reflected worry that most Americans did not use electricity in a meaningful way because of the corporate domination of the utility business. Corporate greed, they thought, not inadequate technology, prevented widespread electrical modernization. Another major strand of continuity was their concern with natural resource development. Public power supporters in the 1920s continued the progressive-conservationist ideal first articulated at the turn of the century. Finally, the reliance on experts represents another tie with the Progressive Era. Morris Cooke, J. D. Ross, and E. F. Scattergood all represented the new class of educated professionals that emerged during this period. These factors together show that the public power movement, which itself first emerged at the beginning of the century, represented a bridge between the Progressive Era and the New Deal.

These four factors—the political debate over modernization, a positive statist role, the continuity between the 1920s and 1930s, and the link between the Progressive Era and the New Deal—combine to reveal the largely neglected political story of electricity in the first decades of the twentieth century. That story, however, did not end in the 1930s. As the twentieth century comes to a close and the twenty-first century begins, the political history of electricity is still being written, with a new chapter devoted to deregulation of the electrical utility industry.

The legislation that became law in the 1920s and 1930s established the political and legal structures that governed much of the electrical generation and distribution in the United States for over sixty years. Since the 1930s private power companies, usually divided along regional monopolies, have continued to generate and distribute most of the electricity used in the United States following the tenets of economics of scale. Stronger state and federal regulations have prevented many of the abuses that so angered the public power movement in the 1920s. The number of towns with public power has remained fairly constant since the 1930s. Public utility districts provide energy for many in the rural West.

The electrical modernization that public power supporters anxiously anticipated in the decades before the New Deal ultimately occurred. In subsequent years the United States became an energy-intensive society. The many uses of electrical energy that seemed so wondrous in the 1920s are now commonplace throughout American society. The American West played a unique role in the political battle for electricity in the first decades of the twentieth century. The vastness of the landscape, the role of the federal government in the area's history and development, the amount of potential hydropower available from undeveloped rivers and streams, and the leadership roles that westerners played made the public power fight especially intense and visible in this region. Although it originated in the late nineteenth century, the public power battle became front-page news in the decade before Franklin Roosevelt's election in the presidency. The public power fight in the twenties helped set the stage for new natural resource policies and the enlargement of the regulatory state during the New Deal.

Appendixes

Appendix 1.1 Percentage of Families with at
Least One Radio in American Cities of
100,000 or More People, 1930

City	Percent
Akron, OH	52.3
Albany, NY	56.0
Atlanta, GA	26.0
Baltimore, MD	49.0
Birmingham, AL	26.7
Boston, MA	56.2
Bridgeport, CT	58.5
Buffalo, NY	54.9
Cambridge, MA	55.1
Camden, NJ	53.3
Canton, OH	50.7
Chattanooga, TN	23.1
Chicago, IL	63.2
Cincinnati, OH	48.7
Cleveland, OH	48.1
Columbus, OH	49.7
Dallas, TX	40.3
Dayton, OH	55.4
Denver, CO	50.8
Des Moines, IA	51.5
Detroit, MI	58.0
Duluth, MN	49.9
Elizabeth, NJ	60.5
El Paso, TX	19.1
Erie, PA	51.4
Evansville, IL	33.8
Fall River, MA	44.5
Flint, MI	52.3
Fort Wayne, IN	61.2
Fort Worth, TX	34.5
Gary, IN	46.4
Grand Rapids, MI	49.4
Hartford, CT	51.4
Houston, TX	31.9
Indianapolis, IN	47.1
Jacksonville, FL	24.7
Jersey City, NJ	63.2
Kansas City, KS	41.8
Kansas City, MO	48.9
Knoxville, TN	24.6
Long Beach, CA	57.8
Los Angeles, CA	58.8
Louisville, KY	33.5
Lowell, MA	40.3
Lynn, MA	64.3
Memphis, TN	26.2
Miami, FL	24.5
Milwaukee, WI	62.8
Minneapolis, MN	59.5
Nashville, TN	28.2
Newark, NJ	54.5

(cont.)

Appendix 1.1 *continued*

City	Percent
New Bedford, MA	37.2
New Haven, CT	54.2
New Orleans, LA	21.0
New York, NY	59.2
Norfolk, VA	32.3
Oakland, CA	57.9
Oklahoma City, OK	36.5
Omaha, NE	52.6
Paterson, NJ	60.3
Peoria, IL	54.7
Philadelphia, PA	56.3
Pittsburgh, PA	52.3
Portland, OR	57.7
Providence, RI	55.1
Reading, PA	56.2
Richmond, VA	33.7
Rochester, NY	55.7
St. Louis, MO	50.2
St. Paul, MN	59.5
Salt Lake City, UT	54.3
San Antonio, TX	26.1
San Diego, CA	51.2
San Francisco, CA	48.7
Scranton, PA	39.2
Seattle, WA	52.3
Somerville, MA	64.1
South Bend, IN	52.3
Spokane, WA	47.9
Springfield, MA	61.1
Syracuse, NY	56.1
Tacoma, WA	48.5
Tampa, FL	14.7
Toledo, OH	61.3
Trenton, NJ	55.7
Tulsa, OK	39.6
Utica, NY	48.5
Washington, DC	53.9
Wichita, KS	37.7
Wilmington, DE	53.6
Worcester, MA	59.9
Yonkers, NY	64.8
Youngstown, OH	45.8
Average for ninety-three cities	53.1

Source: U.S. Bureau of the Census, *Fifteenth Census of the United States: 1930, Population, Vol. 6, Families* (Washington, DC, 1933), Table 76, "Families Having Radio Set, by Color and Nativity of Head, for Cities of 100,000 or More: 1930," 70.

Appendix 2.1 Top Twenty Shareholders of SCE Common Stock as of December 31, 1930

Individual or Business	Title or Affiliation	Number of Shares	Percent of Shares*
John B. Miller	Chairman, SCE	35,507	9.1
A. W. Harris, trustee; N. Harris estate	Director, SCE	24,304	6.2
R. H. Ballard	President, SCE	13,200	3.4
Harry J. Wiegan		11,755	3.0
C. C. Ward	Executive vice president, SCE	10,600	2.7
A. W. Harris, trustee; Harris Trust & Savings Bank	Director, SCE	10,188	2.6
Sun Life Assurance Co. of Canada	Assurance company	87,739	22.5
Weber & Co.	Trust bankers	35,577	9.1
Clark & Co.	General public service corporation	20,190	5.2
E. F. Hutton & Co.	Investment bankers	18,990	4.9
U.S. Electric Light & Power Shares, Inc.	Bank and trust company	15,990	4.1
Woods & Co.		14,500	3.7
Harrigan & Co.	Bank and trust company	13,186	3.4
Dyckman Corp.	Guarantee and trust company	13,135	3.4
A. Iselin & Co.		11,785	3.0
General Electric Employees Securities Corp.	Investment company	11,537	3.0
Blass & Co.	Banking	11,018	2.8
Sigler & Co.	Bank and trust company	10,810	2.8
Ross & Co.		10,010	2.6
E. A. Pierce & Co.	Investment bankers	9,073	2.3
Total number of shares controlled by top twenty stockholders		389,094	100.0

*As a percentage of the top twenty holders of common stock: percentages rounded.
Source: SCE, *1930 Southern California Edison Report to the California Railroad Commission.*

Appendix 3.1   Hearst Newspaper Chain

Newspaper	Year of Acquisition
Albany Times-Union	1923
Atlanta Daily Georgia	1912
Baltimore News	1923
Boston American	1904
Boston Daily Advertiser	1917
Boston Record*	1921
Chicago American	1900
Chicago Examiner	1902
Detroit Times	1921
Los Angeles Examiner	1905
	(cont.)

Appendix 3.1   *continued*

Newspaper	Year of Acquisition
Los Angeles Express†	1931
Los Angeles Herald	1922
Milwaukee Sentinel	1924
New York American	1902
New York Daily Mirror	1922
New York Morning Journal	1895
Oakland Post-Enquirer	1922
Omaha News-Bee	1928
Pittsburgh Sun-Telegraph	1927
Rochester Journal	1922
San Antonio Light	1924
San Francisco Bulletin‡	1929
San Francisco Examiner	1887
San Francisco Morning Call§	1913
Seattle Post-Intelligencer	1921
Syracuse Telegram ||	1922
Washington, D.C., Herald	1922
Washington, D.C., Times	1917
Wisconsin News (Milwaukee)	1918

*Merged with *Daily-Advertiser*
†Merged into *Los Angeles Herald-Express*
‡Merged with *San Francisco Morning Call* into the *Call Bulletin*
§Became the morning paper *Call and Post*
||Merged with *Syracuse Journal* in 1925
Source: John K. Winkler, *William Randolph Hearst: A New Appraisal* (New York: 1955), 7, 8, 119–20, 126, 132, 138, 247–49.

To determine if the editorials that appeared in the *Seattle Post-Intelligencer* were printed in other Hearst newspapers nationwide, as many of the above papers were examined as possible. Microfilm on the following was available: *Baltimore News, Boston Daily Advertiser, Chicago American, Wisconsin News, Detroit Times, New York American, Pittsburgh Sun-Telegraph,* and *San Francisco Examiner.* Almost without exception, either the exact editorials that appeared in the *Post-Intelligencer* or editorials and articles sympathetic to public power appeared in all of the papers as discussed below.

Baltimore News: Hearst's anti-Underwood editorial (December 20, 1924), pro–public power and Boulder Dam editorial (December 30, 1924), and articles discussing Muscle Shoals (May 7 and December 3, 5, 6, 9, 10, 13, 17–19, and 29, 1924).

Boston Daily Advertiser: Muscle Shoals endorsement (May 23, 1924), article and Hearst's anti-Underwood editorial (December 14, 1924), and Muscle Shoals article (December 21, 1924).

Chicago American: Muscle Shoals articles (May 9, 10, 12, 21, and 27, November 11 and 21, and December 2, 4, 10, 15, 16, 17, 18, and 19, 1924), article charging private power held up Boulder Dam legislation (May 23, 1924), Hearst's anti-Underwood editorial (December 20, 1924), Boulder Dam article (February 1, 1928), and Walsh investigation article (February 2, 1928).

Detroit Times: Muscle Shoals articles (May 16 and 18 and December 12 and 21, 1924), Teapot Dome editorial (December 13, 1924), and Boulder Dam editorial (January 1, 1928).

New York American: Muscle Shoals articles (May 22 and 24, 1924), Boulder Dam editorial (May 22, 1924), Teapot Dome editorial (December 13, 1924), three Muscle Shoals articles (December 20, 1924), Hearst's anti-Underwood editorial (December 20, 1924), Muscle Shoals editorial (December 20, 1924), Muscle Shoals editorial cartoon (December 20, 1924), Boulder Dam articles (January 5, 7, and 9, 1928), Boulder Dam editorial cartoons (January 6 and 19, 1928), and Boulder Dam editorials (January 16 and 19, 1928).

Pittsburgh Sun-Telegram: Boulder Dam feature article (January 15, 1928) and Boulder Dam editorial (January 19, 1928).

San Francisco Examiner: Boulder Dam article (May 22, 1924), Boulder Dam editorial (May 22, 1924), Teapot Dome editorial (December 13, 1924), Hearst's anti-Underwood editorial (December 20, 1924), three Muscle Shoals articles (December 20, 1924), Muscle Shoals editorial (December 20, 1924), Muscle Shoals editorial cartoon (December 20, 1924), Boulder Dam articles (January 5, 7, 15, and 17, 1928), and Los Angeles—Boulder Dam editorial (January 17, 1928).

Wisconsin News (Milwaukee): Muscle Shoals article (May 2 and 24, 1924), Teapot Dome editorial (December 15, 1924), two Muscle Shoals article (December 20, 1924), Hearst's anti-Underwood editorial (December 20, 1924), Muscle Shoals editorial (December 22, 1924), and Boulder Dam editorial (January 19, 1928).

Appendix 3.2   Senators Listed by Norris's Office

Name	Party	State	Census Region	Index Score
Barkley, A.	D	KY	South	1.00
Black, H.	D	AL	South	1.00
Blaine, J.	R	WI	North Central	1.00
Borah, W.	R	ID	West	1.00
Bratton, S.	D	NM	West	.86
Brookhart, S.	R	IA	North Central	1.00
Capper, A.	R	KS	North Central	1.00
Connally, T.	D	TX	South	1.00
Couzens, J.	R	MI	North Central	1.00
Cutting, B.	D	NM	West	1.00

(cont.)

Appendix 3.2 *continued*

Name	Party	State	Census Region	Index Score
Frazier, L.	R	ND	North Central	1.00
Glass, C.	D	VA	South	.75
Hatfield, H.	R	WV	South	1.00
Howell, R.	R	NE	North Central	1.00
Johnson, H.	R	CA	West	1.00
La Follette Jr., R.	R	WI	North Central	1.00
McGill, G.	D	KS	North Central	1.00
McKellar, K.	D	TN	South	.89
McNary, C.	R	OR	West	.89
Neely, M.	D	WV	South	1.00
Norbeck, P.	R	SD	North Central	1.00
Norris, G.	R	NE	North Central	1.00
Nye, G.	R	ND	North Central	1.00
Pittman, K.	D	NV	West	.83
Schall, T.	R	MN	North Central	.86
Sheppard, H.	D	TX	South	1.00
Shipstead, H.	Farm-Labor	MN	North Central	1.00
Smith, E.	D	SC	South	1.00
Walsh, T.	D	MT	West	1.00
Wheeler, B.	D	MT	West	1.00
Progressive index: $\bar{X}$ = .97, median = 1.00				

Sources: John P. Robertson to Robert McLendon, May 8, 1931, box 235, folder 9, Norris Papers, and Chapter 3, notes 59–62.

Appendix 4.1 Number and Percentage of Communities Producing or Purchasing Electrical Power, 1894–1930 and 1932

Year	Total	Produce	Produce/ Purchase	Purchase	Percent Produce	Percent Purchase
1894	276	271		5	98.2	1.8
1895	355	348		7	98.0	2.0
1896	423	405		8	98.1	1.9
1897	459	449		10	97.8	2.2
1898	567	556		11	98.1	1.9
1899	623	611		12	98.1	1.9
1900	728	714	1	13	98.1	1.9
1901	783	768	1	14	98.1	1.9
1902	847	831	1	15	98.1	1.9
1903	932	911	1	20	97.7	2.3
1904	1,038	1,010	1	27	97.3	2.7
1905	1,103	1,067	1	35	96.7	3.3
1906	1,177	1,133	2	42	96.3	3.7
1907	1,267	1,215	1	51	95.9	4.1
1908	1,351	1,272	2	77	94.2	5.8
1909	1,414	1,309	6	99	92.6	7.4
1910	1,534	1,390	7	137	90.6	9.4
1911	1,622	1,440	12	170	88.8	11.2
1912	1,730	1,505	16	209	87.0	13.0
1913	1,830	1,558	22	250	85.1	14.9

(cont.)

Appendix 4.1   *continued*

Year	Total	Produce	Produce/ Purchase	Purchase	Percent Produce	Percent Purchase
1914	1,979	1,628	28	323	82.3	17.7
1915	2,149	1,699	34	416	79.1	20.9
1916	2,270	1,728	37	505	76.1	23.9
1917	2,399	1,745	50	604	72.7	27.3
1918	2,498	1,775	57	666	71.1	28.9
1919	2,576	1,789	66	721	69.4	30.6
1920	2,735	1,810	68	857	66.2	33.8
1921	2,836	1,778	77	981	62.7	37.3
1922	3,015	1,785	86	1,144	59.2	40.8
1923	3,066	1,702	102	1,262	55.5	44.5
1924	3,028	1,581	114	1,333	52.2	47.8
1925	2,903	1,434	115	1,354	49.4	50.6
1926	2,630	1,198	115	1,317	45.6	54.4
1927	2,338	988	103	1,247	42.3	57.7
1928	2,170	906	100	1,164	41.8	58.2
1929	2,020	863	98	1,059	42.7	57.3
1930	1,937	835	96	1,006	42.1	56.9
1932	1,851	747	170	934	40.4	59.6

Sources: David Schap, *Municipal Ownership in the Electric Utility Industry: A Centennial View* (New York: 1986), 53; for 1932, see Chapter 3, note 74.

Notes

CHAPTER 1. ELECTRICITY AND POLITICS

1. Richard Rudolph and Scott Ridley, *Power Struggle: The Hundred-Year War over Electricity* (New York, 1986), 23–24.
2. Ibid., 25.
3. Ibid., 27–28. As Rudolph and Ridley point out, Edison and others claimed that the Pearl Street station was the first centralized station, although several other American cities including Cincinnati already had lighting.
4. Thomas Hughes, *Networks of Power: Electrification in Western Society, 1880–1930* (Baltimore, 1983), 81.
5. Ibid., 103–4. Also see ibid., chap. 4, for a complete discussion of the technological problems that plagued the early years of power development.
6. Ibid., 120–23, 274–75. For more on the development of electricity in Chicago at that time see Harold L. Platt, *The Electric City: Energy and the Growth of the Chicago Area, 1880–1930* (Chicago, 1991), especially "Part I: Energy Revolution in the City, 1880–1898."
7. Hughes, *Networks of Power,* 120–23, 274–75.
8. Rudolph and Ridley, *Power Struggle,* 30–32.
9. "Electric Lighting by Municipalities," *New York Record Guide;* copy of article in mss 441, "additions," Richard T. Ely Papers, State Historical Society of Wisconsin, Madison (hereafter Ely Papers). The article contained the following chart listing the cost (in cents) of lighting an arc light for one night (percent of change column added).

City	Private Cost	City Cost	Percent Change
Bay City, MI	27.5	16.0	–41.8
Painesville, OH	19.7	10.6	–46.2
Huntington, IN	39.0	13.7	–64.9
Lewiston, ME	50.0	14.0	–72.0
Auroa, IL	89.5	15.3	–82.9
Average per night	45.1	13.9	–69.2

10. The literature on this subject is immense, but several of the most important works are Alfred Chandler, *The Visible Hand: The Managerial Revolution in American Business* (Cambridge, MA), 1977; Martin J. Sklar, *The Corporate Reconstruction of American Capitalism, 1890–1916: The Market, the Law, and Politics* (New York, 1988); Oliver Zunz, *Making America Corporate, 1870–1920* (Chicago, 1990); Morton Keller, *Regulating a New Economy: Public Policy and Economic Change in America, 1900–1933* (Cambridge, MA, 1990); and David F. Noble, *America by Design: Science, Technology, and the Rise of Corporate Capitalism* (New York, 1977).
11. David E. Nye, *Electrifying America: Social Meaning of a New Technology* (Cambridge, MA, 1990), 169. Nye quotes Thomas Cochran, *American Business in*

the Twentieth Century (Cambridge, MA: Harvard University Press, 1972), 82. For the importance of innovation on the growth of the American economy, see Michael Bernstein, *The Great Depression and Delayed Recovery and Economic Change in America, 1929–1939* (New York, 1987).

12. For more information on Ely, see Benjamin G. Rader, *The Academic Mind and Reform: The Influence of Richard T. Ely in American Life* (Lexington, KY, 1966); Ely's autobiography is Richard T. Ely, *Ground Under Our Feet* (New York, 1938). Rader's work contains a bibliography of Ely's writings. Ely received his Ph.D. from the University of Heidelberg and later taught at Johns Hopkins before moving to the University of Wisconsin in 1892 where he remained until 1925. In 1920 he founded the Institute for Research in Land Economics to study problems arising from land development. In 1925 he changed its name to the Institute for Research in Land Economics and Public Utilities to better reflect the institute's interest in public utility research. Throughout his career Ely held an unwavering belief in the scientific study of economic issues.

13. Richard T. Ely, "The Nature and Significance of Monopolies and Trusts," address delivered before the Philadelphia Ethical Society, December 17, 1899, reprinted in the *International Journal of Ethics* 10 (1900): 274–86; copy in mss 411, box 13a, "Articles–Scrapbook volume 11," Ely Papers.

14. Richard T. Ely, "Municipal Ownership of Natural Monopolies," *North American Review*, March 1901, 445, 452; copy in mss 411, box 7, folder 4, Ely Papers.

15. Richard T. Ely, "The Advantages of Public Ownership and Management of Natural Monopolies," *Cosmopolitan*, March 1901, 557–58; copy in mss 411, box 1, folder 2, Ely Papers.

16. Richard F. Hirsh, *Technology and Transformation in the American Electric Utility Industry* (New York, 1989), examines these issues in detail.

17. Ibid., 18–19.

18. Ibid.

19. Ibid., 22.

20. Rudolph and Ridley, *Power Struggle*, 40.

21. Ibid., 40–41.

22. Hughes, *Networks of Power*, and Hirsh, *Technology and Transformation*.

23. *Statutes at Large* (Washington, DC, 1907), 34: 219–20. The Census Bureau also conducted an electrical census in 1902 as authorized by Congress on March 6, 1902. The act of 1907 amended the 1902 law and required the bureau to take an electrical census every five years. Later censuses, although they contained comparative information with previous ones including the 1907 census, make few if any comparisons with the 1902 census. The 1917 census makes many comparisons with 1907 and 1912, but none with 1902. In fact, in the letter of transmittal for the 1917 census, that census is referred to as "the third report . . . taken in conformity with . . . the act of Congress of June 7, 1906" (page 7). It is noted in the 1922 census that the Census Bureau did not collect any information regarding customers in 1902 (page 5). All of this suggests that the 1902 census may have been less than complete and that the 1907 census was the first complete electrical census.

24. *Congressional Record*, 59th Cong., 1st sess., 40, 2678.

25. U.S. Department of Commerce, Bureau of the Census, Special Reports, *Central Electric Light and Power Stations, 1907* (Washington, DC, 1910). See, for example, the illustrations following pages 96, 98, 104, 106, and 116; chap. 8 contains the technical information.

26. By World War I, for example, California led the nation in the number of high-voltage transmission systems with eight (Hughes, *Networks of Power*, 262–63).

Hughes writes that California had more high-voltage systems then any other region in the world, and all transmitted hydroelectricity (263).

27. Use of the word conservation throughout this work refers to the ideas of people like Theodore Roosevelt and Gifford Pinchot who believed that the nation's resources should be developed to serve the greatest number of people. Those ideas should not be confused with the ideas of John Muir and other preservationists.

28. Samuel P. Hays, *Conservation and the Gospel of Efficiency: The Progressive Conservation Movement, 1890–1920* (Cambridge, MA, 1969), 107–8, and Norris Hundley Jr., *The Great Thirst: Californians and Water, 1770s–1990s* (Berkeley, CA, 1992), 117.

29. For the history of reclamation see Donald J. Pisani, *From Family Farm to Agribusiness: The Irrigation Crusade in California and the West, 1850–1931* (Berkeley, CA, 1984), and *To Reclaim a Divided West: Water, Law, and Public Policy, 1848–1902* (Albuquerque, 1992). Throughout this work the historic name of Hoover Dam will be used for matters of consistency, unless discussed in the present tense. In discussions of the Los Angeles Aqueduct, its historic name, the Owens Valley Aqueduct, also will be used for the same reason.

30. Hays, *Conservation and the Gospel of Efficiency*, 184–86.

31. In the first decades of the twentieth century, electricity commonly was measured in horsepower instead of watts or kilowatts. One horsepower of electricity equals 746 watts of electricity or .746 kilowatts. Today electrical consumption is normally measured in kilowatt hours; a kilowatt of power equals 1.34 horsepower. One kilowatt hour of electricity is required to burn ten 100-watt lightbulbs for one hour. The 6.27 million horsepower that the ten interests controlled equaled 4.6 million kilowatts, or 4.677 megawatts.

32. National Conservation Association, Report of the Minority on Waterpower, December 10, 1913, 1–5, box 522, folder "Answers to some claims made by the power interests," Gifford Pinchot Papers, Library of Congress (hereafter Pinchot Papers).

33. James R. Garfield to Senator Reed Smoot, circa. 1915, box 522, folder "Garfield James R. letter to Senator Smoot," Pinchot Papers. This letter was in reference to a water power bill Smoot introduced.

34. For a concise discussion of the importance of the federal government and Congress, see Hays, *Conservation and the Gospel of Efficiency*, 101–2.

35. Marshall Leighton, chief hydrographer, U.S. Geological Survey, testified during the 1911 National Waterways Commission water power hearings that "the important practicable power sites of the west are now in forest service reserves" (U.S. Senate, *Hearings on the Development and Control of Water Power, Before the National Waterways Commission*, 62d Cong., 2d sess., November 21–24, 1911, S. Doc. 274, serial 6174, 239).

36. Jerome G. Kerwin, *Federal Water-Power Legislation* (New York, 1968), 108–9. The following legislative history is drawn largely from Kerwin.

37. Ibid., 111–12.

38. Ibid., 122–23.

39. Theodore Roosevelt, *Theodore Roosevelt: An Autobiography* (New York, 1913), 394, as cited in Kerwin, *Federal Water-Power Legislation*, 124.

40. Kerwin, *Federal Water-Power Legislation*, 128–29, and Hays, *Conservation and the Gospel of Efficiency*, 164–65.

41. Senate, *Hearings on the Development and Control of Water Power*, 139–46.

42. Ibid., 14–15.

43. Ibid., 275.

44. Ibid., 22–26.

45. Ibid., 100.

46. Ibid., 147–51 (a clear reference to trusts).

47. Ibid., 177–79, 195. Fisher also favored a fifty-year limit on permits.

48. Ibid., 227–28.

49. *Congressional Record*, 63d Cong., 3d sess., 52, 3700, S.R. 544.

50. U.S. Senate, *Electric Power Development in the United States*, 64th Cong., 1st sess., S. Doc. 316, pt. 1, serial 6918, 37, 58–59.

51. Ibid., 12–14.

52. *Congressional Record*, 64th Cong., 1st sess., 53, 2264–73. Kerwin referred to those opposing the printing of the report as the "Old Guard." The report, he wrote, "received wide publicity throughout the country" (*Federal Water-Power Legislation*, 194).

53. Federal involvement at Muscle Shoals started during World War I when the government decided that a synthetic nitrogen plant was needed to ensure a steady supply of the chemical. Production of synthetic nitrogen requires a tremendous amount of electricity, which is why the government authorized a hydroelectric dam at Muscle Shoals and entered into a contract with American Cyanamid Company for production from the company's Muscle Shoals plant (Preston Hubbard, *Origins of the TVA: The Muscle Shoals Controversy, 1920–1932* [New York, 1968], 1–3).

54. U.S. House, *Hearings Before the Committee on Water Power of the House Representatives*, 65th Cong., 2d sess., March 18–May 15, 1918, 20, 23.

55. Ibid., 158.

56. Ibid., 310, 333.

57. Ibid., 450.

58. Richard Lowitt, *George W. Norris: The Persistence of a Progressive, 1913–1933* (Urbana, IL, 1971), 28–31.

59. Kerwin, *Federal Water-Power Legislation*, 154–55.

60. The Federal Water-Power Act, *Statutes at Large* (Washington, DC, 1921), vol. 41, sections 1, 4, 6, 10, and 23. A complete text of the law appears as Appendix 7 in Kerwin, *Federal Water-Power Legislation*, 355–80.

61. Hays deemed the Federal Water Power Act of 1920 a nonconservationist law that signified the "defeat and marked the end of a conservation era" (*Conservation and the Gospel of Efficiency*, 239–40).

62. See, for example, Hughes, *Networks of Power*, Hirsh, *Technology and Transformation*, Nye, *Electrifying America*, and Platt, *The Electric City*.

63. *Electric World*, May, 25, 1929, as cited in Ronald C. Tobey, *Technology as Freedom: The New Deal and the Electrical Modernization of the American Home* (Berkeley, CA, 1996), 12 n. 6. Tobey persuasively argues that electrical modernization occurred only after the federal government intervened during the New Deal.

64. Platt, *The Electric City*, 235.

65. Tobey, *Technology as Freedom*, 5.

66. Nye, *Electrifying America*, 267–68. The four categories of homes in the survey were: "poor homes (industrial), Average homes (price $4500), Modern homes (10–12 years old), [and] Better Class." Perhaps owing to the success of Ford in Detroit, the survey found 2,500 privately owned refrigerators.

67. Tobey, *Technology as Freedom*, 91, Table 3.6, "Appliance Inventory of Electrified Residences, Riverside, 1922."

68. This discussion is drawn from Tobey, *Technology as Freedom*, chap. 1.

69. Ibid., 11.

70. *Electric World*, September 13, 1930, 471, cited in ibid., 10.

71. Tobey, *Technology as Freedom*, 11. Under New Deal legislation the government made low-cost loans available for such improvements under the Home Finance Corporation legislation. Also see David B. Sicilia, "Selling Power: Marketing and Monopoly at Boston Edison, 1886–1929" (Ph.D. diss., Brandeis University, 1991). Sicilia notes that Boston Edison undertook an energetic marketing strategy after 1900 that continued through the 1920s: "But the rate of its diffusion [electricity] was hastened by Boston Edison's comprehensive and aggressive marketing programs. The company's marketing strategy remained fundamentally unchanged since the turn of the century: reaching new customers, lowering market barriers, cultivating demand for electricity by promoting the devices that consumed it" (557). Despite this assertion, 56.2 percent of Boston's 179,200 families had at least one radio in 1930 (see Appendix 1.1).

72. Tobey, *Technology as Freedom*, 29–34, 38, Figure 1.1, "Dwellings Ineligible for Electrical Modernization, 1920–1954."

73. *Sikeston Standard*, March 14, 1930 (Kent Library, State College, Cape Girardeau, Missouri, microfilm); Tobey, *Technology as Freedom*, 16. This debate is examined in more detail in chap. 4. For a different interpretation of this issue, see Sicilia, "Selling Power."

74. Nye, *Electrifying America*, 283.

75. See Appendix 1.1 for a listing of the ninety-three American cities with populations of 100,000 and the percentage of families in each city with at least one radio.

76. U.S. Department of Commerce, Bureau of the Census, *Fifteenth Census of the United States, 1930, Population, Vol. 6, Families* (Washington, DC, 1933), 10; Table 12, "Families Having Radio Set, in Urban, Rural-Farm, and Rural Non-Farm Areas, for the United States, 1930," 52; Table 60, "Families Having Radio Set, in Urban, Rural-Farm, and Rural-Nonfarm Areas, by Divisions and States, 1930," 53; and Table 76, "Families Having Radio Set, by Color and Nativity of Head, for Cities of 100,000 or More," 70. The Census Bureau did not discriminate between radios powered by the transmitted current of batteries; therefore, these numbers probably inflate the degree of electrification and electrical modernization. The low rate of radio ownership in the South points to the imperfect nature of using radios as indicators of electrical modernization. That the South, the most impoverished region in the country, had the fewest number of radios might be due to poverty, which is probably especially true for sharecroppers and tenant farmers. The other explanation is that the area lacked power, thus minimizing poverty as a factor since electricity did not exist even for those who could afford radios.

77. Lizabeth Cohen, *Making a New Deal: Industrial Workers in Chicago, 1919–1939* (New York, 1990), Table 10, "Radio Ownership in Selected Working-class and Middle-class Chicago Neighborhoods," 134.

78. "Technologically capable" means that a home had adequate wiring, switches, and electrical outlets.

79. "Giant Power Bills," January 26, 1926, box 670, folder "Public Utilities, Giant Power Bills Senate"; Gifford Pinchot, "Giant Power," box 946, folder "Articles by Gifford Pinchot on 'Giant Power' Survey Graphic"; and Pinchot to Albert D. Betts, February 12, 1929, box 630, folder B, all in Pinchot Papers; and Gifford Pinchot, "The Householder Carries the Load," *Brotherhood of Locomotive Firemen and Enginemen's Magazine*, May 1928, 389–90, and "My Lord the Kilowatt," January 27, 1929, copies in box 948, folder, "Articles by Gifford Pinchot," Pinchot Papers.

80. George Norris, "Electricity in the Home," box 239, folder "Norris Magazine Articles and Request for," George Norris Papers, Library of Congress (hereafter Norris Papers).

81. *Seattle Star*, May 16, 1927, J. D. Ross, comp., *J. D. Ross Scrapbooks* (Suzzallo Library; Seattle: University of Washington, microfilm), vol. 9 (hereafter *Ross Scrapbooks*). During his tenure as superintendent of City Light, Ross maintained an extensive scrapbook collection of newspaper and journal articles and clippings. Most of the material contained in the scrapbooks originated in Seattle's newspapers, although the scrapbooks do contain some material from out-of-town newspapers and magazines. Ross saved articles that both supported and opposed City Light as well as articles discussing Puget Sound Power and Light (PSP&L). The scrapbooks are useful because they offer insight into the political debate in Seattle between public and private power. In the mid-1920s, as the public power debate became a statewide concern, Ross kept articles representing both sides of that issue.

82. For more information on Ross and Cooke, see Wesley Arden Dick, "Visions of Abundance: The Public Power Crusade in the Pacific Northwest in the Era of J. D. Ross and the New Deal" (Ph.D. diss., University of Washington, 1973), and Jean Christie, "Morris Llewellyn Cooke: Progressive Engineer" (Ph.D. diss., Columbia University, 1963).

84. On the social and intellectual aspects of the decade see, for example, Lynn Dumenil, *The Modern Temper: American Culture and Society in the 1920s* (New York, 1995). For economic and business changes consult Ellis Hawley, *The Great War and the Search for a Modern Order: A History of the American People and Their Institutions, 1917–1933* (New York, 1979).

CHAPTER 2. CONSOLIDATION AND INFLUENCE IN THE 1920s

1. U.S. Department of Commerce, Bureau of the Census, *Census of Electrical Industries, 1927, Central Electric Light and Power Stations* (Washington, DC, 1930), Table 21, "Transmission Lines—Miles of Circuit, by Voltage Capacity, Commercial Establishments: 1927," 35, and *Census of Electrical Industries, 1932, Central Electric Light and Power Stations* (Washington, DC, 1934), Table 17, "Transmission Systems—Miles of Circuit, by Individual Voltage, Commercial Establishments: 1932," 25; and Robert D. Baum, "Power District Legislation," *National Municipal Review* 26 (1937): 28–29. Before 1933, states that passed laws allowing for power districts (although the main focus of the laws was drainage or irrigation) were Idaho (1915), Texas (1919), New Mexico (1921), and Nevada (1923). States that passed laws expressly for power districts were California (1913), Arizona, Nebraska, and Montana (1915), Michigan (1927), Washington (1930), and Oregon, Wisconsin, and Wyoming (1931).

2. Puget Sound Power and Light Company advertisement in *Seattle Post-Intelligencer*, February 18, 1924, *Ross Scrapbooks*, vol. 4.

3. James C. Bonbright, *Public Utilities and the National Power Policies* (New York, 1940), 23.

4. H. S. Raushenbush and Harry W. Laidler, *Power Control* (New York, 1928), 59. Neither Raushenbush nor Laidler were friends of the power trust. In 1929 Raushenbush wrote another book, *High Power Propaganda* (New York, 1929), also published by New Republic that discussed propaganda and public utilities. At that time Raushenbush was serving as secretary for the Committee on Coal and

Giant Power located in New York City. The committee considered itself "an un-official public committee representing the interests of the small consumers and workers in the development of the coal and power industries" (*High Power Propaganda*, front material). Much of the material that they used in the book surfaced during the FTC investigation of the electrical utility industry that Congress authorized in 1925.

5. The Twentieth Century Fund, *Electric Power and Government Policy: A Survey of the Relations Between the Government and the Electric Power Industry* (New York, 1948), 37. Standard Gas and Electric was the country's fifth largest holding company in 1928 and operated in Pittsburgh, the Dakotas, California, Oregon, Kentucky, Louisiana, and Wisconsin (Raushenbush and Laidler, *Power Control*, 74–75).

6. Raushenbush and Laidler, *Power Control*, 68, and Arthur S. Link and William B. Catton, *American Epoch: A History of the United States Since the 1890s* (New York, 1967), 2:331.

7. Raushenbush and Laidler, *Power Control*, 66 n. 6.

8. James C. Bonbright and Gardiner Means, *The Holding Company: Its Public Significance and Its Regulation* (New York, 1932), 111–12.

9. Raushenbush and Laidler noted that majority ownership usually was not needed. By distributing stock ownership in a large number of people, a small group of minority owners could still dictate the holding companies' actions (*Power Control*, 59–60).

10. Bonbright and Means, *The Holding Company*, 112.

11. Middle West Utilities Company stock announcement, July 1926, mss 210, box 15, folder 1, Institute for Research in Land Economics Papers, State Historical Society of Wisconsin, Madison (hereafter IRLE Papers).

12. Ibid.

13. Raushenbush and Laidler, *Power Control*, 78.

14. Ibid., 75.

15. F. L. Greenhouse, "Customer Ownership as Put into Practice by Southern California Edison Company"; copy of article in Stock Sales Bulletins, Literature, Reports, 1917, SCE. William Myers, former archivist for Southern California Edison, graciously made available to me the archival material cited throughout this work. Unfortunately, SCE has since abolished its archives. I will, however, use the citation system that SCE used and refer to the collection as SCE.

16. Letter written by A. N. Kemp, November 1, 1917, Stock Sales Bulletins, Literature, Reports, 1917, SCE.

17. Ibid.

18. Ibid.

19. Ibid.

20. Greenhouse to G. Allan Hancock, November 7, 1923, Stock Sales Bulletins no. 1, Literature, Reports, 1923, SCE. Neither Kemp nor Greenhouse considered electrical usage in the home as a potential market, which was a primary concern of progressives who believed that the electrified home would result in a profound increase in living standards.

21. See Appendix 2.1 for the listing of the top twenty holders of SCE common stock.

22. *1930 Southern California Edison Annual Report to California Railroad Commission*, 24–25. The control of common stock is better understood when compared with the small investor. I have been unable to determine the total number of common stock shares in existence in 1930, but a brief review of some statistics for 1926 provides an indication of the amount of control held by the top twenty common

stock owners. In 1926 the company had 90,000 stockholders of which 60,000 held an investment of less than $300, with the average share costing about $90. An additional 10,000 stockholders held investments between $300 and $500. At the same time, about 1,800 people owned half of the stock, and 450 people owned a third of the stock (N. S. Van Valen, "Power Politics: The Struggle for Municipal Ownership of Electric Utilities in Los Angeles, 1905–1937" [Ph.D. diss., Claremont Graduate School, 1963], 317).

23. Greenhouse letter to district managers and security salesman, dated March 8, 1929, with attached proxy form, Stock Sales Bulletins, Literature, Reports, 1929, SCE.

24. Southern California Edison stock questionnaire, dated February 6, 1926; see questions 9 and 23, Stock Sales Bulletins, Literature, Reports, 1926, SCE.

25. *1930 Southern California Edison Annual Report to the California Railroad Commission*, 24–25, SCE.

26. *1930 Southern California Edison Annual Report to the California Railroad Commission*, Schedule A-16 "Capital Stock," 26–32, SCE. Although preferred stock carried a guaranteed return, people often bought common stock because of the potential higher return and the ability to decide company policy.

27. Bonbright and Means, *The Holding Company*, 12.

28. Ibid., 30, 44.

29. Ibid., 93.

30. Ibid.

31. Ibid.

32. Raushenbush and Laidler, *Power Control*, 51.

33. Bonbright and Means, *The Holding Company*, 92.

34. Raushenbush and Laidler, *Power Control*, 61–64.

35. In the example discussed earlier (Figure 2.1), the operating companies had to make a profit of at least 3.8 percent just to pay the holders of bonds and preferred stock.

36. John Kenneth Galbraith identified poor income distribution, "the bad corporate structure," and "the bad banking structure" as three reasons for the economic crisis that followed the stock market crash. Holding companies and investment trusts had the most vulnerable corporate structures and were in constant danger of reverse leverage. Instead of investing in operating companies after the market crashed, people continued to try and pay dividends, which further cut earnings. Galbraith argues that such activity contributed to the deflationary spiral in *The Great Crash* (Boston, 1988), 177–79. Holding companies also contributed to the poor income distribution by funneling large sums of money into a relatively few hands. The list of SCE stockholders indicates the amount of money investment houses and banks made in utility securities.

37. As measured in kilowatt hours. U.S. Senate, *Utility Corporations, Summary Report of the Federal Trade Commission*, 70th Cong., 1st sess., S. Doc. 92, pt. 71A, serial 8858, pt. 1, 23, 25.

38. *Seattle Star*, June 27, 1923, "Open Electric Session Today, Leonard Welcomes Light and Power Men," *Ross Scrapbooks*, vol. 3.

39. Herbert Hoover led the standardization crusade during his tenure as secretary of commerce. For more on Hoover consult Ellis Hawley, *The Great War and the Search for a Modern Order: A History of the American People and Their Institutions, 1917–1933* (New York, 1979), and Joan Hoff Wilson, *Herbert Hoover: The Forgotten Progressive* (Boston, 1975).

40. Raushenbush and Laidler, *Power Control*, 25; $28 million was double the amount spent in 1922.

41. *Seattle Star*, June 27, 1923, "Open Electric Session Today, Leonard Welcomes Light and Power Men," *Ross Scrapbooks*, vol. 3.

42. *Seattle Star*, February 21, 1924, "Poison Has No Place in Our Schools," *Ross Scrapbooks*, vol. 4.

43. *Seattle Star*, February 25, 1924, "Brockett Talks About Essay," *Ross Scrapbooks*, vol. 4.

44. *Seattle Star*, February 21, 1924, "Poison Has No Place in Our Schools," *Ross Scrapbooks*, vol. 4, and Senate, *Utility Corporations*, S. Doc. 92, pt. 71A, serial 8858, pt. 1, 207.

45. Senate, *Utility Corporations*, S. Doc. 92, pt. 71A, serial 8858, pt. 1, 216–17.

46. Ibid., 218.

47. Ibid., 149, 155.

48. For more on the need for specialized training see Alfred Chandler, *The Visible Hand: The Managerial Revolution in American Business* (Cambridge, MA, 1977). For a different perspective see David F. Noble, *America by Design: Science, Technology, and the Rise of Corporate Capitalism* (New York, 1977).

49. Richard T. Ely and Mary L. Shine, "The Institute for Research in Land Economics and Public Utilities," *Sewanee Review*, February 1924, "additions," mss 411, box 13A, Ely Papers.

50. Richard T. Ely, "Something About the Institute for Research in Land Economics and Public Utilities," mss 210, box 15, folder 1, IRLE Papers.

51. Ely to Martin Insull, March 26, 1924, mss MK, box 87, folder 1, and Martin J. Insull to Ralph E. Heilman, dean, Northwestern University School of Commerce, May 7, 1925, mss MK, box 97, folder 3, Ely Papers. From its inception through July 1, 1930, Ely's institute received $537,895. NELA's contribution represented 18.6 percent of that amount. Additional major contributors included the Carnegie Corporation ($106,875 or 19.9 percent) and the Laura Spelman Rockefeller Memorial fund ($152,500 or 28.4 percent). Other noteworthy contributors directly involved in the electrical utility industry included the Byllesby Engineering and Management Corporation ($21,500); Gerard Swope, president, General Electric Company ($5,000); and General Guy E. Tripp of the Westinghouse Electric and Manufacturing Company ($3,000) (mss 210, box 4, folder 11, IRLE papers).

52. Ely to Walter Dill Scott, president, Northwestern University, June 3, 1930, correspondences, series 3/15/1, box 24, folder 6, Walter Dill Scott Papers, Northwestern University Archives, Evanston, Illinois.

53. Ely to Mr. R. C. Jones, secretary-treasurer, San Antonio Public Service Company, March 12, 1926, mss MK, box 96, folder 7, Ely Papers.

54. Ely to R. H. Ballard, December 14, 1926, mss MK, box 100, folder 9, Ely Papers.

55. Ballard to Ely, December 20, 1926, mss MK, box 101, folder 1, Ely Papers.

56. Ely to Ballard, January 3, 1927, mss MK, box 101, folder 4, Ely Papers.

57. Ely to Ballard, December 14, 1926, mss MK, box 100, folder 9, Ely Papers.

58. G. F. Oxley to Ely, August 8, 1927, mss MK, box 101, folder 4, Ely Papers.

59. Glaeser to Glenn Frank, president, University of Wisconsin, September 5, 1928, box 2, folder 31, Martin G. Glaeser Papers, University of Wisconsin Archives, Madison (hereafter Glaeser Papers). The information contained in this letter became public when Glaeser sent a copy of the letter to FTC commissioner Edgar A. McCulloch. Glaeser initiated contact with the FTC in July 1928 and requested the opportunity to clear his name after it surfaced in regard to NELA, the institute,

and his book. This information is contained in a letter from McCulloch to Glaeser dated July 9, 1928, box 2, folder 31, Glaeser Papers.

60. Glaeser to Frank, September 5, 1928, box 2, folder 31, Glaeser Papers, and Senate, *Utility Corporations*, S. Doc. 92, pt. 71A, serial 8858, pt. 1, 163–64.

61. Ely to Paul S. Clapp, May 29, 1929, mss MK, box 112, folder 7, Ely Papers.

62. Ibid.

63. Ely to the manager of the Public Service Company of Northern Illinois, January 23, 1926, mss MK, box 95, folder 10, Ely Papers. Samuel Insull organized the Public Service Company of Northern Illinois, a holding company, in 1910 and 1911 in order to control five operating companies that served a population of 302,409 people (Platt, *The Electric City*, 183–85).

64. Richard T. Ely, "Chicago: The Public Utility Capital of the United States," written for the *Chicago Tribune Survey;* copy of the manuscript, marked "duplicate unpublished," in "additions," mss 411, box 2, folder 3, Ely Papers. I have found no evidence that the manuscript was ever published, although that does not diminish the insight it provides into Ely's thinking.

65. Robert Healy to Ely, May 21, 1929, mss MK, box 112, folder 5, Ely Papers.

66. Ely to Healy, October 29, 1929, mss MK, box 114, folder 2, Ely Papers.

67. Ely to Pinchot, October 29, 1929, mss MK, box 114, folder 7, Ely Papers.

68. Pinchot to Ely, November 8, 1929, mss MK, box 114, folder 9, Ely Papers. The Northwestern University School of Commerce gave the institute $11,200 between 1927 and 1930, the university's school of liberal arts contributed another $3,123 during the same years, and in 1927 the University of Wisconsin gave $1,012.50 (mss 210, box 4, folder 11, IRLE Papers).

69. Frank Pierce to Ely, May 23, 1928, mss MK, box 114, folder 9, Ely Papers.

70. *Wisconsin State Journal*, September 21, 1924, mss 210, box 23, folder 2, IRLE Papers.

71. Published by the Manufacturers and Merchants Federal Tax League (Chicago, 1925).

72. This narrative is drawn from Richard Lowitt, *George W. Norris: The Persistence of a Progressive, 1913–1933* (Urbana, IL, 1971), chap. 26, and Anne E. Butler and Wendy Wolff, *United States Senate: Election, Expulsion, and Censure Cases, 1793–1990* (Washington, DC, 1995), 323–39.

73. Lowitt, *George W. Norris: The Persistence of a Progressive*, 387–89. In his study of congressional progressives, Erik Olssen notes that rail unions in Pennsylvania solicited Norris's help in campaigning for the democrat William Wilson ("The Progressive Group in Congress, 1922–1929," *Historian* 42 [1980]; reprinted in Joel H. Silbey, ed., *The Congress of the United States, 1789–1989*, 3 vols. [New York, 1991], 2:244–63, 257, n. 59).

74. Lowitt, *George W. Norris: The Persistence of a Progressive*, 392–93.

75. Joseph R. Grundy in an open letter to the "Citizens of Pennsylvania," October 2, 1924, box 43, file "Vare (Penn. 1926–1931)," Norris Papers. Vare wrote the letter on the stationery of the Ways and Means Committee of the Republican National Committee for Pennsylvania, of which he was the chairman-treasurer.

76. Lowitt, *George W. Norris: Persistence of a Progressive*, 393–94.

77. Ibid., 394–95, and Butler and Wolff, *United States Senate*, 330–33.

78. The amendment was attached to S. Res. 329 that also called for an investigation of the tobacco industry.

79. George Kearney, ed., *Official Opinions of the Attorneys General of the United States Advising the President and Heads of Departments in Relation to Their Official Duties* (Washington, DC, 1926), 34:560–62.

80. Ibid., 34:558–64.

81. Ibid., 34:556.

82. Ibid., 34:556–57.

83. Ibid., 34:562.

84. "Don't Shoot We're Coming Down," *Nation,* May 20, 1925, 56.

85. Ibid.

86. George W. Norris, "Boring from Within," *Nation,* September 16, 1926, 297–99. The change in the character and behavior of the FTC is examined in G. Cullom Davis, "The Transformation of the Federal Trade Commission, 1914–1929," *Mississippi Valley Historical Review* 49 (1962): 437–55.

87. U.S. Senate, *Electric-Power Industry, Control of Power Companies,* 69th Cong., 2d sess., S. Doc. 213, serial 8703, xvi.

88. Ibid., 51.

89. Ibid.

90. Ibid., xxiv.

91. For a brief description of the early controversy regarding the Walsh resolution, see Ernest Gruening, *The Public Pays: A Study of Power Propaganda* (New York, 1964), 3–12. The Walsh investigation was one of the major public power issues of the 1920s and is examined at length in Chapter 3.

CHAPTER 3. PUBLIC POWER, NATIONAL POLITICS, AND CONGRESS

1. Norris Hundley Jr., *Water and the West: The Colorado River Compact and the Politics of Water in the American West* (Berkeley, CA, 1975), 51–53, 103.

2. Eugene Clyde La Rue, *Colorado River and Its Utilization* (Washington, DC, 1916), 169–70. The report stated that over two million horsepower could be generated. When translated into megawatts, that equals about 1,492 megawatts; in 1996 the nameplate capacity of Hoover Dam was 2,080 megawatts.

3. Hundley, *Water and the West,* 116–17. Hundley notes that two of the dams would have been above the Grand Canyon and two below, including one in Boulder Canyon. A holding company, the California-Nevada Corporation, controlled Southern Sierras Power.

4. E. F. Scattergood to George Norris, January 26, 1925, box 236, folder "Muscle Shoals and Muscle Shoals Commission (Hoover)," Norris Papers.

5. Hundley, *Water and the West,* 13–14. The lack of fall through a low dam's penstocks would not create enough pressure to drive hydroelectric turbines.

6. *Seattle Times,* June 25, 1923, *Ross Scrapbooks,* vol. 3.

7. The equivalent of about 447,600 kilowatts. Congress passed and President Hoover signed the fourth Swing-Johnson bill in late 1928.

8. *Seattle Post-Intelligencer,* May 22, 1924, *Ross Scrapbooks,* vol. 5. See Appendix 3.1 for a partial listing of Hearst newspapers in existence in the 1920s.

9. *Seattle Union Record,* October 24, 1925, November 15, 1927, and August 30, 1927, *Ross Scrapbooks,* vol. 7.

10. *Seattle Post-Intelligencer,* April 24, 1928, *Ross Scrapbooks,* vol. 7.

11. *Seattle Post-Intelligencer,* January 7, 1928, *Ross Scrapbooks,* vol. 7.

12. "'Speech for Senator McMaster,' 1930 campaign," series C555, folder "'Speech for Senator McMaster,' 1930 campaign," La Follette Family Collection, Library of Congress (hereafter La Follette Collection).

13. Ibid.

14. Norris to B. H. Livesay, June 30, 1930, box 234, folder "L" 26, Norris Papers.

15. Preston J. Hubbard, *Origins of the TVA: The Muscle Shoals Controversy, 1920–1932* (New York, 1968), vii–viii. For more on Norris see his autobiography, *Fighting Liberal* (New York, 1961), and Richard Lowitt, *George W. Norris: The Persistence of a Progressive, 1913–1933,* Urbana, IL, 1971.

16. *Seattle Post-Intelligencer,* December 13, 1924, *Ross Scrapbooks,* vol. 6.

17. *Seattle Post-Intelligencer,* December 20, 1924, *Ross Scrapbooks,* vol. 6.

18. National League of Women Voters bulletin, May 26, 1928, box 226, folder "S.J. Res. 46 Leg," Norris Papers.

19. Norris to J. W. Cowper, February 4, 1929, box 217, folder 8. Norris Papers.

20. Norris to Arthur Capper, August 2, 1928, box 4, folder "1928 Campaign Hoover," Norris Papers.

21. Norris to Pinchot, August 2, 1928, box 4, folder "1928 Campaign Hoover," Norris Papers.

22. Robert M. La Follette Jr., "Dominant Issues in the 1928 Campaign," series C 554, folder "Coolidge Administration 1928," La Follette Collection.

23. "Speech for Senator McMaster," series C 555, folder "Speech for Senator McMaster, 1930 Campaign," La Follette Collection.

24. Norris to C. W. McConaughy, June 2, 1931, box 235, folder 29, Norris Papers.

25. Walter Lippman to Norris, December 22, 1924, and Norris to Lippman, January 19, 1925, box 290, folder "Boulder Dam, 1924–1929 I," Norris Papers.

26. Karl Lee to Norris, March 2, 1927, and Norris to Lee, March 6, 1927, box 290, folder "Boulder Dam, 1924–1929 I," Norris Papers.

27. National Popular Government League, bulletin no. 101, February 11, 1926, series C 422, folder "Muscle Shoals," La Follette Collection.

28. Norris to Hannah P. Morris, December 1, 1928, box 235, folder 31, and Norris to Clark McAdams, April 4, 1931, box 239, folder "Norris Letters," Norris Papers.

29. *St. Louis Post-Dispatch,* March 29, 1931, box 239, folder "Norris Letters," Norris Papers.

30. Pinchot to Norris, February 10, 1928, box 220, folder "Electric Bond and Share Company," Norris Papers. Walsh introduced the resolution in late 1927, but the Senate did not act on it until 1928.

31. Copy of speech by Robert La Follette Jr., series C 422, folder "Muscle Shoals," La Follette Collection.

32. Burton K. Wheeler and Paul F. Healy, *Yankee from the West* (New York, 1977), 307. Wheeler served in the Senate from 1923 to 1947.

33. "Black Raps 'Power Trust' over Radio," *Evening Star,* Washington, DC, February 28, 1930, p. A-6, box 110, folder "Muscle Shoals Lobby," Hugo Black Papers, Library of Congress (hereafter Black Papers).

34. Norris to John T. Duncan, March 25, 1926, box 220, folder 11, and Norris to J. W. Cowper, February 4, 1929, box 217, folder 8, Norris Papers.

35. Judson King, "Comparative Cost of Domestic Electrical Service, United States and Ontario, 1910–1926," copy in box 286, file "Cook, Morris L," Pinchot Papers. King based his study on material contained in *Electrical World,* a trade magazine that was a strong opponent of municipal power, and from bulletins from the Hydro Electric Power Commission of Ontario.

36. Gifford Pinchot, *The Power Monopoly: Its Make-up and Its Menace* (Milford, PA: John R. McFetridge and Sons, 1929); the information cited appears on pages 8 and 9. Copy contained in box 948, folder "Article by Gifford Pinchot, Public Utilities, the Power Monopoly, Its Make-up and Its Menace," Pinchot Papers.

37. Special message by Governor Theodore G. Bilbo to the Extraordinary Session, October 20, 1931, box 235, folder "Mississippi," Norris Papers.

38. *Chattanooga News*, copy of article attached to a letter to Norris from George F. Milton, editor, February 18, 1928, box 235, folder "George Fort Milton," Norris Papers.

39. Norris to Milton, February 7, 1926, box 235, folder "George Fort Milton," Norris Papers.

40. J. W. Harreld to Norris, January 15, 1929, box 246, folder "f, Oklahoma," Norris Papers.

41. Spencer M. DeGolier to Norris, February 10, 1929, box 246, folder "Pennsylvania," Norris Papers. For an account of the influence of the electrical utility industry on the press from a public power perspective, see Ernest Gruening, *The Public Pays: A Study of Power Propaganda* (New York, 1964).

42. "First Blood in the Power War," *New Republic*, February 29, 1928, 56.

43. Felix Frankfurter, "Mr. Hoover on Power Control," *New Republic*, October 17, 1928, 243.

44. *Nation*, January 11, 1928, 38.

45. "Norris's Power Fight," *Nation*, March 28, 1928, 338. For an example of the magazine's reporting of the FTC, see "The Million-Dollar Lobby," *Nation*, May 16, 1928, 554–55.

46. *Congressional Record*, 70th Cong., 1st sess., 1928, 69, 3054.

47. Federal Trade Commission, *Annual Report 1933* (Washington, DC, 1933), 29–30. The seven companies were Pennsylvania Electric Co., Columbia Gas & Electric Corp., New England Gas & Electric Corp., Pennsylvania Electric Co., United Gas Improvement Co., Central Public Service Co., and Utilities Power & Light Co.

48. "What the Power Trust Bought," *New Republic*, October 31, 1928, 289–90.

49. U.S. Senate, *Utility Corporations, Summary Report of the Federal Trade Commission*, 70th Cong., 1st sess., S. Doc. 92, serial 8858, 95 vols.

50. Frankfurter, "Mr. Hoover on Power Control," 242.

51. *New Republic*, October 3, 1928, 165.

52. Ray Lyman Wilbur and Arthur Mastick Hyde, *The Hoover Policies* (New York, 1937), 317–30.

53. Samuel Rosenman, ed., *The Public Papers and Addresses of Franklin D. Roosevelt*, 13 vols. (New York, 1938–1950), 1:727–34, "Campaign Address on Public Utilities."

54. Speech by Senator Norris, March 11, 1931, box 265, folder "Progressive Conference, March 11, 1931," Norris Papers, and the *New York Times*, March 3, 1931.

55. Many members of Congress who were invited could not attend the conference. Two lists indicated those in attendance and those who were invited but could not attend and gave a definitive response. These lists are contained in box 426, folder "Proceedings, Lists and Reports," Norris Papers.

56. Judson King, ed., *Power Records of the Presidential Candidates*, National Popular Government League, bulletin no. 153, March 18, 1932, box 232, folder "Judson King," Norris Papers.

57. See, for example, Carl Thompson to Norris, November 18, 1932, box 3, folder "1932 campaign," Norris Papers.

58. See, for example, Ronald L. Feinman, *Twilight of Progressivism: The Western Republican Senators and the New Deal* (Baltimore, 1981); Ray Tucker and Frederick R. Barkley, *Sons of the Wild Jackass* (Boston, 1932); David E. Nye, *Electri-*

fying America: Social Meaning of a New Technology (Cambridge, MA, 1990), 341; and Hubbard, *Origins of the TVA*, viii.

59. John P. Roberston to Robert McLendon, May 8, 1931, box 235, folder 29, Norris Papers. The list contained thirty-one names; including Norris would have brought the total to thirty-two, a full third of the Senate. Senator Edward Costigan (D-Colo.), however, did not take office until March 4, 1931, and did not vote on any of the legislation examined, which returns the list to thirty-one. Robertson listed both U.S. senators from West Virginia, Henry Hatfield (R) and Matthew Neely (D). Hatfield had defeated Neely in the 1928 elections. In 1930 Neely returned to the Senate after defeating Guy Goff (R) for the other West Virginia Senate seat. Before leaving office in March 1929, Neely supported public power every time he voted (six times). Hatfield, although a Republican, also supported public power each of the three times he voted. Robertson wrote the letter in May 1931, after Neely had been sworn in a second time. See Appendix 3.2 for a complete listing.

60. Because of turnover, more than 96 senators and 435 representatives are included in the analysis of the congressional votes (for the House, a total of 462 seats and for the Senate, 108 seats). Congressmen and congressional seats that did not vote on any of the legislation are excluded. The index equally weighed each vote and party seat. The distribution of the index is bimodal. Considering each party seat equally regardless of the number of votes cast represents both the primary strength and potential weakness of the scaling methodology used. The senator who voted only a couple of times is given the same consideration as the senator who voted nearly every time. To determine if this biased the findings, the index for both the House and Senate for only those seats whose members voted more than half of the time (Senate ≥ 4, House ≥ 3) was calculated. The results were not significantly different from those reported. Of the 108 Senate party seat holders, 93 voted at least four times (86.1 percent). The mean for those 93 seats was .59 and the median was .75, which compares with .57 and .75 for all 108 Senate party seats. In the House, 356 party seat holders voted at least three times (77.1 percent). Their mean was .57 and the median was .63 as compared with a mean of .55 and a median of .60 for all 462 House party seats. For both houses of Congress, studying only those who voted at least half the time would have strengthened the analysis regarding the presence of pro–public power voting behavior in Congress. However, all the seats are included so that every vote cast for the legislation is incorporated into the analysis.

61. The Senate votes: Moses amendment to S. Res. 83, refer utility investigation to Interstate Commerce Committee (public power supporters opposed, y = 40, n = 36, December 19, 1927, *Congressional Record [C.R.]* 69, p. 817); George amendment to S. Res. 83, have the FTC conduct the utility investigation (public power supporters opposed, y = 46, n = 31, February 15, 1928, *C.R.* 69, p. 3053); Harrison amendment to S.J. Res. 46, lease Muscle Shoals to individuals or corporations (public power supporters opposed, y = 26, n = 48, March 13, 1928, *C.R.* 69, p. 4631); pass S.J. Res. 46 (y = 48, n = 25, March 13, 1928, *C.R.* 69, p. 4635); agree to the conference report on S.J. Res. 46 (y = 43, n = 34, May 25, 1928, *C.R.* 69, p. 9842); pass H.R. 5773, construction of Boulder Dam (y = 65, n = 11, December 14, 1929, *C.R.* 70, p. 603); pass S.J. Res. 49: government development of Muscle Shoals (y = 45, n = 23, April 4, 1930, *C.R.* 72, p. 6511); pass conference report on S.J. Res. 49, Muscle Shoals Bill (y = 55, n = 28, February 23, 1931, *C.R.* 72, p. 5716); override presidential veto of S.J. Res. 49 (y = 49, n = 34, March 3, 1931, *C.R.* 72, p. 7098). The House votes: pass S.J. Res. 46 conference report (y = 211, n = 147, May 25, 1928, *C.R.* 69,

p. 9957); Douglas motion to recommit H.R. 5773 (public power supporters opposed, y = 137, n = 219, May 25, 1928, *C.R.* 69, p. 9989); H.R. 5773 conference report (y = 167, n = 122, December 18, 1928, *C.R.* 70, p. 837); Reece amendment to S.J. Res. 49, to lease Muscle Shoals area (public power supporters opposed, y = 186, n = 135, May 28, 1930, *C.R.* 72, p. 9766); pass conference report on S.J. Res. 49, without Reece amendment (y = 216, n = 153, February 20, 1931, *C.R.* 74, p. 5570). The data used were made available by the Inter-University Consortium for Political and Social Research. The U.S. congressional roll call voting records used in this study were originally collected by the Works Progress Administration under the supervision of Clifford Lord and later standardized by the consortium. Neither the collector of the original data nor the consortium bears any responsibility for the analyses or interpretations presented here.

62. Census regions are as follows: Northeast—CT, ME, MA, NH, NJ, NY, PA, RI, VT; North Central—IL, IN, IA, KS, MI, MN, MO, NE, ND, OH, SD, WI; South—AL, AR, DE, FL, GA, KY, LA, MD, MS, NC, OK, SC, TN, TX, VA, WV; and West—AZ, CA, CO, ID, MT, NV, NM, OR, UT, WA, WY. U.S. Department of Commerce, Bureau of the Census, *Fourteenth Census of the United States Taken in the Year 1920, Vol. 1, Population, 1920, Number and Distribution of Inhabitants* (Washington, DC, 1921), Table 35, "Number and Aggregate Population of Urban Places of Specified Sizes, and Population of Rural Districts, by Divisions and States: 1890–1920," 53.

63. Critics of this conclusion might suggest that logrolling accounts for the high degree of noneastern support. Although logrolling cannot be discounted completely, the fact that the votes spanned several years and that large blocs of congressmen existed on each side of the issue mitigates logrolling as an explanation.

64. The literature on the Progressive Era is immense, but some of the works that have discussed the persistence of progressive ideas into the 1920s include Kenneth Campbell MacKay, *The Progressive Movement of 1924* (New York, 1966), 11–12, 244, 253; Arthur S. Link, "What Happened to the Progressive Movement in the 1920s?" *American Historical Review* 64 (1959): 833–51; Clarke A. Chambers, *Seedtime of Reform: American Social Service and Social Action, 1918–1933* (Minneapolis, 1963); Jackson K. Putnam, "The Persistence of Progressivism in the 1920s: The Case of California," *Pacific Historical Review* 35 (1966): 395–411; Paul Glad, "Progressives and the Business Culture of the 1920s," *Journal of American History* 53 (1966): 75–89; Otis Graham, *An Encore for Reform: The Old Progressives and the New Deal* (New York, 1967), 6–7; Peter G. Filene, "An Obituary for 'The Progressive Movement,'" *American Quarterly* 22 (1970): 20–34; Feinman, *Twilight of Progressivism*; and Arthur S. Link and Richard L. McCormick, *Progressivism* (Arlington Heights, IL, 1983).

65. See note 59.

66. U.S. Department of Commerce, Bureau of the Census, *Fifteenth Census of the United States: 1930, Population, Vol. 6, Families* (Washington, DC, 1933), Table 60, "Families Having Radio Set, in Urban, Rural-Farm, and Rural-Nonfarm Areas, by Divisions and States," 53. The Census Bureau did not distinguish between radios powered by batteries or by current supplies from a source outside the home. No attempt is made to distinguish between battery- and non–battery-powered radios, thus using the total number of radios as a determinant of electrical modernization overestimates the number of families served by electrical utilities, either publicly or privately owned. As discussed in Chapter 1, radios are admittedly an imperfect indicator of electrical modernization, but also as shown in Chapter 2 most Americans used few electrical appliances on an everyday basis. The Eta^2 for the three groups is .77.

67. The inclusion in the public power bloc that Norris's office identified of a senator who represented a state with less than 22 percent of families having radios negated Republican opposition to the legislation. Of the thirty-one senators identified by Norris's office, seventeen were Republicans. Thirteen came from North Central states with the remainder evenly split between the West and South (of the thirteen from the North Central region, only one, George McGill, was a Democrat). The thirty-four senators from states with few radios were predominantly from the South (twenty-nine); the other five were from the West.

68. This biographical information is gathered from the *Biographical Directory of the U.S. Congress, 1774–1989, Bicentennial Edition* (Washington, DC, 1989), and the *Official Congressional Directory*, 71st Cong., 3d sess. (Washington, DC, 1931).

69. All population figures are from the 1930 census. U.S. Department of Commerce, Bureau of the Census, *Fifteenth Census of the United States, 1930, Vol. 1, Number and Distribution of Inhabitants* (Washington DC, 1931), Table 5, "Population of Incorporated Places: 1930 and 1920."

70. For more on the rural-urban split in the 1920s, see Charles W. Eagle, *Democracy Delayed: Congressional Reapportionment and Urban-Rural Conflict in the 1920s* (Athens, GA, 1990), especially the conclusion. For state population figures see Bureau of the Census, *Fifteenth Census of the United States, 1930, Vol. 1, Number and Distribution of Inhabitants,* Table 9, "Urban and Rural Population by Divisions and States: 1930 and 1920," 15. When included in the MCA, the value f. for each variable exceeded .05. Examining data from the 1930 census reveals that 267 House party seats had less than 50 percent of their population living in towns of 2,500 or more. The number of party seats from urban districts was 223. The number of rural congressional districts according to the 1930 census was 242, and the number of urban was 193. The data for these tabulations were made available by the Inter-University Consortium for Political and Social Research (historical demographic, economic, and social data). The consortium's staff keypunched the data. The populations of congressional districts were determined by totaling the county level data provided in the 1930 data set or, when necessary, by referring to the 1930 census to determine the population of a specific town or subsection of a city.

71. Robert D. Baum, "Power District Legislation," *National Municipal Review* 26 (1937): 28–29. In some states, PUD referred to people's utility district.

72. Ibid.; also see Chapter 2, note 1, for a listing of the states.

73. David Schap, *Municipal Ownership in the Electric Utility Industry: A Centennial View* (New York, 1986), 23, 51–54.

74. The names of the towns with municipal power were drawn from the following articles by Paul Jerome Raver: "Municipal Ownership in the Last Five Years," *Journal of Land and Public Utility Economics* 9 (1933): 122–34; "Municipally Owned Generating Plants in Existence in the United States as of December 31, 1932," *Journal of Land and Public Utility Economics* 9 (1933): 306–13; and "Municipally Owned Establishments Which Were in Existence in the United States on December 31, 1932, and Which Were Purchasing All Current Distributed on December 31, 1930," *Journal of Land and Public Utility Economics* 9 (1933): 410–17. Raver oversaw the compilation of all of the data for the aforementioned journal, which was first published by the Institute for Research in Land Economics in 1925. The journal appears to be the most comprehensive source for listing towns with municipal power in the late 1920s and early 1930s. Internal memos of the institute reveal that Raver and his colleagues began compiling their information in 1928 from numerous sources published in the 1920s (mss 210, box 18, folder 6, IRLE Papers). In order to ascertain which congressional district represented each town,

I first determined the county in which the towns were located and then each county's congressional district. Altogether, 1,873 towns are included in this study. Some merit may exist to the theories that inadequate private capital or the lack of technology led to municipal power. The number of towns with municipal power declined in the 1920s, although a renewed interest in municipal power developed after the onset of the Depression. The total number of towns with municipal power leveled off at about 1,900 and remained at that number through the 1950s. The more important statistic is the 50-percent-plus number of towns that purchased power wholesale and redistributed it publicly after 1925. This fact strongly indicates that the power to set rates was the issue, since those towns also could have chosen to have the electricity distributed privately.

75. The voting index for the three groups was:

Group	Minimum	Maximum
Strong Opposition	.00	.25
Moderate Support	.33	.67
Strong Support	.75	1.00

$Eta^2 = .95$

CHAPTER 4. THE QUEST FOR INEXPENSIVE ELECTRICITY

1. For the history of the Rural Electrification Administration see D. Clayton Brown, *Electricity for Rural America: The Fight for the REA* (Westport, CT, 1980). Also consult Ronald C. Tobey, *Technology as Freedom: The New Deal and the Electrical Modernization of the American Home* (Berkeley, CA, 1996).

2. For a discussion of several nonpolitical interpretations of municipal power, see David Schap, *Municipal Ownership in the Electrical Utility Industry: A Centennial View* (New York, 1986), chaps. 2 and 3, especially pages 31–32, 63–66, and 102–3. These interpretations involve issues of inadequate technology, finance capital, or potential financial investment return. In each scenario the decision to establish municipal ownership was a last-ditch effort at electrification. As will be shown subsequently, in nearly all of the towns examined in this chapter, the existence of privately owned plants proceeded public ownership. This tendency rules out the idea that lack of private capital forced people to establish public power since private systems had already been built. Technology hastened the move to public distribution systems in some towns since it allowed a municipality to buy power from private companies via high-voltage transmission lines.

3. U.S. Department of Commerce, Bureau of the Census, *Sixteenth Census of the United States, 1940, Population, Second Series, Characteristics of the Population, United States Summary* (Washington, DC, 1943), Table 2, "Population in Groups of Places Classified According to Size, and in Rural Territory, for the United States: 1920 to 1940," 12.

4. The towns examined here do not represent any kind of sample arrived at through formal sampling techniques. Instead, I found information regarding the political debates in these towns in archival collections, namely the Ely and IRLE Papers. For several of the towns I was able to supplement the archival material with information from microfilmed copies of local newspapers. Unfortunately, for most of the towns microfilmed copies of the newspapers are not available, if they exist at all.

5. The population figures for all of the towns examined are from the 1930 census; see source note for Table 4.2 for citations. U.S. Department of Commerce, Bureau of the Census, *Fifteenth Census of the United States, 1930, Agriculture, Vol. 2, Part 1, the Northern States* (Washington, DC, 1932), County Table 10, "Value of Crops, 1929, Value of Livestock, 1930, and Value of Livestock Products, 1929," 786–89 (hereafter *Agricultural Census, 1930*). Bangor election notice, mss UI, box 28, folder "Bangor, Wisconsin, Utilities Case, 1930," O. S. Loomis Papers, State Historical Society of Wisconsin, Madison (hereafter Loomis Papers). The *Bangor Independent* published the notice on October 16, 1930 (State Historical Society of Wisconsin, Madison, microfilm). Unless otherwise noted, subsequent citations to the *Bangor Independent* reference the microfilm copies.

6. *Bangor Independent,* October 30, 1930.

7. Ibid.

8. Ibid.

9. Ibid.

10. Ibid., November 6, 1930.

11. Ibid., January 17, 1929. An advertisement for an RCA Radiola also appeared in this issue.

12. Ibid., January 17, 1929.

13. Ibid., January 24, 1929.

14. Ibid., August 22 and September 19, 1929.

15. Ibid., October 3, 1929.

16. See advertisements in ibid., October 17, November 17, 21, 28, and December 5, 1929.

17. Unfortunately, no copies of the paper exist for January, February, and September 1930.

18. *Bangor Independent,* June 26, August 28, and October 9, 1930. Advertisements for radios also appeared in the October 16, November 27, and December 18, 1930, issues.

19. Ibid., October 9, 1930.

20. *Official Congressional Directory,* 71st Cong., 1st sess. (Washington, DC, 1929), 128. Hull's predecessor in Congress, J. D. Beck, did not vote on the Muscle Shoals conference report, on the motion to recommit the Swing-Johnson bill, or on the Swing-Johnson conference report in 1928.

21. *Agricultural Census, 1930,* 786–89.

22. *Pardeeville-Wyocena Times,* February 2, 1933 (State Historical Society of Wisconsin, Madison, microfilm). In March 1928 a front-page article raised the issue of whether the town should establish municipal power. In the article it was stated that under the present circumstances rates were too high and that the operators of the private plant made a "handsome profit."

23. Ibid., March 2 and 9, 1933.

24. Ibid., March 9 and 16, 1933.

25. Ibid., March 30, 1933.

26. Ibid., April 6, 1933.

27. Ibid., May 18, 1933.

28. Ibid., May 25 and July 27, 1933. A copy of the second article is contained in mss UI, box 27, folder "Pardeeville, Wisconsin, Utilities Case—exhibits, 1933–1944," Loomis Papers.

29. *Pardeeville-Wyocena Times,* June 22, 1933. Another article stressing the same themes appeared on July 20.

30. Ibid., August 10 and 17, 1933. Copies of these article are in mss UI, box 27, folder "Pardeeville, Wisconsin, Utilities Case—exhibits, 1933–1944," Loomis Papers.

31. See, for example, the *Pardeeville-Wyocena Times*, January 1, 13, and 20, 1928.

32. Ibid., June 6, July 6, August 31, and December 21, 1928.

33. Advertisements for electric refrigerators appeared April 6, 1928, and August 6, 1931, in the *Pardeeville-Wyocena Times*. Advertisements for radios appeared in many issues between 1928 and 1933.

34. Ibid., December 12, 1929.

35. Ibid., October 10 and November 6, 13, 20, and 26, 1930.

36. Ibid., June 23, 30, and July 7, 1932, for irons, and November 3 and 24, 1932, for coffeepots.

37. *Biographical Directory of the United States Congress, 1774–1989, Bicentennial Edition* (Washington, DC, 1989), 1286.

38. The information regarding the legal aspect of the Pardeeville case is drawn from a statement that the Pardeeville Village Board issued in April 1941. The board noted that the commission's mistake merely slowed the plant's acquisition, but it expected no further delays in determining the property's value; copy in mss UI, box 27, folder "Pardeeville, Wisconsin, Utilities Case—exhibits, 1933–1944," Loomis Papers.

39. *Agricultural Census, 1930*, 1058–63. Of Missouri's 116 counties, Scott County ranked eleventh in total value of field and other crops and ninth in the value of mules and mule colts.

40. *Sikeston Standard*, January 12, 1932 (Kent Library, State College, Cape Girardeau, Missouri, microfilm). A copy of this article, sent to the Institute for Research in Land Economics and Public Utilities in response to an institute survey conducted regarding municipal power, is in mss 210, box 17, folder 11, IRLE Papers.

41. *Sikeston Standard*, January 10 and 17, 1930. Both an article and an editorial appeared in the January 10 issue.

42. Ibid., January 28 and 31, 1930.

43. *Sikeston Herald*, January 23, 1930 (State Historical Society of Missouri, Columbia, microfilm).

44. Ibid., January 30 and February 6, 1930.

45. *Sikeston Standard*, January 31 and February 4, 1930.

46. *Sikeston Herald*, March 13, 1930.

47. *Sikeston Standard*, March 7 and 18, 1930.

48. *Sikeston Herald*, March 13, 1930.

49. Ibid., March 20, 1930. Another full-page announcement appeared in the following issue on March 27 and emphasized the same themes.

50. *Sikeston Standard*, April 4 and 25, 1930.

51. Ibid., January 12, 1932.

52. Ibid., March 7, 1930.

53. Ibid., March 7 and 11, 1930.

54. Ibid., March 7, 11, and 25, 1930.

55. Ibid., February 25, 1930.

56. See, for example, ibid., March 11 and 18, 1930.

57. This observation is made after examining the *Standard* between January and July 1930 and the *Herald* for 1930 and 1931.

58. David Pepper to Paul J. Raver, March 10, 1932, mss 210, box 17, folder 11, IRLE Papers.

59. *Biographical Directory of the United States Congress, 1774–1989*, 1031.
60. Ibid., 1807.
61. Mss 210, box 17, folder 11, IRLE Papers.
62. Paul J. Raver, research associate, IRLE, to city clerk, Sullivan, Missouri, March 8, 1932, mss 210, box 7, folder 5, IRLE Papers. The clerk's response was handwritten on the information sheet.
63. *Agriculture Census, 1930*, 1058–63. Franklin County was eleventh in the value of dairy products and twenty-fifth in field crop value among the state's 116 counties.
64. *Biographical Directory of the United States Congress, 1774–1989*, 739.
65. Mss 210, box 17, folder 11, IRLE Papers.
66. Ibid.
67. *LeVang's Weekly*, January 5, 1928 (Minnesota Historical Society, St. Paul, microfilm).
68. Ibid., March 1, 1928.
69. Ibid., March 8, 1928. The first question dealt with agriculture relief.
70. Ibid., March 15, 1928.
71. Ibid., April 12 and May 3, 1928.
72. Ibid., June 14, July 19, and August 9, 1928.
73. Ibid., January 1, February 23, and March 1 and 8, 1928.
74. Ibid., March 8 and May 24, 1928.
75. Ibid., October 13, 20, November 4, and December 6, 1928.
76. Ibid., October 25 and November 29, 1928.
77. *Agriculture Census, 1930*, 866–69. The county ranked third in the value of livestock, thirteenth in the value of livestock products, and fifteenth in the value of crops.
78. *Biographical Directory of the United States Congress, 1774–1989*, 1035.
79. Ibid., 774–75.
80. Mss 210, box 17, folder 11, IRLE Papers.
81. *Agricultural Census, 1930*, 1363–67; *Biographical Directory of the United States Congress, 1774–1989*, 1857.
82. Mss 210, box 17, folder 11, IRLE Papers.
83. U.S. Department of Commerce, Bureau of the Census, *Fifteenth Census of the United States, 1930, Agriculture, Vol. 2, Part 2, the Southern States* (Washington, DC, 1932), County Table 10, "Value of Crops, 1929, Value of Livestock, 1930, and Value of Livestock Products, 1929," 1569. Yoakum is situated in Lavaca County.
84. *Biographical Directory of the United States Congress, 1774–1989*, 1420.
85. See Appendix 4.1.
86. See Schap, *Municipal Ownership in the Electric Utility Industry*.

CHAPTER 5. SEATTLE AND WASHINGTON STATE

1. In 1997 Puget Sound Power and Light merged with Washington Natural Gas to form Puget Sound Energy.
2. Carlos A. Schwantes, *Radical Heritage: Labor, Socialism, and Reform in Washington and British Columbia, 1885–1917* (Seattle, 1979), 10.
3. Gordon B. Dodds, *The American Northwest: A History of Oregon and Washington* (Arlington Heights, IL, 1986), 101.
4. U.S. Department of Commerce, Bureau of the Census, *Twelfth Census of the United States Taken in the Year 1900, Vol. 1, Population* (Washington, DC, 1901), Table

5, "Population of States and Territories by Minor Civil Divisions: 1890 and 1900," 404.

5. Dodds, *The American Northwest*, 134–35 and 194–95. For a general history of the Pacific Northwest, also see Carlos A. Schwantes, *The Pacific Northwest: An Interpretive History* (Lincoln, NE, 1996).

6. Schwantes, *Radical Heritage*, 18–19. For more on this subject see William Robbins, *Colony and Empire: The Capitalist Transformation of the American West* (Lawrence, KS, 1994).

7. Schwantes, *Radical Heritage*, 36–37, 80.

8. Ibid., 94–95.

9. Ibid., 152–55.

10. Dana Frank, *Purchasing Power: Consumer Organizing, Gender, and the Seattle Labor Movement, 1919–1929* (New York, 1994), 15–16, 21.

11. Ibid., 21–31.

12. Ibid., 34–39.

13. Lynn Dumenil, *The Modern Temper: American Culture and Society in the 1920s* (New York, 1995), 219–20.

14. Nell Irvin Painter, *Standing at Armageddon: The United States, 1877–1919* (New York, 1987), termed the year 1919 "The Great Unrest." See ibid., chap. 12.

15. Frank, *Purchasing Power*, 244.

16. In some states the districts were called people's utility districts.

17. J. D. Ross's career with City Light and his appointment to head the Bonneville Power Administration are examined in Wesley Arden Dick, "Visions of Abundance: The Public Power Crusade in the Pacific Northwest in the Era of J. D. Ross and the New Deal," (Ph.D. diss., University of Washington, 1973). I wish to thank the anonymous readers of the *Pacific Northwest Quarterly* who commented on an earlier version of the material presented in this chapter. A good general history of Seattle is Richard C. Berner, *Seattle in the 20th Century*, vol. 1, *Seattle, 1900–1920: From Boomtown, Urban Turbulence, to Restoration* and vol. 2, *Seattle, 1921–1940: From Boom to Bust* (Seattle, 1991, 1992).

18. It is beyond the scope of this book to determine Ross's exact degree of importance to City Light and public power in Washington. City Light was already in existence before his employment, although during his tenure as superintendent he oversaw its continued growth and in doing so gained a huge public following and national recognition. After his departure City Light continued to expand, and under his successors the company purchased PSP&L's holdings within Seattle's city limits.

19. *Seattle Star*, December 15, 1915, as quoted in Dick, "Visions of Abundance," 243.

20. *Seattle Sunday Times*, October 20, 1929, *Ross Scrapbooks*, vol. 13 (see Chapter 1, note 81, for a brief discussion of J. D. Ross's scrapbooks).

21. Berner, *Seattle, 1921–1940*, 49.

22. In 1930 nine West Coast cities had populations greater than 100,000. In terms of the percentage of families with at least one radio, Seattle was fifth among the nine cities. Los Angeles, the only other of the nine towns with municipal power, had the greatest percentage of families with at least one radio (58.8 percent), and Spokane had the smallest (47.9 percent). U.S. Department of Commerce, Bureau of the Census, *Fifteenth Census of the United States, 1930, Population, Vol. 6, Families* (Washington, DC, 1933), 10; Table 12, "Families Having Radio Set, in Urban, Rural-Farm, and Rural-Nonfarm Areas, for the United States, 1930," 52; Table 60, "Families Having Radio Set, in Urban, Rural-Farm, and Rural-Nonfarm Areas, by

Divisions and States, 1930," 53; and Table 76, "Families Having Radio Set, by Color and Nativity of Head, for Cities of 100,000 or More," 70. See Appendix 1.1 for a complete listing of the percentages of families with radios in the cities with populations of 100,000 people or more. Without detailed housing stock records, it is difficult to determine which Seattle homes had ranges or radios. It is possible, however, that newer homes, built since the population explosion of the 1910s, were better outfitted to use electrical appliances. Other, older homes in the city may have been wired inadequately to use the new appliances of the 1920s and were not rewired until the New Deal programs made it economically possible.

23. Between 1900 and 1910 Seattle's population increased from 80,671 to 237,194. In 1920, 315,312 people lived in Seattle. U.S. Department of Commerce, Bureau of the Census, *Thirteenth Census of the United States Taken in the Year 1910, Vol. 3, Population* (Washington, DC, 1913), 286, and *Fourteenth Census of the United States Taken in the Year 1920, Vol. 3, Population* (Washington, DC, 1921), 656.

24. A. W. Leonard, "Seattle Finds Efficient Aid in Electricity," *Seattle Post-Intelligencer*, November 6, 1926, *Ross Scrapbooks*, vol. 7. Leonard was PSP&L's president in the 1920s. The history of Seattle City Light is explored in William Sparks, "J. D. Ross and Seattle City Light, 1917–1932" (M.A. thesis, University of Washington, 1964); Wesley Arden Dick, "The Genesis of Seattle City Light" (M.A. thesis, University of Washington, 1965); and Dick, "Visions of Abundance."

25. Robert C. Wing, ed., *A Century of Service: The Puget Power Story* (Seattle, 1987), 44–48.

26. B. C. Forbes, "Romance Lies Behind Stone-Webster Move," *Seattle Post-Intelligencer*, June 28, 1929, *Ross Scrapbooks*, vol. 12.

27. Wing, *A Century of Service*, 24.

28. Fred Vincent, "Why Light and Power Are Cheap in Seattle," *Pearson's Magazine*, August 1916, 109–11, *Ross Scrapbooks*, vol. 16.

29. *Northwest Magazine*, "Seattle City Light Plant Is a Complete Success," April 16, 1913, *Ross Scrapbooks*, vol. 1, and Berner, *Seattle 1900–1920*, 47.

30. *Northwest Magazine*, "Seattle City Light Plant Is a Complete Success," April 16, 1913, *Ross Scrapbooks*, vol.1.

31. *Pacific Builder and Engineer*, April 4, 1914, *Ross Scrapbooks*, vol. 1. Both Dick and Sparks refer to the use of potential electricity to attract new business and industry as "city building." City building is also a theme in Harold L. Platt, *The Electric City: Energy and the Growth of the Chicago Area, 1880–1930* (Chicago, 1991).

32. *San Francisco Examiner*, "Best Lighting Boast in Seattle," July 26, 1917, *Ross Scrapbooks*, vol. 1. Wesley Arden Dick also noted that before public power, electricity cost twenty cents per kilowatt hour in Seattle, and "City Light served as a 'yardstick' and competitive rate regulator from its inception" ("Visions of Abundance," 243). It is important to keep in mind that private rates dropped throughout the period studied. Friends of public power believed that direct competition hastened that decline.

33. This summary of the *Electric World* article is drawn from "Seattle's Light Plant," *Seattle Post-Intelligencer*, August 2, 1912, *Ross Scrapbooks*, vol. 1. The *Seattle Post-Intelligencer* generally opposed public power until 1920, when William Randolph Hearst, who strongly supported public power projects in the 1920s, purchased the paper (see Chapter 3).

34. J. L. Engdahl, "Seattle Breaks Grip of Light Trust and Reaps Big Profit on City Plant," *Milwaukee Leader*, December 5, 1913, *Ross Scrapbooks*, vol. 1.

35. Copies contained in *Ross Scrapbooks*, vol. 1.

36. "Power Charges Too High, Rate Base Is All Wrong, Seattle Expert Aserts," *Walla Walla Union,* April 30, 1924 (Northwest and Whitman College Archives, Penrose Memorial Library, Walla Walla, Washington, microfilm; hereafter Northwest and Whitman College Archives).

37. Dick, "Visions of Abundance," 245, 251.

38. "City Saves Much Money, Says Mayor," *Seattle Union Record,* January 6, 1919, *Ross Scrapbooks,* vol. 2.

39. "City Cutting Its Power Plant Debt," *Seattle Times,* March 23, 1919, and "Order Skagit Work Started," *Seattle Star,* September 6, 1919, *Ross Scrapbooks,* vol. 2. When Ross made this statement, the first Skagit project was not yet on-line and had only acquired the rights to the project in late 1917. He believed that a second project needed to be considered to meet Seattle's growing electrical needs.

40. Robert L. Hill, "Power and Politics in Seattle," *Nation,* March 2, 1932, 254, and Berner, *Seattle, 1900–1920,* 261–62. The *Nation* erroneously published the year as 1918. For more on the Skagit River projects, consult Paul C. Pitzer, *Building the Skagit: A Century of Upper Skagit Valley History, 1870–1950* (Portland, 1978).

41. J. D. Ross, "After Thirty Years," *Public Service Journal,* August 16, 1935, 1 (copy in *Ross Scrapbooks,* vol. 18). Gill was elected in 1910, although he was recalled in 1911 following corruption charges. He successfully ran for mayor in 1914 and survived another recall drive in January 1917. In February 1917 he finished third in the primary election to Ole Hanson, who later won the general election, and James Bradford. Gill had opposed municipal power in his earlier terms, although in 1917 he supported municipal power, as did all three mayoral candidates. In early 1917 Gill, the police chief, and the sheriff were acquitted on charges that they accepted bribes from bootleggers (Berner, *Seattle, 1900–1920,* 231, 234, 249, 324).

42. Berner, *Seattle, 1900–1920,* 261–64.

43. "Hydro-Electric Resources Will Mean Cheaper Power," *Seattle Post-Intelligencer,* August 8, 1920, *Ross Scrapbooks,* vol. 2. The argument evidently was that hydroelectric development could now continue unabated since the Federal Water Power Act had resolved the legal issue involving compensation and length of terms (see Chapter 1).

44. Berner, *Seattle, 1921–1940,* 42.

45. Until the completion of the Cushman Dam plant, northwest of Tacoma, in 1923, the city continually faced the potential problem of power shortages, as did Seattle until the completion of the first Skagit plant in 1924 (ibid., 42).

46. "Attack Power Scheme," *Seattle Star,* August 1, 1922, and "Ross Opposes Leonard Offer of Power Line," *Seattle Post-Intelligencer,* August 2, 1922, *Ross Scrapbooks,* vol. 3.

47. "Proposal of Light Co. Is Turned Down," *Seattle Post-Intelligencer,* August 12, 1922, *Ross Scrapbooks,* vol. 3.

48. Jay Brigham, "Nine Renegade Senators, Democratic Isolationist Senators, and F.D.R." (M.A. thesis, University of Maryland, 1986), 20.

49. "Fight on City Power Selling Tax Opposed," *Seattle Post-Intelligencer,* January 11, 1923, and "Big Interests Attempt to Defeat Power Bill," *Seattle Star,* January 31, 1923, *Ross Scrapbooks,* vol. 3.

50. Berner, *Seattle, 1921–1940,* 67.

51. The *Seattle Star* called Davis's bill "a page in history" that never would have passed because of poor language. See "Power Crisis Due This Week," *Seattle Star,* February 5, 1923, *Ross Scrapbooks,* vol. 3.

52. "City Power Supporters to Demand Initiative," *Seattle Star,* February 15, 1923, *Ross Scrapbooks,* vol. 3, and Wing, *A Century of Service,* 68.

53. "City Light Rate Slash Is Voted by Committee," *Seattle Post-Intelligencer*, April 21, 1923, and "Power Facilities Here Ample, Rates Compare with Lowest," *Seattle Times*, July 12, 1923, *Ross Scrapbooks*, vol. 3.

54. "Launch State Power Fight," *Seattle Star*, June 13, 1923, and "Hold Power for People," *Seattle Post-Intelligencer*, July 25, 1923, *Ross Scrapbooks*, vol. 3.

55. "People Own Utilities," *Seattle Times*, June 28, 1923, *Ross Scrapbooks*, vol. 3.

56. "Skagit Project May Turn Out White Elephant," *Seattle Times*, July 8, 1923, *Ross Scrapbooks*, vol. 3.

57. "Rude Awakening," *Seattle Times*, July 24, 1923, *Ross Scrapbooks*, vol. 3.

58. *Seattle Post-Intelligencer*, January 18, 1924; *Seattle Times*, January 18, 1924; and "Cheap Power—Not Taxes," *Seattle Post-Intelligencer*, January 23, 1924, all in *Ross Scrapbooks*, vol. 4.

59. *Seattle Post-Intelligencer*, May 4, 1924, *Ross Scrapbooks*, vol. 4.

60. The advertisement discussed here appeared in the *Seattle Times*, May 6, 1924, *Ross Scrapbooks*, vol. 5.

61. "Why This Fear?" *Seattle Post-Intelligencer*, May 29, 1924, *Ross Scrapbooks*, vol. 5.

62. "Power Bill for Public Good," *Seattle Post-Intelligencer*, May 31, 1924, *Ross Scrapbooks*, vol. 5.

63. "Rally Gives Demo's Help," *Seattle Post-Intelligencer*, June 15, 1924, *Ross Scrapbooks*, vol. 5.

64. The issue of debt for both the city and PSP&L was an integral part of the public power fight in Seattle. In his two-volume history of Seattle, Berner traces the origins of the debt debate to the city's purchase of PSP&L's streetcar lines in 1919. The city paid PSP&L too much for the overvalued streetcar system, and in subsequent years charges of fraud often surfaced. The debt issue became paramount during the entire public power debate in the city through the 1920s. The city's purchase of the streetcars and the Skagit River project increased its indebtedness considerably. Stone and Webster anticipated that the city would default on its bond obligations, at which time it could regain the rights to the Skagit River. Berner further notes that "to impede the completion" of the Skagit "became a matter of highest priority" for Stone and Webster (*Seattle in the Twentieth Century*, 1:235, 260–70, and 2:50–55).

65. "Labor to Fight for La Follette, Bone Backing Also Pledged, Active State Campaign Planned," *Seattle Post-Intelligencer*, October 21, 1924, and "Bone Flays 'Power Trust' in Debate, Brockett Cites Tax Loss in Argument," *Seattle Post-Intelligencer*, October 20, 1924, *Ross Scrapbooks*, vol. 5.

66. The vote was 217,393 to 139,492. The bill did well in both Seattle and Tacoma, although it fared poorly in rural areas. The Reed bill lost by more than two to one, 208,809 to 99,450 (Berner, *Seattle, 1921–1940*, 72).

67. Dick, "Visions of Abundance," 77.

68. U.S. Senate, *Utility Corporations, Summary Report of the Federal Trade Commission*, 70th Cong., 1st sess., S. Doc. 92, serial 8858, pt. 35, 27, and pt. 81–A, 5–6.

69. "Rate Hearings Scheduled for This Morning," *Walla Walla Union*, August 8, 1925, Northwest and Whitman College Archives. The other towns participating in the suit (the population for those towns incorporated in 1920 is given in parentheses) were: Babton, Benton City, Beverly, Burbank, Dixie, Grandview (1,011), Granger (412), Huntsville, Kahlotus (151), Kiona, Moxee, Naches, Othello (649), Outlook, Pomeroy (1,804), Prescott (559), Prosser (1,697), Richmond, Selah, Sunnyside (1,809), Toppenish (3,120), Union Gap (332), Wallual, Wapato (1,128), White Bluffs, and Zillah; U.S. Department of Commerce, Bureau of the Census,

Fifteenth Census of the United States, 1930, Population, Vol. 1, Number and Distribution of Inhabitants (Washington, DC, 1931), Table 5, "Population of Incorporated Places, 1930 and 1920," 1158–59.

70. "Hearings on Rate Reduction Open Tuesday Morning," *Walla Walla Daily Bulletin,* August 11, 1925, Washington State Library, Olympia, microfilm, (hereafter Washington State Library). The correct date of the paper is probably Monday, August 10, rather than August 11, which was a Tuesday and for which a separate issue appeared.

71. "Calculations Inflated to Force Charges Up Local Board Claims," *Walla Walla Union,* April 20, 1924, *Ross Scrapbooks,* vol. 16.

72. "Power Charges Too High, Rate Base Is All Wrong, Seattle Expert Asserts," and "Cut Announced in Light Rates by Power Firm," *Walla Walla Union,* April 30, 1924, Northwest and Whitman College Archives. Ross later appeared as an expert witness for the plaintiffs.

73. "Fight for Low Rates Goes On," *Walla Walla Union,* May 1, 1924, Northwest and Whitman College Archives.

74. "Hearings on Rate Reduction Open Tuesday Morning," *Walla Walla Daily Bulletin,* August 11, 1925, Washington State Library; "City Scores a Point in First Day of Session of Big Rate Hearing," *Walla Walla Union,* August 12, 1925, Northwest and Whitman College Archives; and "Laing Reveals Defense Program of P-P-L," *Walla Walla Daily Bulletin,* August 19, 1925, Washington State Library.

75. "City Scores a Point in First Day Session of Big Rate Hearing," *Walla Walla Union,* August 12, 1925, Northwest and Whitman College Archives.

76. "City Scores a Point in First Day Session of Big Rate Hearing," "Capital Stock, Bonds in District Far Exceed Value of Local Plants," and "Plants Not Used in Rate Base," *Walla Walla Union,* August 12 and 13, 1925, Northwest and Whitman College Archives.

77. "Watered Stock Revealed at Rate Hearing," *Walla Walla Daily Bulletin,* August 12, 1925, Washington State Library.

78. "Power Case Likely Will End Tonight," *Walla Walla Union,* August 19, 1925, 1; and "Hearing Ends on Valuation of Property," *Walla Walla Union,* August 20, 1925, Northwest and Whitman College Archives.

79. "Million Lopped Off P-P-L Co. Rate Base," *Walla Walla Daily Bulletin,* December 31, 1925, Washington State Library.

80. Berner, *Seattle, 1921–1940,* 77–84.

81. Ibid., 82.

82. Sparks, "J. D. Ross and Seattle City Light," 153–55, and Berner, *Seattle, 1921–1940,* 92–94.

83. Sparks, "J. D. Ross and Seattle City Light," 155–61, 163–67.

84. Ibid., 180–81.

85. Dick, "Visions of Abundance," 262.

86. Ibid., 263.

87. Marion Zioncheck as quoted in Berner, *Seattle, 1921–1940,* 129.

88. "Ross Appeals for Municipal Light Plant," *Colorado Springs Telegraph,* July 18, 1923; and "Ross Report on Power Predicts Cut in Cost," *Colorado Springs Gazette,* July 19, 1923, *Ross Scrapbooks,* vol. 16.

89. "Municipal Ownership Came After 10-Year Campaign by Citizens," *Colorado Springs Sunday Gazette and Telegraph,* October 11, 1925, *Ross Scrapbooks,* vol. 17.

90. T. B. Miller to Frank Edwards, July 27, 1928, box 87, folder 6, Seattle Lighting Department.

91. Walter A. Scott to Frank Edwards, November 30, 1930, box 87, folder 7, Seattle Lighting Department.

92. Lucy Knowles Caldwell to "The Mayor of Seattle," November 18, 1931, box 87, folder 8, Seattle Lighting Department. The article had appeared in *Golden Age Magazine*. The reference to electric ranges again points to the importance of electrical modernization.

93. G. R. Camo to "Mayor of Seattle," January 3, 1933, box 87, folder 10, Seattle Lighting Department.

94. Alvin C. Reis, secretary, Wisconsin Legislative Interim Committee on Water Power, to superintendent, Municipal Water and Light Company, Seattle, October 19, 1928, and copy of the questionnaire with Ross's response, box 102, folder 28, Seattle Lighting Department. Dick also discussed the national stature that Ross had obtained by 1924 and noted that Norris invited Ross to testify during the 1924 Muscle Shoals hearing ("Visions of Abundance," 257). As the previous material indicates, even people in smaller municipalities across the United States were aware of Ross's and City Light's reputation.

95. R. B. Bermann, "Puget Power Plans Battle on City Light," *Seattle Post-Intelligencer*, October 6, 1927, *Ross Scrapbooks*, vol. 9.

96. Bone to Ross, October 7, 1927; and Bone to Ross, October 26, 1927, box 57, folder 32, Seattle Lighting Department.

97. "Survey Shows Utilities in Bad Shape; Who Financed It? Oh, That's a Secret," *Seattle Star*, January 3, 1927, and "League Will Give Findings on Utilities," *Seattle Post-Intelligencer*, January 4, 1927, *Ross Scrapbooks*, vol. 9.

98. "Minutes of Meeting of Public Policy Committee, National Electric Light Association," box 75, folder 16, "NELA," Seattle Lighting Department. R. H. Ballard, president of Southern California Edison, chaired the committee. Martin Insull was among those in attendance. Robert T. Healy, FTC chief counsel, told Ross about the NELA scheme in a letter dated January 3, 1929 (Dick, "Visions of Abundance," 258 n. 54; for a brief discussion of the NELA plan see page 258). The *Seattle Post-Intelligencer* broke the story on April 30, 1928, and used part of the quoted material in its article (*Ross Scrapbooks*, vol. 10). The quote also appears in Wing, *A Century of Struggle*, 87.

99. Scattergood to Ross, June 13, 1928, box 71, folder 15, Seattle Lighting Department. A copy of the Stoess letter of June 6, 1928, and Scattergood's reply to Stoess regarding the original statement are attached to the letter from Scattergood to Ross.

100. Judson King to Ross, December 21, 1928, box 75, folder 19, Seattle Lighting Department.

101. Copy of letter sent from Ross to P. C. Stoess, May 25, 1928, box 100, folder 12, Seattle Lighting Department.

102. City of Seattle, Department of Lighting, "Annual Report, Year Ending December 31, 1928," p. 8, box 124, folder 7, Seattle Lighting Department.

103. Dick, "Visions of Abundance," 258.

104. "Puget Power Aids Quiz of City Light," *Seattle Post-Intelligencer*, January 15, 1928, *Ross Scrapbooks*, vol. 10.

105. Wing, *A Century of Service*, 85.

106. "Monopoly in Electricity Proposed by Councilman," *Seattle Times*, March 17, 1927, and "City Light Would Acquire P.S.P.&L. System," *Seattle Star*, June 10, 1927, *Ross Scrapbooks*, vol. 9.

107. "City Urged to Buy Out Puget Power," *Seattle Post-Intelligencer*, March 23, 1928, *Ross Scrapbooks*, vol. 9.

108. For a brief recap of the Oregon public power fight and the career of one

of its leading proponents, George W. Joseph, see Dick, "Visions of Abundance," 85–92. Following the November 1930 election of public power candidate Julius Meier and the passage of the People's Utility Law (similar to Washington's Grange bill), an article in the *Nation* argued that the success of public power in Oregon in the recent campaign was due to the loss of businesses in the state to either Seattle, Tacoma, or Los Angeles, all of which had public power. The implication is clear that high private rates in Oregon hurt the state when trying to attract new businesses (as discussed in Dick, "Visions of Abundance, 89).

109. The paper reported that Ross received "prolonged applause" ("Brockett and Ross Argue Power Issue," *Seattle Post-Intelligencer*, June 29, 1929, *Ross Scrapbooks*, vol. 12). Before 1934 any discussion of Seattle City Light acquiring Puget Sound Power and Light property was usually limited to possessions within the city and several hydroelectric sites. In 1934 Ross significantly raised the stakes when he proposed that the city buy all of PSP&L. If the purchase had occurred, the city would have owned property stretching from Canada to Oregon and from central Washington to Puget Sound. Ross believed that a thirty-year, $95 million bond could finance the purchase. Little support developed for his proposal, and the following year, when Ross became a member of the Securities and Exchange Commission, the idea became a memory. The question of duplicate systems in Seattle continued until 1951, when City Light finally purchased PSP&L's property in the city (Wing, *A Century of Service*, 85–91).

110. Dick, "Visions of Abundance," 81. In some states PUD stood for people's utility district.

111. *Seattle Times*, January 29, 1929, *Ross Scrapbooks*, vol. 12.

112. Berner, *Seattle, 1921–1940*, 144.

113. *Seattle Times*, January 29, 1929, *Ross Scrapbooks*, vol. 12.

114. *Seattle Star*, January 30, 1929, *Ross Scrapbooks*, vol. 12.

115. Ibid.

116. "Leonard Bans Grange Battle," *Seattle Post-Intelligencer*, October 31, 1929, *Ross Scrapbooks*, vol. 13.

117. Senate, *Utility Corporations*, 70th Cong., 1st sess., S. Doc. 92, pt. 70, serial 8858, 930.

118. Dick, "Visions of Abundance," 81.

119. "Consumers, How Do You Like—To Pay Propaganda Bills?" *Seattle Post-Intelligencer*, March 30, 1929, *Ross Scrapbooks*, vol. 12.

120. Fred J. Chamberlin, "Discusses the District Power Bill," *Grange News*, March 5, 1930, *Ross Scrapbooks*, vol. 14.

121. Wing, *A Century of Service*, 68–69.

122. The ten states that enacted PUD laws between 1927 and 1936 were Alabama, Mississippi, Nevada, South Dakota, Tennessee, Michigan, Oregon (where they were called people's utility districts), Wisconsin, Wyoming, and South Carolina (Organization of Municipal Power Districts, box, 24, folder "Wisconsin Development Authority," Loomis Papers). Also see Robert D. Baum, "Power District Legislation," *National Municipal Review* 26 (1937): 28–29. Governors favoring public power elected or reelected in 1930 included Franklin Roosevelt (D-N.Y.), Gifford Pinchot (R-Pa.), Julius Meier (I-Ore.), and Theodore Bilbo (D-Miss.). The Republican candidate in the 1930 Oregon election was George Joseph, who also favored public power. However, he died before that general election and was replaced by Phil Metchan, who did not endorse Joseph's public power platform. Joseph supporters then urged Meier, a lifelong Republican and public power supporter, to enter the race as an Independent.

CHAPTER 6. LOS ANGELES AND PUBLIC POWER

1. For a concise history of early Spanish interests in the Southwest, see David J. Weber, "The Spanish-Mexican Rim," in Clyde A. Millner II, Carol A. O'Connor, and Martha A. Sandweiss, eds., *The Oxford History of the American West* (New York, 1994), 45–77. During the voyage Cabrillo died, but his chief pilot, Bartolomé Ferrer, continued on as far north as present-day Oregon.

2. Ibid., 67. San Jose was founded in 1777, and what developed into Santa Cruz, in 1797. Also see Andrew Rolle, *Los Angeles: From Pueblo to City of the Future* (San Francisco, 1981), 7–12.

3. Carol A. O'Connor, "A Region of Cities" in Millner, O'Connor, and Sandweiss, *The Oxford History of the American West*, 548.

4. Carey McWilliams, *Southern California: An Island on the Land* (Salt Lake City, 1973), 150.

5. O'Connor, "A Region of Cities," 251.

6. McWilliams, *Southern California*, 14, 118–21. Los Angeles grew tremendously between 1880 and 1950, and part of the expansion in territory occurred as it annexed smaller towns. The growth in population and territory is as follows:

Los Angeles Population and Territorial Growth, 1880–1950

Year	Population	Percent Change	Territory (sq. mi.)	Percent Change
1880	11,183	—	30.3	—
1890	50,395	350.6	30.3	0.0
1900	102,479	103.4	44.4	46.4
1910	319,198	211.5	85.3	92.2
1920	576,673	80.7	363.9	326.8
1930	1,238,048	114.7	441.7	21.4
1940	1,504,277	21.5	450.8	2.1
1950	1,970,358	31.0	453.5	0.6

Source: Los Angeles Department of Water and Power, Public Affairs Division, *Water and Power Facts: A Brief Summary of Important Historical Data and Current Facts Concerning the Municipally Owned Department of Water and Power, City of Los Angeles* (Los Angeles, 1985), 11–18.

7. Kevin Starr, *Material Dreams: Southern California Through the 1920s* (New York, 1990); see especially chap. 4. Mike Davis notes that Los Angeles was "the creature of real-estate capitalism" (*City of Quartz: Excavating the Future in Los Angeles* [New York, 1990], 25).

8. Starr, *Material Dreams*, 85.

9. The *Los Angeles Times* was a leading booster newspaper and vehemently attacked any notions of unionism as did the Los Angeles Chamber of Commerce and the Merchants and Manufacturers Association.

10. Morrow Mayo, *Los Angeles* (New York, 1933), quoted in Davis, *City of Quartz*, 30.

11. McWilliams, *Southern California*, 278–83.

12. For a controversial history of the *Los Angeles Times*, see William Bonelli, *Billion Dollar Blackjack* (Beverly Hills, CA, 1954); for a more recent work consult

Robert Gottlieb and Irene Wolt, *Thinking Big: The Story of the Los Angeles Times, Its Publishers, and Their Influence on Southern California* (New York, 1977).

13. Frederick L. Bird and Frances M. Ryan, *Public Ownership on Trial: A Study of Municipal Light and Power in California* (New York, 1930), 141–48.

14. Despite the conservative nature of Los Angeles, historians have long recognized the existence of a strong progressive reform tradition in California. Hiram Johnson may be the individual most closely associated with California reform during his tenure as governor. Johnson, however, was only one of many California progressives. An excellent overview is William Deverell and Tom Sitton, eds., *California Progressivism Revisited* (Berkeley, CA, 1994). Especially relevant to the examination of Los Angeles is Tom Sitton, "John Randolph Haynes and the Left Wing of California," in *California Progressivism Revisited*, which is drawn from Sitton's larger work, *John Randolph Haynes, California Progressive* (Stanford, CA, 1992). Despite the presence of progressive reform in Southern California on issues related to public power and conservationism, a strong conservative element did exist and manifested itself, in addition to requiring a two-thirds vote on bonds, in the city's strong anti-labor attitude. Starr, in *Material Dreams*, his history of Los Angeles in the 1920s, examines the WASP oligarchy that dominated the city (see chap. 6).

15. The rise of the West in the twentieth century has been the subject of several of Gerald Nash's works; see, for example, *The American West in The Twentieth Century: A Short History of an Urban Oasis* (Albuquerque, 1977); *The American West Transformed: The Impact of the Second World War* (Bloomington, IN, 1985); *World War II and the West: Reshaping the Economy* (Lincoln, NE, 1990); and *Creating the West: Historical Interpretations, 1890–1990* (Albuquerque, 1991).

16. The history of Los Angeles in the 1920s and the role of city boosters in its growth is examined in Starr, *Material Dreams*. Starr's favorable history emphasizes how the city fathers' visions became a reality through a combination of private political power and public money. Although the development of public power in Los Angeles and the city's successful attempts to import water and power are examined herein, it is important to note that San Francisco took similar steps to guarantee its economic future when it secured the rights to Hetch Hetchy's water in Yosemite National Park. For more on Los Angeles also consult Robert Fogelson, *The Fragmented Metropolis: Los Angeles, 1850–1930* (Cambridge, MA, 1967), and Jules Tygiel, *The Great Los Angeles Swindle: Oil, Stocks, and Scandals During the Roaring Twenties* (New York, 1994).

17. Thomas Hughes, *Networks of Power: Electrification in Western Society, 1880–1930* (Baltimore, 1983), 263, 281. The state had eight high-voltage transmission systems. See Chapter 4 for a brief discussion of the technological explanation of municipal power. For a comprehensive history of energy in California, see James C. Williams, *Energy and the Making of Modern California* (Akron, 1997).

18. McWilliams, *Southern California*; the original title was *Southern California Country: An Island on the Land*.

19. Sitton, *John Randolph Haynes*, 120.

20. Some of the major works that discuss the Owens Valley controversy are Mary Austin, *The Ford* (Boston, 1917); McWilliams, *Southern California*; Mayo, *Los Angeles*; Remi Nadeau, *The Water Seekers* (New York, 1960); Vincent Ostrom, *Water and Politics: A Study of Water Policies and Administration in the Development of Los Angeles* (Los Angeles, 1953); Nelson S. Van Valen, "Power and Politics: The Struggle for Municipal Ownership of Electric Utilities in Los Angeles, 1905–1937" (Ph.D. diss., Claremont Graduate School, 1965); Abraham Hoffman, *Vision or Villainy: Origins of the Owens Valley–Los Angeles Water Controversy* (College Station,

TX, 1981); and William Kahrl, *Water and Power: The Conflict over Los Angeles' Water Supply in the Owens Valley* (Berkeley, CA, 1982). Kahrl's work contains an excellent bibliography. For works that examine the importance of water in California and the entire West (including Southern California), consult Donald Worster, *Rivers of Empire: Water, Aridity, and the Growth of the American West* (New York, 1985); Marc Reisner, *Cadillac Desert: The American West and Its Disappearing Water* (New York, 1986); John Walton, *Western Times and Water Wars: State, Culture, and Rebellion in California* (Berkeley, CA, 1992); Donald J. Pisani, *From Family Farm to Agribusiness: Crusade in California and the West, 1850–1931* (Berkeley, CA, 1984), and *To Reclaim a Divided West: Water, Law, and Public Policy, 1848–1902* (Albuquerque, 1992); and Norris Hundley Jr., *The Great Thirst: Californians and Water, 1770s–1990s* (Berkeley, CA, 1992). For an analysis of the conspiracy theory see Hoffman, chap. 7.

21. Nelson S. Van Valen, "A Neglected Aspect of the Owens River Aqueduct Story: The Inception of the Los Angeles Municipal Electric System," *Southern California Quarterly* 59 (1977): 88. This article is based in part on Van Valen's doctoral dissertation, "Power Politics."

22. *Los Angeles Times*, August 6, 1905, as quoted in Van Valen, "A Neglected Aspect of the Owens River Aqueduct Story," 87–88, and Hoffman, *Vision or Villainy*, 145. Hoffman also argues that "people could envision the aqueduct project as an idea in tune with the progressive spirit of the times" (145). The *Times* supported the construction of the aqueduct for both water and power purposes. The paper's conservative editor, Otis Chandler, strongly opposed the establishment of the municipally owned generating system, and the *Times* threw its considerable weight against the numerous ballot measures required to build and expand the municipal power distribution system in Los Angeles. Chandler and other opponents of the project believed that the power generated should be sold to private companies for distribution.

23. Los Angeles Board of Water Commissioners, "Fourth Annual Report," 6, as quoted in Van Valen, "A Neglected Aspect of the Owens River Aqueduct Story," 88–89.

24. Quoted from Van Valen, "A Neglected Aspect of the Owens River Aqueduct Story," 92.

25. Kahrl, *Water and Power*, 136–44.

26. Roosevelt to Hitchcock, June 25, 1906, reprinted in Elting E. Morison, ed., *The Letters of Theodore Roosevelt* (Cambridge, MA: Harvard University Press, 1952), 5: 315–16, as quoted in Kahrl, *Water and Power*, 140.

27. Van Valen, "Power Politics," 26, 46, 50.

28. Sitton, *John Randolph Haynes*, 120.

29. Van Valen, "Power Politics," 62. Sitton also cites Van Valen on this and many of the other ballot measures.

30. Ibid., 50–51.

31. Van Valen, "A Neglected Aspect of the Owens River Aqueduct Story," 100–103.

32. Sitton, *John Randolph Haynes*, 51–52; Sitton cites Fogelson, *The Fragmented Metropolis*, 229–30. Starr notes that the aqueduct's progressive nature of using a resource to serve the greatest number of people strengthened the city's case, something that "the most energetic of the ever-energetic Progressives, President Theodore Roosevelt," deeply believed (*Material Dreams*, 55). He examines the building of the aqueduct in chap. 3 of *Material Dreams*.

33. Van Valen, "Power Politics," 14–15, and "Southern California Edison Company of Los Angeles, U.S.A., and Its Gigantic Electric Construction Project,

Plans of Financing, and Its Organization as of May 1st, 1924," Stock Sales Bulletins no. 2, Literature, Reports, 1924, SCE. The Los Angeles Gas and Electric Corporation was a subsidiary of the Pacific Lighting Company of San Francisco.

34. Boyle Workman, *The City That Grew* (Los Angeles, 1935), 331–33.

35. Sitton, *John Randolph Haynes*, 51–54. Haynes and the *Examiner* supported organized labor in the city. The staunchly conservative *Times* opposed labor and pejoratively referred to Haynes and Hearst as "doc" and "willie" (ibid., 55).

36. *Los Angeles Times*, April 16, 1914, as quoted in Van Valen, "Power Politics," 102–3.

37. Van Valen, "Power Politics," 106.

38. Workman, *The City That Grew*, 334. Workman was a banker by profession and also served on the city's public service commission in 1916 and 1917 (*The National Cyclopedia of American Biography* [New York, 1944], 31: 407–8).

39. Bird and Ryan, *Public Ownership on Trial*, 109.

40. Hughes, *Networks of Power*, 281.

41. Letter that A. N. Kemp wrote, November 1, 1917, Stock Sales Bulletins, Literature, Reports, 1917, SCE. This letter and others of a similar nature are discussed in greater detail in Chapter 2.

42. Committee on Municipal Ownership of the City Club of Los Angeles, "Report on Government Ownership of Public Utility Service Undertakings" (Los Angeles, 1917), 1–8.

43. Ostrom, *Water and Politics*, 60–61.

44. Sitton, *John Randolph Haynes*, 170–71.

45. George P. Clements, "Parceling Out the Colorado River," *Southern California Business*, January 1923, 13. Clements served as the manager of the Chamber of Commerce's agricultural department.

46. Ibid., 23.

47. Ibid., "Southern California Leads in Farm Electrification," November 1928, 27, 45.

48. Ibid., June 1927, 8.

49. Ibid., May 1928, 48.

50. John Lewis Brock, "Ten Minutes at the Boulder Dam Site," ibid., October 1925, 15.

51. Lucius K. Chase, "The C. of C. Plan for Colorado River," ibid., November 1925, 13. See also "The Chamber's Stand on Colorado River Project," ibid., February 1928. A high dam would not have been necessary for only flood control or irrigation.

52. Burdett Moody, "Industries Make Huge Power Demand," ibid., January 1925, 9–10. Burdett was a business agent for the Los Angeles Bureau of Power and Light. Other articles in *Southern California Business* stressing the importance of power for industrial growth include Edgar Lloyd Hampton, "Cheap Power as a City Developer," May 1923, and "Water and Power Attract Industries," March 1925.

53. R. H. Ballard, "Getting Ahead of Power Needs," ibid., February 1925, 22, 38.

54. Advertisements of this nature appeared in ibid., April 1927, 8, and June 1927, 8.

55. Ibid., March and September 1926; both advertisements appeared inside the back cover. Other advertisements of this type appeared in the August and December 1926 issues of the magazine.

56. "Telling the Story About Industrial Los Angeles," ibid., July 1927, 26–27.

57. See Chapter 3 for a complete discussion of this issue.

58. Van Valen, "Power Politics," 245, and Ostrom, *Water and Politics*, 66.

59. Van Valen, "Power Politics," 254, and Ostrom, *Water and Politics*, 67. The actual vote was 117,035 to 14,436.

60. Ostrom, *Water and Politics*, 67. Federal approval of the Colorado River Compact became part of the Swing-Johnson legislation when it passed Congress in 1928.

61. Ibid., 66–67.

62. *Los Angeles Examiner*, August 26, 1921, quoted in Ostrom, *Water and Politics*, 65.

63. Ostrom, *Water and Politics*, 65.

64. See Chapter 2 for a more complete analysis of SCE stock holdings in the 1920s.

65. Circular letter no. 164, August 20, 1917, Stock Sales Bulletins, Literature, Reports, 1917, SCE.

66. "Report of Committee on Sale of Company Securities to Customers and Resident Citizens" (New York City, 1920); copy contained in Stock Sales Bulletins, Literature, Reports, 1920, SCE. The convention was held in Pasadena; F. L. Greenhouse and A. N. Kemp were two of the five members of the committee that wrote the report.

67. This information is drawn from the minutes of a meeting of SCE stock salespeople held November 5, 1921. A copy of the minutes entitled "Stock Salesmen Meeting Held in Assembly, Edison Building on November 5, 1921" is in Stock Sales Bulletins, Literature, Reports, 1921, SCE.

68. Letter from W. L. Frost, general commercial manager, SCE, to department heads, May 11, 1925, in Stock Sales Bulletins, Literature, Reports, 1925, SCE.

69. Edison stock questionnaire, February 6, 1926, question 20; copy contained in Stock Sales Bulletins, Literature, Reports, 1926, SCE.

70. Van Valen, "Power Politics," 317–18. It is not clear where Van Valen obtained information about SCE stock ownership distribution. A Los Angeles Lawyers Club "Report," page 19, provided the information about the number of voters in Los Angeles.

71. *Southern California Business*, June 1927, 8.

72. Van Valen, "Power Politics," 292. The passage of the Federal Water Power Act removed many of the problems that had existed in securing land on which to build the Owens Valley Aqueduct. In order to build the aqueduct Los Angeles purchased land extending from the city into the eastern Sierras. The city still retains ownership of this land. In the case of the Boulder Dam transmission lines, the city only had to secure right-of-way privileges but did not actually purchase land.

73. Ostrom, *Water and Politics*, 71, and Van Valen, "Power Politics," 343–44.

74. Van Valen, "Power Politics," 269, 275.

75. Ostrom, *Water and Politics*, 71–72. Ostrom notes in his discussion of the suit that under the 1911 franchise agreement the company could only sell power for lighting, not heat or power. An injunction would be filed preventing the company from using "public streets and rights of way unless a new franchise was secured."

76. Ostrom, *Water and Politics*, 72.

77. Van Valen, "Power Politics," 367. The most recent agreement had been signed in 1932 (ibid., 342).

78. Starr, *Material Dreams*, 157.

CHAPTER 7. POLITICS, ELECTRICITY, AND THE NEW DEAL

1. Preston Hubbard, *Origins of the TVA: The Muscle Shoals Controversy, 1920–1932* (New York, 1968), 300–315; for King's pamphlet see box 232, folder "Judson King," Norris Papers; for Norris's view on the Muscle Shoals legislation in 1932, see Norris to Congressman Ralph Horr, June 27, 1932, box 225, folder "S.J. 15, 72nd Congress and S.J. 49, 71st Congress," Norris Papers; and John P. Robertson to Harvey McMillion, November 22, 1932, box 3, folder "1932 Campaign," Norris Papers. Also see Harold L. Platt, *The Electric City: Energy and the Growth of the Chicago Area, 1880–1930* (Chicago, 1991), especially chap. 10, for more on Insull's fall from power and the national importance of electricity in 1930.

2. For example, see V. O. Key Jr., "A Theory of Critical Elections;" *Journal of Politics* 17 (1955): 3–18; and Walter Dean Burnham, "The Changing Shape of the American Political Universe," *American Political Science Review* 59 (1965): 7–28, and *Critical Elections and the Mainsprings of American Politics* (New York, 1970). Allan J. Lichtman presents an opposing view in "Critical Election Theory and the Reality of American Presidential Politics, 1916–1940," *American Historical Review* 81 (1976): 317–51. For an overview of realignment literature, see Richard L. McCormick, "The Realignment Synthesis in American History," reprinted in *The Party Period and Public Policy: American Politics from the Age of Jackson to the Progressive Era* (New York, 1986).

3. When TVA passed by a vote of 63 to 20 in the spring of 1933, 46 of 67 veteran senators voted for the legislation (73.0 percent of all yea votes) as did all 17 recently sworn-in senators. In the House, of the 306 yea votes cast, 172 came from veteran representatives (56.2 percent), against 92 total nay votes. When the House passed the TVA conference report, 142 out of 258 yea votes came from nonfreshman congressmen (55.0 percent), against 112 nay votes. In each instance, the number of votes from veteran legislators was enough to pass the legislation. See Jay Brigham, "New Deal–Old Deal: Old Representatives and Senators in the New Deal," unpublished paper delivered at the American Society for Environmental History Meeting, March 1997.

Bibliography

MANUSCRIPT COLLECTIONS

Black, Hugo. Papers. Library of Congress.
Borah, William. Papers. Library of Congress.
Connally, Tom. Papers. Library of Congress.
Ely, Richard T. Papers. State Historical Society of Wisconsin, Madison.
Glaeser, Martin G. Papers. University of Wisconsin Archives, Madison.
Institute for Research in Land Economics and Public Utilities. Papers. State Historical Society of Wisconsin, Madison.
La Follette Family Collection. Library of Congress.
Loomis, O. S. Papers. State Historical Society of Wisconsin, Madison.
McNary, Charles. Papers. Library of Congress.
Norris, George. Papers. Library of Congress.
Pinchot, Gifford. Papers. Library of Congress.
Scott, Walter Dill. Papers. Northwestern University Archives, Evanston, Illinois.
Seattle Lighting Department. Records. University of Washington, Seattle.
Southern California Edison. Records. El Monte, California.

GOVERNMENT DOCUMENTS

Butler, Anne E., and Wendy Wolff. *United States Senate: Election, Expulsion, and Censure Cases, 1793–1990.* Washington, DC: Government Printing Officed, 1995.
Biographical Directory of the United States Congress, 1774–1989, Bicentennial Edition. Washington, DC: Government Printing Office, 1989.
The Colorado River Commission of the State of California. *Colorado River and the Boulder Canyon Project.* Sacramento: California State Publishing Office, 1931.
Congressional Record. 59th Cong., 1st sess., 1906, vol. 40; 63d Cong., 3rd sess., 1916, vol. 52; 64th Cong., 1st sess., 1916, vol. 53; and 69th Cong., 1st sess., 1926, vol. 67–72nd Cong., 2d sess., 1933, vol. 76.
Kearney, George, ed. *Official Opinions of the Attorney General of the United States Advising the President and Heads of Departments in Relation to Their Official Duties.* Vol. 34. Washington, DC: Government Printing Office, 1926.
La Rue, Eugene Clyde. *Colorado River and Its Utilization.* Washington, DC: Government Printing Office, 1916.
Los Angeles Department of Water and Power, Public Affairs Division. *Water and Power Facts: A Brief Summary of Important Historical Data and Current Facts Concerning the Municipally Owned Department of Water and Power, City of Los Angeles.* Los Angeles: Department of Water and Power, 1985.
The Statutes at Large of the United States of America. Vols. 34 and 41. Washington, DC: Government Printing Office, 1907 and 1921.
United States Congress, 67th Congress, 1st session, through 72nd Congress, 2nd session, Official Congressional Directory. Washington, DC: Government Printing Office, 1921–1933.

U.S. Congress. House. *Hearings Before the Committee on Water Power of the House of Representatives.* 65th Cong., 2d sess., 1918.

U.S. Congress. Senate. *Electric Power Development in the United States.* 64th Cong., 1st sess., 1916, S. Doc. 316. Serial 6918–20.

————. *Electric-Power Industry, Control of Power Companies.* 69th Cong., 2d sess., 1927. S. Doc. 213. Serial 8703.

————. *Hearings on the Development and Control of Water Power, Before the National Waterways Commission.* 62d Cong., 2d sess., 1911. S. Doc. 274. Serial 6174.

————. *Utility Corporations, Summary Report of the Federal Trade Commission.* 70th Cong., 1st sess., 1928. S. Doc. 92, pts. 15, 35, 66, 70, 71A, 81A, and 84D. Serial 8858.

U.S. Department of Commerce. Bureau of the Census. *Census of Electrical Industries, 1922, Central Electric Light and Power Stations.* Washington, DC: Government Printing Office, 1925.

————. *Census of Electrical Industries, 1927, Central Electric Light and Power Stations.* Washington, DC: Government Printing Office, 1930.

————. *Census of Electrical Industries, 1932, Central Electric Light and Power Stations.* Washington, DC: Government Printing Office, 1934.

————. *Twelfth Census of the United States Taken in the Year 1900, Vol. 1, Population.* Washington, DC: Government Printing Office, 1901.

————. *Thirteenth Census of the United States Taken in the Year 1910, Vol. 3, Population.* Washington, DC: Government Printing Office, 1913.

————. *Fourteenth Census of the United States Taken in the Year 1920, Vol. 1, Population, 1920, Number and Distribution of Inhabitants.* Washington, DC: Government Printing Office, 1921.

————. *Fifteenth Census of the United States, 1930, Agriculture, Vol. 2, Part 1, the Northern States.* Washington, DC: Government Printing Office, 1932.

————. *Fifteenth Census of the United States, 1930, Agriculture, Vol. 2, Part 2, the Southern States.* Washington, DC: Government Printing Office, 1932.

————. *Fifteenth Census of the United States, 1930, Vol. 1, Number and Distribution of Inhabitants.* Washington, DC: Government Printing Office, 1931.

————. *Fifteenth Census of the United States, 1930, Population, Vol. 6, Families.* Washington, DC: Government Printing Office, 1933

————. *Sixteenth Census of the United States, 1940, Population, Second Series, Characteristics of the Population, United States Summary.* Washington, DC: Government Printing Office, 1943.

————. Special Reports. *Central Electric Light and Power Stations, 1907.* Washington, DC: Government Printing Office, 1910.

U.S. Federal Emergency Administration of Public Works. *Municipally Owned Electric Utilities in the United States, 1934.* Washington, DC: Government Printing Office, 1934.

U.S. Federal Trade Commission. *Annual Report,* 1927–1934. Washington, DC: Government Printing Office, 1927–1935.

U.S. Public Works Administration. *Municipally Owned Electric Utilities in the United States.* Washington, DC: Government Printing Office, 1934.

BOOKS

Ashby, LeRoy. *The Spearless Leader: Senator Borah and the Progressive Movement in the 1920s.* Urbana: University of Illinois Press, 1972.

Austin, Mary. *The Ford.* Boston: Houghton Mifflin, 1917.

Belgen, Theodore C. *Minnesota: A History of the State*. Minneapolis: University of Minnesota Press, 1963.

Berner, Richard C. *Seattle in the 20th Century*. Vol. 1, *Seattle, 1900–1920: From Boomtown, Urban Turbulence, to Restoration*. Vol. 2, *Seattle, 1921–1940: From Boom to Bust*. Seattle: Charles Press, 1991, 1992.

Bernstein, Michael. *The Great Depression and Delayed Recovery and Economic Change in America, 1929–1939*. New York: Cambridge University Press, 1987.

Bird, Frederick L., and Frances M. Ryan. *Public Ownership on Trial: A Study of Municipal Light and Power in California*. New York: New Republic, 1930.

Bonbright, James C. *Public Utilities and the National Power Policies*. New York: Columbia University Press, 1940.

Bonbright, James C., and Gardiner Means. *The Holding Company: Its Public Significance and Its Regulation*. New York: McGraw-Hill, 1932.

Bonelli, William. *Billion Dollar Blackjack*. Beverly Hills, CA: Civic Research Press, 1954.

Brown, D. Clayton. *Electricity for Rural America: The Fight for the REA*. Westport, CT: Greenwood Press, 1980.

Burnham, Walter Dean. *Critical Elections and the Mainsprings of American Politics*. New York: Norton, 1970.

Caro, Robert A. *The Years of Lyndon Johnson: The Path to Power*. New York: Vintage Books, 1981.

Chambers, Clarke A. *Seedtime of Reform: American Social Service and Social Action, 1918–1933*. Minneapolis: University of Minnesota Press, 1963.

Chandler, Alfred. *The Visible Hand: The Managerial Revolution in American Business*. Cambridge, MA: Harvard University Press, 1977.

Chrislock, Carl H. *The Progressive Era in Minnesota, 1899–1918*. St. Paul: Minnesota Historical Society, 1971.

City Club of Los Angeles, Committee on Municipal Ownership. *Report on Government Ownership of Public Utility Service Undertakings*. Los Angeles: City Club of Los Angeles, 1917.

Cohen, Lizabeth. *Making a New Deal: Industrial Workers in Chicago, 1919–1939*. New York: Cambridge University Press, 1990.

Conkin, Paul. *The New Deal*. Arlington Heights, IL: AHM Publishing, 1967.

Cronon, William. *Nature's Metropolis: Chicago and the Great West*. New York: Norton, 1991.

Davis, Mike. *City of Quartz: Excavating the Future in Los Angeles*. New York: Vintage Books, 1990.

Dawley, Alan. *Struggles for Justice: Social Responsibility and the Liberal State*. Cambridge, MA: Harvard University Press, 1991.

Deverell, William, and Tom Sitton, eds. *California Progressivism Revisited*. Berkeley: University of California Press, 1994.

Dierdorff, John. *How Edison's Lamp Helped Light the West: The Story of Pacific Power and Light Company and Its Pioneer Forebears*. Portland: Pacific Power and Light, 1971.

Dodds, Gordon B. *The American Northwest: A History of Oregon and Washington*. Arlington Heights, IL: Forum Press, 1986.

Dorau, Herbert B. *The Changing Character and Extent of Municipal Ownership in the Electric Light and Power Industry*. Chicago: Institute for Research in Land Economics and Public Utilities, 1930.

———. *Materials for the Study of Public Utility Economics*. New York: Macmillian, 1930.

Dumenil, Lynn. *The Modern Temper: American Culture and Society in the 1920s*. New York: Hill and Wang, 1995.

Eagle, Charles W. *Democracy Delayed: Congressional Reapportionment and Urban-Rural Conflict in the 1920s*. Athens: University of Georgia Press, 1990.

Ely, Richard T. *Ground Under Our Feet*. New York: Macmillian, 1938.

Fairbanks, Carol, and Bergine Haakenson. *Writings of Farm Women: An Anthology*. New York: Garland Publishing, 1990.

Federal Writers Project of the Works Progress Administration. *Minnesota: A State Guide*. 1938. Reprint, New York: Hastings House, 1978.

Feinman, Ronald L. *Twilight of Progressivism: The Western Republican Senators and the New Deal*. Baltimore: Johns Hopkins University Press, 1981.

Fischer, Claude. *America Calling: A Social History of the Telephone to 1940*. Berkeley: University of California Press, 1992.

Fite, Gilbert C. *George N. Peek and the Fight for Farm Parity*. Norman: University of Oklahoma Press, 1954.

Fitzgerald, F. Scott. *The Great Gatsby*. 1915. Reprint, New York: Scribner's, 1980.

Fogelson, Robert. *The Fragmented Metropolis: Los Angeles, 1850–1930*. Cambridge, MA: Harvard University Press, 1967.

Forbath, William E. *Law and the Shaping of the American Labor Movement*. Cambridge, MA: Harvard University Press, 1991.

Frank, Dana. *Purchasing Power: Consumer Organizing, Gender, and the Seattle Labor Movement, 1919–1929*. New York: Oxford University Press, 1994.

Freidel, Frank. *Franklin D. Roosevelt: A Rendezvous with Destiny*. Boston: Little, Brown, 1990.

Galbraith, John Kenneth. *The Great Crash*. 1954. Reprint, Boston: Houghton Mifflin, 1988.

Glaeser, Martin G. *Outlines of Public Utility Economics*. New York: Macmillan, 1927.

———. *Public Utilities in American Capitalism*. New York: Macmillan, 1957.

Gottlieb, Robert, and Irene Wolt. *Thinking Big: The Story of the Los Angeles Times, Its Publishers, and Their Influence on Southern California*. New York: Putnam, 1977.

Graham, Otis. *An Encore for Reform: The Old Progressives and the New Deal*. New York: Oxford University Press, 1967.

Gruening, Ernest. *Many Battles: The Autobiography of Ernest Gruening*. New York: Liveright, 1973.

———. *The Public Pays: A Study of Power Propaganda*. 1931. Reprint, New York: Vanguard Press, 1964.

Hamilton, David E. *From New Day to New Deal: American Farm Policy from Hoover to Roosevelt, 1928–1933*. Chapel Hill: University of North Carolina Press, 1991.

Hansen, John Mark. *Gaining Access: Congress and the Farm Lobby, 1919–1981*. Chicago: University of Chicago Press, 1991.

Hawley, Ellis. *The Great War and the Search for a Modern Order: A History of the American People and Their Institutions, 1917–1933*. New York: St. Martin's Press, 1979.

Hays, Samuel P. *Conservation and the Gospel of Efficiency: The Progressive Conservation Movement, 1890–1920*. 1959. Reprint, Cambridge, MA: Harvard University Press, 1969.

———. *Response to Industrialization*. Chicago: University of Chicago Press, 1957.

Hirsh, Richard F. *Technology and Transformation in the American Electric Utility Industry*. New York: Cambridge University Press, 1989.

Hoffman, Abraham. *Vision or Villainy: Origins of the Owens Valley–Los Angeles Water Controversy*. College Station: Texas A&M Press, 1981.

Hofstadter, Richard. *The Age of Reform: From Bryan to F.D.R.* New York: Vintage Books, 1955.

———. *The American Political Tradition and the Men Who Made It.* 1948. Reprint, New York: Vintage Books, 1973.

Hubbard, Preston. *Origins of the TVA: The Muscle Shoals Controversy, 1920–1932.* 1961. Reprint, New York: Norton, 1968.

Hughes, Thomas. *Networks of Power: Electrification in Western Society, 1880–1930.* Baltimore: Johns Hopkins University Press, 1983.

Hundley, Norris, Jr. *The Great Thirst: Californians and Water, 1770s–1990s.* Berkeley: University of California Press, 1992.

———. *Water and the West: The Colorado River Compact and the Politics of Water in the American West.* Berkeley: University of California Press, 1975.

Jorgensen, Emil Oliver. *False Education in Our Colleges and Universities.* Chicago: Manufacturers and Merchants Federal Tax League, 1925.

Kahrl, William. *Water and Power: The Conflict over Los Angeles' Water Supply in the Owens Valley.* Berkeley: University of California Press, 1982.

Kasson, John F. *Amusing the Million: Coney Island at the Turn of the Century.* New York: Hill and Wang, 1978.

Keller, Morton. *Regulating a New Economy: Public Policy and Economic Change in America, 1900–1933.* Cambridge, MA: Harvard University Press, 1990.

Kelley, Robert, *The Shaping of the American Past.* Englewood Cliffs, NJ: Prentice-Hall, 1986.

Kerwin, Jerome G. *Federal Water-Power Legislation.* 1926. Reprint, New York: Ames Press, 1968.

Kleinsorge, Paul Lincoln. *The Boulder Canyon Project: Historical and Economic Aspects.* Stanford, CA: Stanford University Press, 1941.

Kolko, Gabriel. *The Triumph of Conservatism.* New York: Free Press, 1963.

Kramer, Dale. *The Wild Jackasses: The American Farmer in Revolt.* New York: Hastings House, 1956.

Lee, Kai N., and Donna Lee Klemka. *Power and the Future of the Pacific Northwest.* Seattle: University of Washington Press, 1980.

Leuchtenburg, William. *Franklin D. Roosevelt and the New Deal.* New York: Harper and Row, 1963.

———. *The Perils of Prosperity, 1914–1932.* Chicago: University of Chicago Press, 1958.

Levins, Jack. *Power Ethics.* New York: Alfred Knopf, 1931.

Link, Arthur S., and William B. Catton. *American Epoch: A History of the United States Since the 1890s.* 3 vols. New York: Alfred Knopf, 1967.

Link, Arthur S., and Richard L McCormick. *Progressivism.* Arlington Heights, IL: Harlan Davidson, 1983.

Lowitt, Richard. *George W. Norris: The Persistence of a Progressive, 1913–1933.* Urbana: University of Illinois Press, 1971.

MacKay, Kenneth Campbell. *The Progressive Movement of 1924.* New York: Octagon Books, 1966.

MacMahon, Edna C. *Municipal Electric Plant Managers, Their Selection, Training, Salaries and Tenure, with a List of Municipally Owned Plants in the United States.* Chicago: Public Service Administration, 1934.

Malott, Orth E. *Forces Affecting Municipally Owned Electric Plants in Wisconsin.* Chicago: Institute for Research in Land Economics and Public Utilities, 1930.

Martis, Kenneth C. *The Historical Atlas of Political Parties in the United States Congress, 1789–1989.* New York: Macmillian, 1989.

————. *The Historical Atlas of United States Congressional Districts, 1789–1983*. New York: Free Press, 1982.

Mayo, Morrow. *Los Angeles*. New York: Alfred Knopf, 1933.

McCormick, Richard L. *The Party Period and Public Policy: American Politics from the Age of Jackson to the Progressive Era*. New York: Oxford University Press, 1986.

McDonald, Forrest. *Insull*. Chicago: University of Chicago Press, 1962.

McGeary, M. Nelson. *Gifford Pinchot, Forester-Politician*. Princeton: Princeton University Press, 1960.

McWilliams, Carey. *Southern California: An Island on the Land*. 1946. Reprint, Salt Lake City: Peregrine, 1973.

Meyers, William A. *Iron Men and Copper Wires: A Centennial History of the Southern California Edison Company*. Corona Del Mar, CA.: Trans-Anglo Books, 1983.

Millner, Clyde A., II, Carol A. O'Connor, and Martha A. Sandweiss. eds. *The Oxford History of the American West*. New York: Oxford University Press, 1994.

Montgomery, David. *The Fall of the House of Labor: The Workplace, the State, and American Labor Activism, 1865–1925*. New York: Cambridge University Press, 1987.

Nadeau, Remi. *The Water Seekers*. New York: Doubleday, 1960.

Nash, Gerald. *The American West in the Twentieth Century: A Short History of An Urban Oasis*. Albuquerque: University of New Mexico, 1977.

————. *The American West Transformed: The Impact of the Second World War*. Bloomington: Indiana University Press, 1985.

————. *Creating the West: Historical Interpretations, 1890–1990*. Albuquerque: University of New Mexico Press, 1991.

————. *World War II and the West: Reshaping the Economy*. Lincoln: University of Nebraska Press, 1990.

Nash, Roderick. *The Nervous Generation: American Thought, 1917–1930*. 1970. Reprint, Chicago: Ivan R. Dee, 1990.

The National Cyclopedia of American Biography. Vol 31. New York: James T. White, 1944.

Neal, Steve. *McNary of Oregon: A Political Biography*. Portland: Western Imprints, 1985.

Noble, David F. *America by Design: Science, Technology, and the Rise of Corporate Capitalism*. New York: Oxford University Press, 1977.

Norris, George. *Fighting Liberal: The Autobiography of George W. Norris*. 1945. Reprint, New York: Collier Books, 1961.

Nye, David E. *Electrifying America: Social Meaning of a New Technology*. Cambridge, MA: MIT Press, 1990.

O'Neill, Eugene O. "Dynamo." In *The Plays of Eugene O'Neill*. New York: Scribner's, 1935.

Ostrom, Vincent. *Water and Politics: A Study of Water Policies and Administration in the Development of Los Angeles*. Los Angeles: Haynes Foundation, 1953.

Painter, Nell Irvin. *Standing at Armageddon: The United States, 1877–1919*. New York: Norton, 1987.

Pattison, Mary. *Principle of Domestic Engineering*. New York: Trow Press, 1915.

Pisani, Donald J. *From Family Farm to Agribusiness: Crusade in California and the West, 1850–1931*. Berkeley: University of California Press, 1984.

————. *To Reclaim a Divided West: Water, Law, and Public Policy, 1848–1902*. Albuquerque: University of New Mexico Press, 1992.

Pitzer, Paul C. *Building the Skagit: A Century of Upper Skagit Valley History, 1870–1950*. Portland: Galley Press, 1978.

Platt, Harold L. *The Electric City: Energy and the Growth of the Chicago Area, 1880–1930.* Chicago: University of Chicago Press, 1991.

Powell, Bolling R., Jr. *Compilation and Analysis of Congressional Debates on the Right of the Federal Government to Operate Power Projects and on Related Subjects.* St. Louis: St. Louis Publishing, 1935.

The Public Ownership League of America. *Public Ownership: A Brief History of the Public Ownership League and What It Has Done to Protect and Promote Municipal and Public Utilities and National Resources.* Chicago: Public Ownership League of America, 1929.

Rader, Benjamin G. *The Academic Mind and Reform: The Influence of Richard T. Ely in American Life.* Lexington: University Press of Kentucky, 1966.

Ramsey, M. L. *Pyramids of Power: The Story of Roosevelt, Insull, and the Utility Wars.* 1937. Reprint, New York: Da Capo Press, 1975.

Raushenbush, H. S. *High Power Propaganda.* New York: New Republic, 1929.

Raushenbush, H. S., and Harry W. Laider. *Power Control.* New York: New Republic, 1928.

Raver, Paul Jerome. *Recent Technological Developments and the Municipally Owned Power Plant.* Chicago: Institute for Economic Research, 1932.

Raver, Paul Jerome, and Marion R. Sumner. *Municipally Owned Electric Utilities in Nebraska.* Chicago: Institute for Economic Research, 1932.

Ready, L. S., and H. G. Butler, eds. *Report to the Committee of Fifteen of the Los Angeles Chamber of Commerce on Certain Phases of the Power Situation in Los Angeles and Southern California.* San Francisco: n.p., 1925.

Reisner, Marc. *Cadillac Desert: The American West and Its Disappearing Water.* New York: Penguin, 1986.

Robbins, William. *Colony and Empire: The Capitalist Transformation of the American West.* Lawrence: University Press of Kansas, 1994.

Rolle, Andrew. *Los Angeles: From Pueblo to City of the Future.* San Francisco: Boyd and Fraser, 1981.

Roosevelt, Theodore. *Theodore Roosevelt: An Autobiography.* 1913. Reprint, New York: Scribner's and Sons, 1926.

Rose, Mark H. *Cities of Light and Heat: Domesticating Gas and Electricity in Urban America.* University Park: Pennsylvania State University Press, 1995.

Rosenman, Samuel, ed. *The Public Papers and Addresses of Franklin D. Roosevelt.* 13 vols. New York: Random House, 1938–1950.

Rudolph, Richard, and Scott Ridley. *Power Struggle: The Hundred-Year War over Electricity.* New York: Harper and Row, 1986.

Ruggles, C. O. *Public Utilities: A Survey of the Extent of Instruction in the Field of Public Utilities in Colleges and Universities; the Industry's Demand for College Graduates; the Character of the Opportunities in the Industry Open to College Men; and the Willingness and Ability of the Utilities to Cooperate with Colleges and Universities in the Training of Men for the Industry and in the Study of Public Utility Problems.* New York: National Electric Light Association, 1929.

Saloutos, Theodore, and John D. Hicks. *Twentieth-Century Populism in the Middle West, 1900–1939.* Lincoln: University of Nebraska Press, 1964.

Scattergood, E. F. *The Boulder Dam Project.* Los Angeles: Department of Water and Power, 1935.

Schacht, John, ed. *Three Progressives from Iowa: Gilbert Haugen, Herbert C. Hoover, Henry A. Wallace.* Iowa City: University of Iowa Press, 1980.

Schap, David. *Municipal Ownership in the Electric Utility Industry: A Centennial View.* New York: Praeger, 1986.

Schlesinger, Arthur S., Jr. *The Age of Roosevelt*. 3 vols. Boston: Houghton Mifflin, 1957–1960.

Schwantes, Carlos A. *The Pacific Northwest: An Interpretative History*. Lincoln: University of Nebraska Press, 1996.

———. *Radical Heritage: Labor, Socialism, and Reform in Washington and British Columbia, 1885–1917*. Seattle: University of Washington Press, 1979.

Sitton, Tom. *John Randolph Haynes: California Progressive*. Stanford, CA: Stanford University Press, 1992.

Sklar, Martin J. *The Corporate Reconstruction of American Capitalism, 1890–1916: The Market, the Law, and Politics*. New York: Cambridge University Press, 1988.

Starr, Kevin. *Material Dreams: Southern California Through the 1920s*. New York: Oxford University Press, 1990.

Staudenmaier, John M. *Technology's Storytellers: Reweaving the Human Fabric*. Cambridge, MA: MIT Press, 1985.

Steeter, John. *Politics and Technology*. New York: Guilford Press, 1992.

Stevens, Joseph E. *Hoover Dam: An American Adventure*. Norman: University of Oklahoma Press, 1988.

Thelen, David P. *Paths of Resistance: Tradition and Dignity in Industrializing Missouri*. New York: Oxford University Press, 1986.

———. *Robert M. La Follette and the Insurgent Spirit*. Boston: Little, Brown, 1976.

Thompson, Carl D. *Confessions of the Power Trust*. New York: E. P. Dutton, 1932.

Tobey, Ronald C. *Technology as Freedom: The New Deal and the Electrical Modernization of the American Home*. Berkeley: University of California Press, 1996.

Tucker, Ray, and Frederick R. Barkley. *Sons of the Wild Jackass*. Boston: L. C. Page, 1932.

The Twentieth Century Fund. *Electric Power and Government Policy: A Survey of the Relations Between the Government and the Electric Power Industry*. New York: Twentieth Century Fund, 1948.

Tygiel, Jules. *The Great Los Angeles Swindle: Oil, Stocks, and Scandals During the Roaring Twenties*. New York: Oxford University Press, 1994.

Walton, John. *Western Times and Water Wars: State, Culture, and Rebellion in California*. Berkeley: University of California Press, 1992.

Weatherson, Michael A., and Hal Boehim. *Hiram Johnson: A Bio-Biography*. New York: Greenwood Press, 1988.

Weinstein, James. *The Corporate Ideal in the Liberal State, 1900–1918*. Boston: Beacon Press, 1968.

Wheeler, Burton K., and Paul F. Healy. *Yankee from the West*. 1962. Reprint, New York: Octagon, 1977.

Wiebe, Robert H. *The Search for Order, 1877–1920*. New York: Hill and Wang, 1967.

Wilbur, Ray Lyman, and Arthur Mastick Hyde. *The Hoover Policies*. New York: Scribner's, 1937.

Williams, James C. *Energy and the Making of Modern California*. Akron: University of Akron Press, 1997.

Wilson, Joan Hoff. *Herbert Hoover: The Forgotten Progressive*. Boston: Little, Brown, 1975.

Wing, Robert C., ed. *A Century of Service: The Puget Power Story*. Seattle: Puget Sound Power and Light, 1987.

Winkler, John K. *William Randolph Hearst: A New Appraisal*. New York: Hasting House, 1955.

Winner, Langdon. *Autonomous Technology: Technics-Out-of-Control as a Theme in Political Thought*. Cambridge, MA: MIT Press, 1977.

Workman, Boyle. *The City That Grew*. Los Angeles: Southland Publishing, 1935.
Works Progress Administration. *Minnesota: A State Guide*. 1938. Reprint, New York: Hastings House, 1978.
Worster, Donald. *Rivers of Empire: Water, Aridity, and the Growth of the American West*. New York: Pantheon, 1985.
Zunz, Oliver. *Making America Corporate, 1870–1920*. Chicago: University of Chicago Press, 1990.

SIGNED ARTICLES

Ashby, Darrel Leroy. "Progressivism Against Itself: The Senate Western Bloc in the 1920s." *Mid-America* 50 (1968); reprinted in *The Congress of the United States, 1789–1989*, ed. Joel H. Silbey, 3 vols. New York: Carlson, 1991.
Ballard, R. H. "Getting Ahead of Power Needs." *Southern California Business*, February 1925, 22, 38–39.
Barber, Earl H. "Toward an Electrified America." *Journal of Land and Public Utility Economics* 11 (1935): 248–55.
Baum, Robert D. "Power District Legislation." *National Municipal Review* 26 (1937): 28–29.
Bender, Thomas. "Wholes and Parts: The Need for Synthesis in American History." *Journal of American History* 74 (1986): 120–36.
Brock, John Lewis. "Ten Minutes at the Boulder Dam Site." *Southern California Business*, October 1925, 15, 45, 50.
Bruere, Martha Bensley. "What Is Giant Power for?" *Annals of the American Academy of Political and Social Science* 118 (1925): 120–23.
Budlong, Julia. "Portland Votes No." *Nation*, May 23, 1928, 587–88.
Burnham, Walter Dean. "The Changing Shape of the American Political Universe." *American Political Science Review* 59 (1965): 7–28.
Butterfield, Kenyon L. "The Farm Problem Made Clear: The Farmers' Problems and Solutions." *Current History* 29 (1928): 265–81.
Chase, Lucius K. "The C. of C. Plan for Colorado River." *Southern California Business*, November 1925, 13, 40–41.
Claggett, William et al. "Walter Dean Burnham and the Dynamics of America Politics." *Social Science History* 10 (1986): 204–314.
Clements, George P. "Parceling Out the Colorado River." *Southern California Business*, January 1923, 13–14, 50.
Cochran, Thomas. "The 'Presidential Synthesis' in American History." *American Historical Review* 53 (1948): 748–59.
Davis, G. Cullom. "The Transformation of the Federal Trade Commission, 1914–1929." *Mississippi Valley Historical Review* 49 (1962): 437–55.
DeGraff, Leonard. "Corporate Liberalism and Electric Power System Planning in the 1920s." *Business History Review* 64 (1990): 1–31.
Eastman, George L., and A. G. Arnoll. "The Chamber's Stand on the Colorado River Project." *Southern California Business*," February 1928, 24.
Feinman, Ronald L. "The Progressive Republican Senate Bloc and the Presidential Election of 1932." *Mid-America* 59 (1977): 73–91.
Frankfurter, Felix. "Mr. Hoover on Power Control." *New Republic*, October 17, 1928, 240–43.
Galambos, Louis. "The Emerging Organizational Synthesis in Modern American History." *Business History Review* 44 (1970): 279–90.

————. "Technology, Political Economy, and Professionalization: Central Themes of the Organizational Synthesis," *Business History Review* 57 (1983): 471–93.

Glad, Paul. "Progressives and the Business Culture of the 1920s." *Journal of American History* 53 (1966): 75–89.

Glaeser, Martin G. "The Los Angeles Bureau of Power and Light." 4 parts. *Journal of Land and Public Utility Economics* 6–9 (1930–1933).

Hampton, Edgar Lloyd. "Cheap Power as a City Developer." *Southern California Business*, May 1923, 12–13, 42.

————. "Water and Power Attract Industries." *Southern California History*, March 1925, 12–13, 42–43.

Hart, Joseph K. "The Place of Leisure in Life." *Annals of the American Academy of Political and Social Science* 118 (1925): 112–15.

Heggie, Helen E. "Developments in Municipal Ownership of Electrical Plants in Minnesota." *Journal of Land and Public Utility Economics* 4 (1928): 289–94.

Hill, Robert L. "Power Politics in Seattle." *Nation*, March 2, 1932, 253–54.

Johnson, Hiram. "Converting the Colorado River into a National Asset." *Current History* 29 (1929): 786–92.

Kahrl, William L. "The Politics of California Water: Owens Valley and the Los Angeles Aqueduct, 1900–1927." *California Historical Quarterly* 55 (1976): 2–25, 98–121.

Key, V. O., Jr. "A Theory of Critical Elections." *Journal of Politics* 17 (1955): 3–18.

Kousser, J. Morgan. "Toward 'Total Political History': A Rational-Choice Research Program." *Journal of Interdisciplinary History* 20 (1990): 521–60.

Leuchtenburg, William E. "The Pertinence of Political History: Reflections on the Significance of the State in America." *Journal of American History* 73 (1986): 585–600.

Lichtman, Allan J. "Critical Election Theory and the Reality of American Presidential Politics, 1916–1940." *American Historical Review* 81 (1976): 317–51.

Link, Arthur S. "What Happened to the Progressive Movement in the 1920s?" *American Historical Review* 64 (1959): 833–51.

Lowitt, Richard. "A Neglected Aspect of the Progressive Movement: George W. Norris and Public Control of Hydroelectric Power, 1913–1919." *Historian* 27 (1965): 350–65.

McNinch, Frank R. "The Evolution of Federal Control of Electric Power." *Journal of Land and Public Utility Economics* 12 (1936): 111–19.

Moody, Burdett. "Industries Make Huge Power Demand." *Southern California Business*, January 1925, 9, 38–40.

Norris, George W. "Boring from Within." *Nation*, September 16, 1926, 297–99.

————. "Hope for Progressives." *Nation*, December 19, 1928, 679–80.

O'Brien, Patrick G. "A Reexamination of the Senate Farm Bloc, 1921–1922." *Agricultural History* 68 (1972); reprinted in *The Congress of the United States, 1789–1989*, ed. Joel H. Silbey, 3 vols. New York: Carlson, 1991.

Olssen, Erik. "The Progressive Group in Cong., 1922–1929." *Historian* 42 (1980); reprinted in *The Congress of the United States, 1789–1989*, ed. Joel H. Silbey, 3 vols. New York: Carlson, 1991.

Pattison, Mary. "The Abolition of Household Slavery." *Annals of the American Academy of Political and Social Science* 118 (1925): 124–27.

Pinchot, Gifford. "Message to the General Assembly of the Commonwealth of Pennsylvania, February 17, 1925"; reprinted as "Giant Power, Large Scale Electrical Development as a Social Factor." *Annals of the American Academy of Political and Social Science* 118 (1925): vii–xii.

————. "Who Owns Our Rivers?" *Nation,* January 18, 1928, 64–66.

Posner, Russell. "The Progressive Voters League, 1923–26." *California Historical Society Quarterly* 36 (1957): 251–61.

Putnam, Jackson K. "The Pattern of California Politics." *Pacific Historical Review* 61 (1992): 23–52.

————. "The Persistence of Progressivism in the 1920s: The Case of California." *Pacific Historical Review* 35 (1966): 395–411.

Raver, Paul Jerome. "Municipal Ownership in the Last Five Years." *Journal of Land and Public Utility Economics* 9 (1933): 122–34.

————. "Municipally Owned Generating Plants in Existence in the United States as of December 31, 1932." *Journal of Land and Public Utility Economics* 9 (1933): 306–13.

————. "Municipally Owned Establishments Which Were in Existence in the United States on December 31, 1932, and Which Were Purchasing All Current Distributed on December 31, 1930." *Journal of Land and Public Utility Economics* 9 (1933): 410–17.

Shammas, Carole. "A New Look at Long-Term Trends in Wealth Inequality in the United States." *American Historical Review* 98 (1993): 412–31.

Tobey, Ronald C. "How Urbane Is the Urbanite? An Historical Model of the Urban Hierarchy and the Social Motivation of Service Classes." *Historical Methods Newsletter* 7 (1974): 59–75.

Van Valen, Nelson S. "A Neglected Aspect of the Owens River Aqueduct Story: The Inception of the Los Angles Municipal Electric System." *Southern California Quarterly* 59 (1977): 85–109.

UNSIGNED ARTICLES

"Behind the Power Lobby." *Nation,* May 18, 1928, 57.

"Business Is Not Business." *Nation,* October 31, 1928, 442.

"The Chamber's Stand on Colorado River Project." *Southern California Business,* February 1928, 24.

"The Cradle of Electric Energy: Los Angeles Lays Claim to Being the Pioneer City in Many of the Utilities That Use Hydro-Electric Power." *Southern California Business,* February 1923, 13–14, 35.

"Don't Shoot We're Coming Down." *Nation,* May 20, 1925, 563.

"First Blood in the Power War." *New Republic,* February 29, 1928, 56–57.

"The Million-Dollar Lobby." *Nation,* May 16, 1928, 554–55.

Nation, January 11, 1928, 38; and April 18, 1928, 420.

New Republic, October 3, 1928, 162–63.

"Norris's Power Fight." *Nation,* March 28, 1928, 338.

"The Power Lobby Wins." *Nation,* February 29, 1928, 229.

"Power Mergers and the Public." *Nation,* August 14, 1928, 150.

"Smith as Political Expert." *New Republic,* October 3, 1928, 164–66.

Southern California Business, January 1923, 23; March 1926, 8; September 1926, 8; April 1927, back cover; June 1927, 8, back cover; and May 1928, 48 (advertisements from these issues cited).

"Southern California Leads in Farm Electrification." *Southern California Business,* November 1927, 27, 45.

"Telling the Story About Industrial Los Angeles." *Southern California Business,* July 1927, 26–27.

"Water and Power Attract Industries." *Southern California Business*, March 1925, 12–13, 42–43.
"What Price Electricity?" *New Republic*, February 22, 1928, 6–7.
"What the Power Trust Bought." *New Republic*, October 31, 1928, 289–90.

UNPUBLISHED MATERIAL

Brigham, Jay. "Nine Renegade Senators, Democratic Isolationist Senators, and F.D.R." M.A. thesis, University of Maryland, 1986.
Christie, Jean. "Morris Llewellyn Cooke: Progressive Engineer." Ph.D. diss., Columbia University, 1963.
Dick, Wesley Arden. "The Genesis of Seattle City Light." M.A. thesis, University of Washington, 1965.
————. "Visions of Abundance: The Public Power Crusade in the Pacific Northwest in the Era of J. D. Ross and the New Deal." Ph.D. diss., University of Washington, 1973.
Dollar, Charles Mason. "The Senate Progressive Movement, 1921–1933: A Roll Call Analysis." Ph.D. diss., University of Kentucky, 1966.
Olssen, Erik. "Dissent from Normalcy: Progressives in Congress, 1918–1925." Ph.D. diss., Duke University, 1969.
Ross, J. D., comp. *J.D. Ross Scrapbooks.* 19 vols. Suzzallo Library; Seattle: University of Washington. Microfilm.
Sicilia, David B. "Selling Power: Marketing and Monopoly at Boston Edison, 1886–1929." Ph.D. diss., Brandeis University, 1991.
Sparks, William. "J. D. Ross and Seattle City Light, 1917–1932." M.A. thesis, University of Washington, 1964.
Van Valen, Nelson S. "Power and Politics: The Struggle for Municipal Ownership of Electric Utilities in Los Angeles, 1905–1937." Ph.D. diss., Claremont Graduate School, 1965.

NEWSPAPERS

Baltimore News, May 1924, December 1924, January 1928. Albert S. Cook Library, Towson State College, Baltimore. Microfilm.
Bangor Independent, 1929–1930. State Historical Society of Wisconsin, Madison. Microfilm.
Boston Daily Advertiser, May 1924, December 1924. Library of Congress. Microfilm.
Chicago American, May 1924, December 1924, January 1928. Illinois State Historical Library, Old State Capitol, Springfield. Microfilm.
Daily Wisconsin-News (Milwaukee), May 1924, December 1924, January 1928. State Historical Society of Wisconsin, Madison. Microfilm.
Detroit Times, May 1924, December 1924, January 1928. Detroit Public Library. Microfilm.
LeVang's Weekly, 1928. Minnesota Historical Society, St. Paul. Microfilm.
New York American, May 1924, December 1924. Library of Congress. Microfilm.
New York Times.
Pardeeville-Wyocena Times, January–August 1933. State Historical Society of Wisconsin, Madison. Microfilm.
Pittsburgh Sun Telegraph, January 1928. Hillman Library, University of Pittsburgh. Microfilm.

Sikeston Herald, 1930–1931. State Historical Society of Missouri, Columbia. Micro-film.

Sikeston Standard, January–May 1930, January 1932. Kent Library, State College, Cape Girardeau, Missouri. Microfilm.

Walla Walla Daily Bulletin. Washington State Library, Olympia. Microfilm.

Walla Walla Union. Northwest and Whitman College Archives, Penrose Library, Walla Walla. Microfilm.

Index